REVOLUTION 101
MANJUNATHISM

MANJUNATH AREKERE
CHIKKAHUCHHAIAH

TRUE SIGN
PUBLISHING HOUSE

Published by True Sign Publishing House
Address: SY. No. 21/2 & 21/3, Sonnenahalli,
Krishnarajapura, Bengaluru,
Karnataka - 560049 India
E-mail: truesignbooks@gmail.com
Website: www.truesign.in

Revolution 101: Manjunathism

Author: Manjunath Arekere Chikkahuchhaiah

ISBN: 978-93-5988-845-3

First Edition: 2023

Publisher's Note

The views, thoughts, and opinions expressed in this book belong solely to the author and do not necessarily reflect the perspectives of True Sign Publishing House. The publisher has remained committed to ensuring the integrity of the author's voice and has not influenced or edited the content beyond standard publication processes.

ॐ असतो मा सद्गमय।
तमसो मा ज्योतिर्गमय।
मृत्योर्मा अमृतं गमय।
ॐ शान्तिः शान्तिः शान्तिः॥

Lead us from the unreal to the real
Lead us from darkness to light
Lead us from death to immortality
Aum peace, peace, peace!

ನಮ್ಮನ್ನು ಅವಾಸ್ತವದಿಂದ ವಾಸ್ತವದೆಡೆಗೆ ಕರೆದೊಯ್ಯಿರಿ
ಕತ್ತಲೆಯಿಂದ ಬೆಳಕಿನೆಡೆಗೆ ನಮ್ಮನ್ನು ನಡೆಸು
ನಮ್ಮನ್ನು ಸಾವಿನಿಂದ ಅಮರತ್ವದೆಡೆಗೆ ನಡೆಸು
ಓಮ್ ಶಾಂತಿ, ಶಾಂತಿ, ಶಾಂತಿ!

"Allah makes the impossible possible."

The one who fears is not made perfect in love. Psalm 31:24

Yada yada hi dharmasya glanirbhavati bharata।
Abhythanamadharmasya tadatmanam srijamyaham।।
Paritranaya sadhunang vinashay cha dushkritam।
Dharmasangsthapanarthay sambhabami yuge yuge।।

ಯದಾ ಯದಾ ಹಿ ಧರ್ಮಸ್ಯಗ್ಲಾನಿರ್ಭವತಿ ಭಾರತ।
ಅಭ್ಯುತ್ಥಾನಮಧರ್ಮಸ್ಯತದಾತ್ಮಾನಂ ಸೃಜಾಮ್ಯಹಂ।।
ಪರಿತ್ರಾಣಾಯ ಸಾಧೂನಾಂ ವಿನಾಶಾಯ ಚ ದುಷ್ಕೃತಾಂ।
ಧರ್ಮಸಂಸ್ಥಾಪನಾರ್ಥಾಯ ಸಂಭವಾಮಿ ಯುಗೇ ಯುಗೇ।।

ಯಾವಾಗ ಧರ್ಮದ ಅವನತಿಯಾಗುವುದೋ ಅಧರ್ಮದ ಉನ್ನತಿಯಾಗುವುದೋ ಆಗ ನಾನು ಅವತಾರ ಮಾಡುತ್ತೇನೆ. ಸಾಧುಗಳ ರಕ್ಷಣೆಗಾಗಿ, ದುಷ್ಟರ ವಿನಾಶಕ್ಕಾಗಿ ಮತ್ತು ಧರ್ಮದ ಸಂಸ್ಥಾಪನೆಗಾಗಿ ಪ್ರತಿಯುಗದಲ್ಲೂ ಅವತರಿಸುತ್ತೇನೆ.

- ಭಗವಾನ್ ಶ್ರೀಕೃಷ್ಣ, ಭಗವದ್ಗೀತೆ.

Whenever there is a decline in righteousness or the rise of unrighteousness, then I incarnate. I will incarnate in every age for the protection of innocent and good, for the destruction of the wicked and for the establishment of order and peace.

- Lord Krishna, Bhagavad Gita.

REVOLUTION 101 - Manjunathism

by - Manjunath Arekere Chikkahuchhaiah

"I promise 'The Five Pillars' to all Indians:
Peace, Land, Education, Healthcare, and Jobs
with minimum wages for all."

What is the ape to man? A laughing-stock, a thing of shame. And just the same shall man be to the Superman: a laughing-stock, a thing of shame. "Ye have made your way from the worm to man, and much within you is still worm."

Friedrich Wilhelm Nietzsche

Manjunath Arekere Chikkahuchhaiah, Indian Revolutionary, Existentialist Philosopher.

It's time for Indians to overcome mediocrity
and now one becomes what one is.

CONTENTS

Preface

We are about to kick-start a movement, one that aims to uproot the corrupt political establishment and pave the way for fresh ideas, a new culture, new norms, and a new socio-political-economic order. We've had our fill of the theatrics from these political parties who engage in the blame game and resort to playing the God, religion, and caste cards to win favor with the uneducated masses. Without revolutionary theory, there can be no revolutionary movement. We must gear up to combat this corrupt system with unwavering courage, determination, and boundless energy.

Our social order is in shambles, our economic system is in disarray, our political structure is flawed, and there's a lack of discipline. We lack proper law and order, and everything seems to be tailored to the rich man's whims. We need jobs to pay our bills, we need minimum wages to balance our expenses, and we need a free centralized universal education system to ensure our youth receives proper education, and we need an universal healthcare system.

In the vibrant history of India, where tradition and modernity intersect, where the past and present coexist, and where a multitude of voices clamour for change, this book finds its place. It is a journey through the myriad currents of thought, action, and transformation that define contemporary India.

Our focus, unapologetically, is on the issues that India faces today. From the struggles that simmer beneath the surface of society to the urgent need for change, this book delves into the heart of the matter.

It calls upon each reader to be a revolutionary, not necessarily in the sense of armed conflict but in the commitment to drive meaningful transformation within our society.

The pages ahead explore a spectrum of revolutions, from the historical to the contemporary, both in India and across the globe. By examining the catalysts, drivers, and underlying philosophies of these revolutions, we aim to illuminate the paths to change and the reasons for their occurrence.

In the midst of these discussions, we traverse the philosophical landscapes of Friedrich Nietzsche, exploring his dichotomy of master morality and slave morality. Nietzsche's ideas provide a lens through which we can view the dynamics of power and ethics that shape societies and revolutions.

We also delve into the unique and home-grown ideology of Manjunathism, a revolutionary movement that has sparked conversations and inspired action in India. Through the lens of Manjunathism, we unearth the potential for grassroots change and the transformative power of individual agency.

Finally, our journey culminates in an exploration of Martin Heidegger's profound philosophical work, "Being and Time." Explained by Simon Critchley a philosopher, he teaches at The New School in New York:This examination invites readers to ponder the profound questions of existence, meaning, and authenticity, providing a philosophical foundation for the transformation we seek.

As you turn the pages of this book, we invite you to embark on a thought-provoking and enlightening journey. It is a call to action, an invitation to participate in the ongoing transformation of India, and an exploration of the philosophical underpinnings that shape our world. We hope that, in our collective pursuit of change, we can find clarity, inspiration, and the path to a more just and equitable society.

The Indian Dream

In the spirit of **"Let a Thousand flowers bloom,"** we envision a landscape where a multitude of ideas and educational opportunities flourish. Our vision is to establish a thousand schools of thought across rural India, breaking away from a centralized high-class coaching system. We believe in nurturing a diversity of intellectual growth, where ideas and innovation can thrive.

"Dare to think, dare to speak, dare to act" resonates as a powerful call to action. It echoes a campaign that encourages peasants to come together in collective farms, urging them to fearlessly express their thoughts and take bold steps towards progress and self-sufficiency.

"To rebel is justified," which accompanied by "smash the four olds," we recognize the need to break free from outdated norms. It urges us to challenge old ideas, customs, culture, and habits, fostering a revolutionary spirit that seeks to reshape our society for the better.

To **"seek truth from facts"** remains a guiding principle. We emphasize the importance of emancipating our minds, grounding ourselves in reality, and integrating theory with practice. This commitment is essential for the smooth execution of our socialist modernization program.

"Have fewer children, raise more GOATs" acknowledges the imperative of environmental sustainability. We understand that our planet is under strain, and it is our responsibility to ensure a balanced future by conserving resources and nurturing our environment.

In our pursuit of a **"harmonious society,"** we prioritize democracy, the rule of law, equity, justice, sincerity, amity, and vitality. We emphasize respect for the legal and justice systems, recognizing that upholding the law and adhering to regulations is essential for maintaining order and justice. We are committed to addressing any breaches of rules or instances of corruption through peaceful and legal means.

In their work, our grand judges and grand procurators always hold supreme the party's cause, the people's interest, and the constitution and law. Their unwavering commitment ensures that our nation's principles remain intact and that the rights of its citizens are protected, fostering a just and equitable society for all.

Message to millennials

The world is yours, as well as ours, but in the last analysis, it is yours. You young people, full of vigour and vitality, are in the bloom of life, like the sun at eight or nine in the morning. Our hope is placed on you ... the world belongs to you. India's future belongs to you.

"We want cultural struggle, we do not want armed struggle" and "The masses do not want civil war."

Message to the student leaders:

“You are invited to involve in the cultural-socio-political-economical revolution: struggle-criticism-transformation. Now, first, you're not struggling; second, you're not criticizing; and third, you're not transforming. Or rather, you are struggling, but it's a struggle against societal repression. The people are not happy, the workers are not happy, city residents are not happy, most people in schools are not happy, most of the students even in your schools and colleges are not happy. Even within the faction that supports you, there are unhappy people. Is this the way to unify the world? By publicly denouncing another religion? By denouncing the poor and protecting the rich, by building walls to cover slums? We have traitors within our country they are corrupt politicians and government officials who take bribes, commission and encourage corruption they are the black sheep and they must be exiled or put in jail for lifetime for betraying their people and their country

The revolution has to be a permanent process, constantly kept alive through unending class struggles. Hidden enemies in the society and intellectual circles have to be identified and removed. Conceived of as a "revolution to touch people's souls," the aim of the Cultural Revolution is to attack the Four Olds-- old ideas, old culture, old customs, and old habits--in order to bring the areas of education, healthcare, jobs, minimum wages, art and literature in line with socialist ideology. Anything that is suspected of being feudal, superstitious, imperial or pretentiousness is to be destroyed.

"Our Primary Target: Eliminating Corrupt Politicians, Corrupt Government Officials, and Religious Bigots."

He who does not deliberately close his eyes cannot fail to see that the new "Critical" trend of disintegrating society that the corrupt politicians and government officials are involved in commercial profiteering, fictitious deals, exploitation of natural resources, lobbying for family members, adulteration of foodstuffs, cheating, official embezzlement, theft, burglary and daylight robbery, the corrupt political society itself falls victim to direct and limitless degeneration, for its innermost law of life is the profoundest of immoralities, namely the exploitation of man by man. The revolution will have to struggle with this enemy and be an instrument of counter-revolution on every hand. It is a two-edged sword.

Corrupt politicians, including all elected officials from local panchayat members to the highest offices of the land such as President, Prime Minister, Chief Ministers, Governors, MLAs, and MPs, if found involved in corrupt practices that harm our state or nation, should be held accountable for their actions.

Such individuals can be seen as betraying the trust of their motherland, compromising their values and morals, and failing to uphold the interests of the people they are meant to serve. They have, in essence, betrayed their country and its citizens, including their own families.

It is essential that we, as responsible citizens, label corrupt politicians for their unethical behaviour and the harm they cause to our nation's farmers, labourers, underprivileged, women, and children. However, we should strive to hold them accountable through legal means and must promote hate against corruption and the people involved in it. It is our collective duty to demand transparency, accountability, and ethical governance from our elected representatives."

Corrupt politicians – pimp's who pimped our motherland

Politicians found involved in corrupt practices that harm our state or nation, should be held accountable for their actions.They will be considered as PIMP'S who whored their MOTHER (motherland), who whored their wife (their values and morals) and their daughters (The people of the State)- (and the family who support these corrupt politicians are fit to be called like that without hesitation.) So hereby, I call all the people of this country to label corrupt politicians as PIMP's who pimped their mother, wife and daughters.

They have PIMPED their motherland for the money which rightly belongs to farmers, laborers, poor, woman and children of this country. And they have not only betrayed their country, they have also betrayed the people of this country and their family and they don't deserve to live among us.

Corrupt Government officials and Public-Private contractors – are the Pimp's who pimped their Mother, their wife and their daughters.

Corruption among government officials and public-private contractors is a serious concern. When individuals employed by state or central governments engage in corrupt practices or accept bribes, they betray the trust of their positions and harm the interests of the nation.

It is crucial that such individuals be held accountable for their actions. We, as responsible citizens, should label and expose corrupt practices and demand transparency, integrity, and ethical conduct from all government employees and contractors.

It is our collective responsibility to safeguard the integrity of our nation and ensure that public funds are used for the benefit of the people.

Any person who is employed by the state and the central government if they are involved in corruption or bribery: even they will be considered, branded and labeled as PIMP'S who whored their mother, wives and their daughters and we shall not allow them to live among us with the money they have earned by whoring their MOTHERLAND – they must be exiled.

"Politicians who involve religion, God, and caste in politics are traitors who betray our country through religious bigotry."

The integration of religion, god, and caste into politics is a matter of significant concern. When political leaders, parties, famous personalities, and citizens utilize these factors for political gain, they may inadvertently mislead people, divert their attention from important issues, and hinder the nation's progress.

It is crucial to recognize that India is a diverse and pluralistic nation with a multitude of castes, religions, and beliefs. Attempting to divide the nation along these lines is not only impractical but also contrary to the spirit of unity and progress that we should strive for.

We cannot establish separate governments for each caste, religion, or God, as this would undermine the stability and effectiveness of our democratic system. Instead, it is the responsibility of one government to protect the welfare and rights of all citizens, regardless of their background.

Our true identity is as citizens of India, bound by the principles of love and brotherhood. Those who exploit caste, religion, and God for political purposes may inadvertently undermine the sovereignty of our nation and the principles laid out in the Indian Constitution.

As responsible citizens, we should be committed to preserving the sovereignty of India and upholding the values of the Indian Constitution. It is our duty to resist attempts to divide our nation and promote unity, equality, and progress for all.

Political leaders, political parties, any leaders, any famous personalities and the people,

anyone who involves religion, God and caste in politics is trying to mislead people into ignorance, and they are influencing people to ignore science and technology and they clearly don't want to develop the nation in the name of unity, they are clearly trying to divide the nation in the name of religion, caste and God.

We cannot be divided in the name of caste because we have 2500 castes, we cannot be divided in the name of religion because we have 10s of religion, we cannot divide in the name of God because we have 33 million Hindu gods + Allah and Jesus.

We cannot form 2500 government for 2500 castes.

We cannot form 10s of government for 10s of religion.

We cannot form 33 million governments for 33 million Gods.

We can form only one government and it is the duty of this one government to protect the welfare of the people who belong to all castes, all religions and all Gods.

We consider our primary allegiance to our nation, India, and our core values are rooted in love and brotherhood.

Those who exploit caste, religion, and God for political purposes go against the principles of national unity and the Indian Constitution.

Their actions can be seen as undermining the sovereignty of India.

We are committed to safeguarding the sovereignty of our country and upholding the principles of the Indian Constitution. We are ready to stand up and defend these values, even if it means making the ultimate sacrifice."

The Declaration of Rights of Every Indian

"Nature inherently grants freedom and equality to all individuals, with distinctions among them primarily determined by their overall contributions to society."

"Every person is born with inherent and inalienable rights, including the right to property, the protection of their dignity and life, full control over their own body and abilities, the pursuit of well-being, and the ability to resist oppression."

"Every Indian citizen by birth has the right to free education, free healthcare, jobs with minimum wages, the right to own property, and the right to live in a prejudice-free society. These are our birthrights, and if we're denied these rights, we must fight tooth and nail to secure them, for as the saying goes, 'Where there's a will, there's a way.'"

"No one should face persecution for their religion, beliefs, or the expression of their thoughts through speech, writing, or printing, except when such actions disrupt the peace of the community through slanderous or harmful acts."

"In today's governance, every government's primary objective is the well-being of its citizens. The separation of powers among the legislative, executive, and judicial branches is fundamental, ensuring that no entity or individual holds authority that doesn't directly stem from the collective will of the nation."

“Legislative authority is exercised by representatives elected by the people, drawn from diverse districts, through transparent, frequent, and fair elections.”

“Judicial power is focused on upholding the law, with proceedings conducted openly and justice administered without bias or delay.”

Laws are designed to be clear, precise, and applicable uniformly to all members of society.”

“Subsidies are allocated openly and proportionally, fostering transparency and fairness in their distribution."

"As society advances and evolves, adapting to changing norms and addressing the needs of each new generation, it becomes imperative to consider mechanisms within our constitutional framework that allow for occasional, exceptional gatherings of representatives. These gatherings would have the singular purpose of reviewing and, if deemed necessary, revising the structure of our government."

"We recognize these fundamental truths to be self-evident: that all individuals are inherently equal, each endowed with certain unassailable rights, including the right to life, liberty, and the pursuit of happiness. To safeguard these rights, societies establish governments that derive their legitimate authority from the consent of the governed.

In cases where any form of government deviates from its purpose of preserving these rights and instead threatens them, it is the prerogative of the people to consider altering or replacing it. Such a new government should be founded on principles that prioritize the well-being and security of its citizens.”

“Certainly, careful consideration should be given to long-standing governments, and changes should not be made lightly or for trivial reasons. History shows that people are often more inclined to endure hardships that can be endured than to disrupt established systems. However, when a sustained pattern of abuses and usurpations reveals a deliberate intention to subject the populace to absolute tyranny, it becomes not only a right but a duty for the people to cast aside such a government and establish new safeguards for their future security."

The **Declaration of Rights of Every Indian** refers to the fundamental rights and freedoms guaranteed to the citizens of India by the Constitution of India. These rights are enshrined in Part III of the Constitution and are often referred to as "Fundamental Rights." They are considered the cornerstone of Indian democracy and provide protection and safeguards to individuals against arbitrary actions of the state. Here is a brief overview of the fundamental rights guaranteed to every Indian:

1. **Right to Equality (Articles 14-18):** This includes the right to equality before the law, prohibition of discrimination on grounds of religion, race, caste, sex, or place of birth, and equality of opportunity in public employment.
2. **Right to Freedom (Articles 19-22):** This includes the right to freedom of speech and expression, the right to assemble peacefully and without arms, the right to form associations or unions, the right to move freely throughout the territory of India, and the right to reside and settle in any part of the country.
3. **Right Against Exploitation (Articles 23-24):** These articles prohibit trafficking in human beings and forced labour. They also provide for the prohibition of employment of children in hazardous industries.
4. **Right to Freedom of Religion (Articles 25-28):** These articles guarantee the freedom of conscience and the right to freely profess, practice, and propagate religion. They also ensure that religious institutions have the autonomy to manage their own affairs.
5. **Cultural and Educational Rights (Articles 29-30):** These rights protect the interests of minorities by allowing them to conserve their distinct language, script, or culture. Article 30 grants the right to minorities to establish and administer educational institutions of their choice.
6. **Right to Constitutional Remedies (Article 32):** This article empowers individuals to approach the Supreme Court of India for the enforcement of their fundamental rights. It is often considered the "heart and soul" of the Constitution.
7. **Right to Privacy (Not explicitly mentioned but inferred from other fundamental rights):** The Supreme Court of India, in various judgments, has recognized the right to privacy

as a fundamental right inherent in the right to life and personal liberty (Article 21).

These fundamental rights are justiciable, meaning that citizens can approach the courts if their rights are violated by the state or any other entity. However, these rights are not absolute and are subject to reasonable restrictions in the interest of the sovereignty and integrity of India, security of the state, friendly relations with foreign countries, public order, decency, and morality.

In addition to these fundamental rights, the Constitution of India also includes Directive Principles of State Policy (Part IV), which provide guidelines for the government in matters of policy and governance. While these principles are not enforceable by the courts, they are meant to guide the state in creating a just and equitable society.

"To rebel in order to build our nation and enlighten our people is a revolutionary act."

Manjunath Arekere Chikkahuchhaiah

The Duties of the Revolutionary towards Himself

1. "The revolutionary is a blessed individual. Their personal interests revolve around socio-economic and political change, while their primary mission is the establishment of equality. India holds a special place in their heart, and their attachment is deeply rooted in their love for their motherland. The revolutionary operates without personal gain or the pursuit of fame. Their entire being is wholly dedicated to the singular purpose of revolution and societal reform."
2. "The revolutionary, in the very core of their being, has severed all ties with the oppressive social order, rejecting its laws, moralities, and customs. They stand as a relentless adversary against caste-based discrimination and imperialism. If they coexist with these systems, it is solely to hasten their destruction. Their sole mission is the abolition of the caste system and the unification of the entire nation under a single identity: 'INDIAN.' Let us acknowledge the truth that we are one, and we shall remain united as one."
3. "The revolutionary holds public opinion in contempt and harbors a deep aversion to the current state of social morality in all its

forms. For them, morality is defined by anything that advances the cause of the revolution. They view the creation of a New Order, a New Culture, and New Ideas as paramount, regardless of the obstacles presented by the existing norms."

4. "The revolutionary is a resolute individual, unyielding in the face of unfounded discrimination related to caste and religion, as well as in opposition to an immoral social order. They harbor no expectations of mercy from their adversaries and extend none to them in return. There exists between them, whether openly declared or concealed, an unrelenting and irreconcilable conflict that may extend to the very end. The revolutionary must be prepared to endure hardships and adversity."
5. "The revolutionary, even while being exacting with themselves, must exhibit unrelenting resolve in confronting corrupt politicians, government officials, and the immoral social order. They must suppress tender emotions like kinship, love, friendship, gratitude, and honour, replacing them with a cold and unwavering passion for the cause of revolution. Their sole source of pleasure, consolation, reward, and satisfaction should be the success of the revolution.
6. Night and day, their singular focus should be the merciless dismantling of corrupt administration. They must work tirelessly and with a clear mind towards this goal, ready to obliterate the tyrannical social order, corrupt politicians and their associates, and be prepared to personally remove any obstacles that hinder the path to revolution and reform."
7. "The true revolutionary is characterized by their resolute and unemotional approach, devoid of sentimentality, romanticism, infatuation, or exaltation. They must also eliminate any personal feelings of hatred and revenge. Revolutionary zeal, cultivated as a constant practice, should be applied with deliberate and rational calculation.

In all circumstances and places, the revolutionary should act not on personal impulses but solely in the service of the revolutionary cause, which includes eradicating the caste system, discrimination, inequality, and corruption. Their unwavering commitment extends to working collaboratively for the development of India, its infrastructure, and its socio-economic-political framework, with the aim of establishing an administration and institutions that provide free education, free medical care, and jobs with minimum wages for all."

The Relations of the Revolutionary towards his Comrades

"The true revolutionary should avoid establishing formal friendships or attachments, except with individuals who have proven their unwavering commitment to the cause of revolution through their actions. The depth of friendship, loyalty, and responsibility to such comrades should be determined exclusively by their effectiveness in furthering the objective of completely dismantling the caste system, eradication of discrimination and inequality, and challenging the existing socio-economic-political order."

1. "Solidarity among revolutionaries is not just a mere concept; it is the very foundation of revolutionary strength. Comrades who share the same revolutionary fervor and comprehension should, to the greatest extent possible, engage in collective deliberation on important matters, striving for unanimous consensus. Once a plan is finalized, however, the revolutionary must primarily depend on their own actions. When carrying out actions aimed at dismantling the caste system and combating corruption, each individual should act autonomously, turning to others for advice and support only when such collaboration is imperative for the plan's advancement."
2. "All revolutionaries should mentor and support less initiated comrades, considering them as an integral part of the shared revolutionary effort. These less experienced individuals represent a valuable resource that should be utilized judiciously to ensure the greatest possible benefit for the revolution. The committed revolutionary should see themselves as dedicated capital, pledged to the triumph of the revolution. However, decisions regarding the allocation of this capital cannot be made in isolation; they must receive unanimous consent from fully initiated comrades."

The Relations of the Revolutionary towards Society

1. The new member, having given proof of his loyalty not by words but by deeds, can be received into the society only by the unanimous agreement of all the members.

2. "The revolutionary immerses themselves in the world of the state, the privileged classes, and what is conventionally known as civilization, all with the sole objective of expediting the total eradication of caste-based discrimination and corruption. They cannot be considered a true revolutionary if they harbor any sympathy for corrupt politicians or corrupt government officials. The revolutionary should be ready to take legal action against any individual or entity involved in corruption without hesitation. Their aversion to all forms of corruption and corrupt individuals should be unwavering and equal. They cease to uphold the revolutionary spirit if they allow themselves to be influenced by sentiments associated with the current corrupt socio-economic-political order."

3. "In the pursuit of an unwavering revolution, the revolutionary may find it necessary, and indeed frequently essential, to live within society while assuming a false identity that differs significantly from their true self. This disguise allows them to gain access to a wide range of social strata, including the upper classes, the burgeoning middle class, commercial enterprises, places of worship, the residences of wealthy and corrupt politicians, bureaucratic circles, the world of literature, military institutions, as well as the domains of politics and legislation."

4. This filthy social order can be split up into several categories. The first category comprises those who must be sent to jail without delay. Comrades should compile a list of those to be condemned according to the relative gravity of their political-social-economic- bureaucratic corruption; their assets and property, their sons and daughter's assets and property, their grandsons and granddaughter's assets and property must be confiscated by the new government and the executions should be carried out according to the prepared order.

   When a list of those who are corrupt and those who are involved in corruption in any way (has betrayed their motherland and its people) is made, and the order is prepared, no private sense of outrage should be considered, nor is it necessary to pay attention to the hatred provoked by these people among the comrades or the people. Hatred and the sense of outrage may even be useful insofar as they incite the masses to self-awareness. It is necessary to be guided only by their relative usefulness of these charges for the sake of reform of social-political-economic system. Above all, those who are especially inimical to the revolutionary organization must be destroyed;

5. The second group comprises those who will be spared for the time being in order that, by a series of exposing corrupt policies and hypocrisy of society, they may drive the people into an inevitable protest.
6. The third category consists of a great many corrupt brutes in high positions, distinguished neither by their cleverness nor their energy, while enjoying riches, influence, power, and high positions by virtue of their rank. These must be exploited in every possible way; they must be implicated and embroiled in our affairs, their dirty secrets must be ferreted out, and they must be transformed into slaves. Their power, influence, and connections, their wealth and their energy, will be snatched from them and they will be put in jail for betrayal of their motherland and their people.
7. The fourth category comprises of corrupt ambitious office-holders and corrupt government officials having various shades of opinion. The revolutionary must pretend to collaborate with them, blindly following them, while at the same time, prying out their secrets until they are completely in his power. They must be so compromised that there is no way out for them, and then they can be put in jail based on the evidence provided by whistle blowers.
8. The fifth category consists of those doctrinaires, conspirators, and corrupt officers who cut a great figure on paper or in their cliques. They must be constantly driven on to make compromising declarations: as result, the majority of them will be destroyed, while a minority will become genuine revolutionaries.

The Attitude of Society towards People

1. Society has no aim other than the complete liberation and happiness of the masses - i.e., of the people who live by manual labor. Convinced that their emancipation and the achievement of this happiness can only come about as a result of an all-

destroying popular protest, society will use all its resources and energy towards exposing the evils and miseries of the corrupt administration until at last people's patience is exhausted and they are driven to a general questioning.

2. By a revolution, society does not mean an orderly protest according to the classic western model -a protest which always stops short of attacking the rights of property and the traditional social systems of a so-called civilization and morality. Until now, such revolution has always limited itself to the overthrow of one political form in order to replace it by another, thereby attempting to bring about a so-called revolutionary state. The only form of revolution beneficial to the people is one which destroys the entire corrupt system to its roots and exterminates all the discrimination, inequality and corrupt social order, institutions, and classes in India.

3. With this end in view, society therefore refuses to impose any new organization from above. Any future organization will doubtless work its way through the movement and life of the people; but this is a matter for future generations to decide. Our task is terrible, total, universal, and merciless destruction of corruption, corrupt politicians, corrupt government officials, system of bribery, discrimination and inequality and elimination of laziness, idleness and weakness.

4. Therefore, in drawing closer to the people, we must above all make common cause with those elements of the masses which, since the foundation of the state of India, have never ceased to protest, not only in words but in deeds, against everything directly or indirectly connected with the state: against the feudalism, the bureaucracy, the Temples, the exploiters, and the parasitic middlemen (Broker).

5. We must unite with the all adventurous caste and religion and fight as one, we are the only genuine revolutionaries in India.

6. To weld the people into one single unconquerable and all destruction of any kind of corruption, any kind of discrimination and any kind of inequality –this is our aim, our conspiracy, and our task.

Who is a Revolutionary?

A revolutionary is someone who seeks significant and often radical change in the political, social, or economic structures of a society. The strength of the movement lies in the awakening of the masses (principally the industrial workers) and the weakness lies in the lack of consciousness and initiative among the revolutionary leaders.

Here are some key aspects of the job of a revolutionary:

Identifying and Highlighting Injustice: Revolutionaries often start by identifying and highlighting existing injustices, inequalities, or oppressive conditions within a society. They may use various means, such as public speeches, writings, or activism, to raise awareness about these issues.

Mobilizing Support: Revolutionaries aim to mobilize support from individuals and groups who share their concerns and goals. This may involve organizing protests, rallies, or other forms of collective action to build a movement.

Advocating for Change: Revolutionaries advocate for change by proposing new ideas, policies, or systems that they believe will address the underlying issues causing injustice. They may participate in political debates, engage with policy-makers, or draft and promote reform proposals.

R**esisting the Status Quo:** Revolutionaries often engage in acts of resistance against the existing power structures. This can range from non-violent civil disobedience to more militant actions, depending on their beliefs and the circumstances.

Building Alliances: Revolutionaries may seek to build alliances with other groups or movements that share common goals or enemies. Collaboration can amplify their efforts and resources.

Creating Alternative Institutions: In some cases, revolutionaries may establish alternative institutions or systems to demonstrate their vision for a better society. This can include community-based organizations, cooperative businesses, or even parallel governance structures.

Challenging Authority: Revolutionaries challenge the authority of the ruling establishment and may engage in acts of civil resistance or disobedience to undermine the existing power structures.

Propaganda and Communication: Revolutionaries use various forms of propaganda and communication to disseminate their ideas and messages, including pamphlets, posters, social media, and other means.

Adapting Strategies: Revolutionaries often need to adapt their strategies and tactics based on changing circumstances, including government repression, shifts in public opinion, or emerging opportunities for change.

Sacrifice and Risk: Engaging in revolutionary activities can be risky, and many revolutionaries are prepared to make personal sacrifices, including facing arrest, imprisonment, or physical harm, for their cause.

Leadership and Organization: Some revolutionaries take on leadership roles within revolutionary movements, helping to coordinate activities and strategize for change.

Negotiation and Transition: In some cases, when revolutionary movements achieve their objectives or when there is an opportunity for peaceful transition, revolutionaries may engage in negotiations with existing authorities to facilitate a transition to a new political order.

What triggers a need for revolution within a country?

A revolution is a fundamental and often sudden and dramatic change in the way a society, government, or system operates. It typically involves a significant shift in political, social, economic, or cultural norms and structures. Revolutions can take many forms, including political revolutions, social revolutions, and technological revolutions, among others.

Key characteristics of a revolution may include:

Overthrow of the Existing Order: Revolutions often involve the overthrow or significant disruption of the existing political or social order. This can be achieved through protests, uprisings, or armed conflicts.

Change in Leadership: Revolutions frequently result in a change in leadership, such as the removal of a ruling monarch, dictator, or government officials.

Shift in Ideology or Values: Revolutionaries typically advocate for new ideologies, principles, or values that they believe will lead to a better society. These may include concepts like democracy, equality, or freedom.

Mass Mobilization: Successful revolutions often require the support and active participation of a significant portion of the population. Mass mobilization through protests, strikes, and other forms of collective action is common.

Long-lasting Impact: Revolutions can have far-reaching and long-lasting effects on a society, reshaping its political, economic, and social structures for years or even generations.

Notable historical examples of revolutions include the **American Revolution** (1775-1783), the **French Revolution** (1789-1799), the **Russian Revolution** (1917), and the **Chinese Communist Revolution** (1949). These revolutions had profound impacts on the countries and regions in which they occurred and influenced global history.

It's important to note that not all movements for change are successful in achieving their revolutionary goals, and the outcomes of revolutions can vary widely. Some revolutions lead to greater freedom, justice, and prosperity, while others result in instability, authoritarianism, or conflict. The success of a revolution often depends on a complex interplay of factors, including the level of popular support, the strategies employed by revolutionaries, and the response of existing authorities.

Here are some key developments and influences that contributed to the origin of the modern concept of revolution:

Enlightenment Ideas: The Enlightenment, an intellectual movement in the 17th and 18th centuries, played a crucial role in shaping the concept of revolution. Enlightenment thinkers like John Locke, Jean-Jacques Rousseau, and Montesquieu articulated ideas about natural rights, social contracts, and the limits of governmental authority. These ideas laid the groundwork for the notion that people have the right to revolt against oppressive rulers and seek a better form of government.

The American Revolution: The American Revolution (1775-1783) was a pivotal event that demonstrated the possibility of achieving independence and self-governance through armed struggle against colonial rule. It served as a model and source of inspiration for subsequent revolutionary movements around the world.

The French Revolution: The French Revolution (1789-1799) was a watershed moment in the history of revolutions. It not only led to the overthrow of the French monarchy but also articulated revolutionary principles such as liberty, equality, and fraternity. The

French Revolution's impact extended beyond France and inspired movements for change in other countries.

Industrialization: The Industrial Revolution, which began in the late 18th century and continued into the 19th century, brought about significant economic and social changes. Urbanization, the growth of the working class, and the concentration of wealth in the hands of industrialists contributed to social and class tensions that could fuel revolutionary movements.

Nationalism: The rise of nationalism in the 19th century played a role in the origin of revolutions. Nationalist movements sought to unite people based on shared language, culture, and history, often in opposition to imperial or colonial rule. Nationalist revolutions and uprisings occurred in various parts of the world.

Colonial Independence Movements: Throughout the 19th and 20th centuries, many colonized regions and nations sought independence from European colonial powers. These anti-colonial struggles were often framed as revolutionary movements, aiming to overthrow colonial rule and establish self-determination.

Socialism and Communism: The emergence of socialist and communist ideologies in the 19th and early 20th centuries provided intellectual frameworks for revolutionary change. These ideologies called for the overthrow of capitalist systems and the establishment of more equitable and classless societies.

Globalization: In the modern era, revolutions have often been influenced by global events, such as the spread of revolutionary ideas, the role of international actors, and the impact of global economic systems. The interconnectedness of the world in the 20th and 21st centuries has reshaped the dynamics of revolution.

Revolution has been shaped by a combination of philosophical ideas, historical events, economic and social transformations, and the aspirations of people seeking to challenge oppressive systems and create a more just and equitable world.

The European Colonial System

The European colonial system was a complex and often brutal system of domination and exploitation that began in the late 15th century and continued through most of the 20th century. It involved European powers establishing and maintaining control over territories in Asia, the Americas, and Africa. The methods and impact of colonialism varied across regions and over time, but there were some common elements in how the European colonial system worked and how it exploited these continents:

Exploration and Conquest:

European explorers like Christopher Columbus, Vasco da Gama, and Hernán Cortés sailed to Asia, the Americas, and Africa in search of new trade routes and resources.

They often established contact with indigenous people and, in many cases, used military force to conquer and subjugate them.

Establishment of Colonies:

European powers established colonies in these regions, claiming the land as their own.

Colonies were governed by European officials, and indigenous populations were often subjected to discriminatory laws and harsh treatment.

Resource Extraction:

One of the primary motives for colonialism was the exploitation of valuable resources, such as gold, silver, spices, timber, and agricultural products.

Native populations were often forced to work in mines, plantations, and other resource-extraction industries under brutal conditions.

Slave Trade:

In Africa and the Americas, European colonial powers engaged in the trans-atlantic slave trade, forcibly capturing and transporting millions of Africans to work as slaves on plantations and in mines.

This system of slavery was particularly cruel and a dehumanizing form of exploitation.

Economic Exploitation:

European powers established economic systems that benefited their home countries at the expense of the colonies. This included monopolizing trade, levying heavy taxes, and controlling local industries.

The colonies were often forced to produce cash crops and raw materials for export, which resulted in economic dependency and impoverishment.

Cultural and Religious Domination:

European colonial powers often sought to impose their culture, religion, and language on the indigenous populations.

Missionaries played a significant role in spreading Christianity, while indigenous cultures and traditions were often suppressed or eradicated.

Land Dispossession:

Indigenous people frequently lost their ancestral lands through land seizures and dispossession.

Land was often redistributed to European settlers or used for commercial agriculture.

Violence and Exploitation:

European colonialism was marked by violence, including wars of conquest, massacres, and the suppression of indigenous revolts.

The exploitation and subjugation of indigenous populations resulted in immense suffering and loss of life.

It is important to note that the impact of colonialism varied widely across different colonies and regions. While some regions experienced economic development and modernization under colonial rule, many others suffered long-lasting social, economic, and political consequences. The legacy of colonialism continues to shape the political and economic landscape of many former colonies to this day.

Industrialisation of America

European colonization played an important role in the industrialization of the Americas, particularly in North America, but it was often accompanied by exploitation from Africa and Asia. Here's how this process unfolded:

Access to Resources: European colonizers, particularly the British, Spanish, French, and Portuguese, established colonies in the Americas to exploit the vast natural resources available. This included agricultural products like tobacco, cotton, and sugar, as well as minerals like gold and silver. These resources were essential for European industries.

Labour Force: The colonization of the Americas led to the enslavement and exploitation of millions of Africans. African slaves were forced to work on plantations, mines, and in various other labour-intensive industries. Their forced labour provided the cheap workforce needed for the cultivation of cash crops and extraction of resources, contributing to the profitability of these industries.

Market Expansion: The colonies in the Americas provided European powers with new markets for their manufactured goods. This economic expansion created demand for European products and helped stimulate industrialization in Europe.

Capital Accumulation: The wealth generated from the exploitation of the Americas, as well as the trans-atlantic slave trade, contributed to capital accumulation in Europe. This capital was then reinvested in European industries, including the emerging textile and manufacturing sectors.

Innovation and Technological Transfer: As European settlers established colonies, they introduced new agricultural practices and technologies to increase productivity. This transfer of knowledge and technology had a positive impact on the agricultural and industrial sectors in the Americas.

Infrastructure Development: European colonial powers invested in infrastructure, such as roads, ports, and transportation networks, to facilitate the movement of goods and resources. These investments often benefited the development of industry and trade.

Economic Policies: European colonial powers implemented economic policies that favoured their own industries and trade interests. For example, they restricted the colonies' ability to trade with other nations, ensuring that the colonies primarily served as sources of raw materials and markets for European manufactured goods.

Intellectual Exchange: Colonization facilitated the exchange of ideas, knowledge, and technology between Europe and the Americas, contributing to scientific and technological advancements that supported industrialization.

It is essential to recognize that the benefits of industrialization in the Americas were often enjoyed by the European colonial powers and the European settlers rather than the indigenous people and enslaved Africans who faced exploitation, forced labour, and harsh living conditions. Additionally, the exploitation and suffering endured by Africans and indigenous populations during colonization were significant human rights abuses and had lasting social, economic, and cultural impacts that persist to this day. The legacy of colonialism is complex, with both positive and negative consequences for different groups of people and regions.

Exploitation of India by British

India experienced significant exploitation during the period of European colonization, primarily by the British, Portuguese, Dutch, and French. Here are some key points in which India was exploited:

Economic Exploitation:

Resource Extraction: India was rich in valuable resources such as spices, textiles, indigo, cotton, and precious metals. European colonizers extracted these resources for export to Europe, which contributed to significant wealth for European nations.

Monopoly on Trade: European powers established monopolies on key trade routes and commodities, limiting India's ability to trade with other regions and forcing them to buy and sell goods at unfavourable terms.

Heavy Taxation: The British, in particular, imposed heavy taxes on Indian farmers and industries, extracting revenue to support their colonial administration.

Deindustrialization:

India had a thriving textile industry that was renowned worldwide. However, British colonial policies systematically destroyed this industry to protect the interests of British manufacturers. Indian weavers were forced to buy British-made textiles, resulting in the collapse of the indigenous textile sector and widespread unemployment.

Landownership and Revenue Policies:

British landownership policies favoured the landlords and the colonial administration, often leading to the dispossession of farmers from their lands. The British implemented the **Zamindari** and **Ryotwari systems**, which exploited farmers and led to indebtedness.

Exploitative Labour Practices:

The British exploited Indian labourers, particularly in industries like agriculture, mining, and manufacturing. Indentured labourers from India were sent to work on plantations in various British colonies, including the Caribbean, Africa, and Southeast Asia.

Working conditions in factories and mines were often deplorable, with long hours, low wages, and minimal workers' rights.

Impact on Agriculture:

British policies favoured cash crops like indigo, opium, and jute, which were profitable for export but had negative consequences for Indian agriculture and food security.

The promotion of cash crops often led to food shortages and famines in India.

Cultural and Educational Suppression:

European colonizers often sought to undermine Indian culture and heritage, promoting Western education and values while devaluing indigenous languages and traditions.

This cultural exploitation aimed to create a sense of inferiority among the Indian population.

Divide and Rule:

The British employed a "divide and rule" strategy, exploiting existing religious and regional divisions to maintain control. This strategy exacerbated tensions between different communities and regions.

Imposition of Taxes and Tariffs:

British authorities imposed tariffs and taxes on Indian goods, making Indian products less competitive in international markets.

Export of Wealth:

Much of the wealth generated in India, whether through taxes, resource extraction, or trade, was exported to Europe, benefiting the European colonial powers at the expense of the Indian population.

Political Exploitation:

The British ruled India directly from 1858, exploiting its vast resources and strategic importance within the British Empire.

It's important to note that the exploitation of India during colonial rule had profound and lasting impacts on the country's social, economic, and political development. Many of these exploitative practices left a legacy that continues to influence modern India. After gaining independence in 1947, India faced the daunting task of overcoming the economic and social inequalities left by centuries of colonial exploitation.

"Understanding historical revolutions"

The French Revolution

The French Revolution, which occurred between 1789 and 1799, had a multitude of interconnected causes that contributed to its outbreak. These causes can be broadly categorized into the following:

Social Inequality: France in the late 18th century was characterized by significant social inequality. The society was divided into three estates: **the clergy, the nobility, and the common people (the Third Estate).** The clergy and nobility enjoyed various privileges and exemptions from taxation, while the common people bore the brunt of the tax burden.

Financial Crisis: France faced a severe financial crisis due to extravagant spending by the monarchy, costly wars (especially the American Revolutionary War), and a regressive tax system. The state was nearly bankrupt, and attempts to reform the fiscal system faced resistance from the privileged classes.

Intellectual Enlightenment: Enlightenment ideas, which emphasized r**eason, liberty, and equality,** had gained popularity in France. Prominent philosophers like **Voltaire, Rousseau, and Montesquieu** had a significant influence on public opinion, challenging the traditional authority of the monarchy and the Church.

Ineffectual Monarchy: King Louis XVI and his queen, Marie Antoinette, were seen as ineffective rulers. Their perceived extravagance and poor governance undermined the monarchy's legitimacy.

Food Shortages: Poor harvests in the late 1780s led to widespread food shortages and rising bread prices. This exacerbated the suffering of the common people and fuelled discontent.

Fiscal Reforms: Attempts by the government to address the financial crisis, such as the convening of the Estates-General in 1789 and proposed tax reforms, led to demands for political representation and a constitutional monarchy.

Political Radicalization: As the Estates-General transformed into the National Assembly in 1789, the political climate became increasingly radical. The Third Estate, representing commoners, formed the National Assembly and declared itself the legitimate government of France.

Storming of the Bastille: The symbolic event that marked the beginning of the revolution occurred on July 14, 1789, when a Parisian mob stormed the Bastille, a royal prison, in search of weapons and to protest against royal tyranny.

Spread of Revolutionary Ideas: The revolutionary fervour quickly spread throughout France and was fuelled by the publication of key revolutionary documents like the **Declaration of the Rights of Man and of the Citizen.**

Foreign Involvement: As the revolution progressed, it faced opposition from other European monarchies who feared the spread of revolutionary ideals. This led to the outbreak of wars, further destabilizing France.

These causes, among others, created a volatile and explosive atmosphere in France, ultimately leading to a series of events that resulted in the **overthrow of the monarchy, the Reign of Terror, and the rise of Napoleon Bonaparte.** The French Revolution had a profound impact on France and the world, influencing subsequent revolutionary movements and political developments

The American Revolution

The American Revolution, which occurred between 1775 and 1783, was primarily driven by a combination of political, economic, and ideological factors that led the American colonists to seek independence from British rule. Some of the key reasons for the American Revolution include:

Taxation without Representation: One of the most well-known slogans of the American Revolution was,"No taxation without representation." The American colonists believed that they were being unfairly taxed by the British government without having a say in the policies and decisions that affected them. **TheSugar Act (1764), Stamp Act (1765), Townshend Acts (1767),** and other taxes imposed by the British Parliament were met with resistance from the colonists.

Trade Restrictions: The British government imposed various trade restrictions and regulations on the American colonies, such as the **Navigation Acts,** which limited colonial trade with countries other than Britain. These restrictions hampered the economic interests of the colonists and hindered their ability to engage in free trade.

British Military Presence: The presence of British troops in the American colonies, particularly in the aftermath of the French and Indian War (1754-1763), created tensions. The **Quartering Act of 1765** required colonists to house and feed British soldiers, which was resented by many.

Ideological Influences: Enlightenment ideas, particularly those of thinkers like **John Locke, Montesquieu and Voltaire,** played a significant role in shaping the American revolutionary thought. These ideas emphasized concepts of natural rights, individual liberty, and the idea that government should derive its authority from the consent of the governed.

Incidents and Conflicts: Events like t**he Boston Massacre (1770) and the Boston Tea Party (1773)** further heightened tensions between the American colonists and the British government. These incidents demonstrated the willingness of some colonists to resist British authority.

Continental Congress: The convening of the **Continental Congress in 1774** brought together representatives from the American colonies to address their grievances and discuss a unified response to British policies. The **First Continental Congress (1774)** and the **Second Continental Congress (1775)** were instrumental in coordinating resistance efforts.

Military Conflict: The outbreak of open hostilities at the **Battles of Lexington** and **Concord** in April 1775 marked the beginning of the armed conflict between American colonial forces and British troops. This armed confrontation further galvanized the colonists' desire for independence.

Common Cause: As the conflict escalated, more colonists began to rally around the idea of independence and self-governance. Thomas Paine's pamphlet "Common Sense" (1776) played a pivotal role in advocating for independence and convincing many colonists of the need to break away from British rule.

Foreign Support: The American colonists received support from foreign powers, most notably France, which provided military assistance and recognized American independence in 1778. This assistance bolstered the American cause.

These factors, among others, converged to ignite the American Revolution, ultimately leading to the **Declaration of Independence** in 1776 and the subsequent establishment of the United States as an independent nation. The American Revolution had a profound impact on the course of world history, inspiring other independence movements and shaping the principles of democracy and individual rights.

The Russian Revolution

The Russian Revolution, which took place in 1917, was a complex and multifaceted event driven by a combination of political, economic, social, and ideological factors. The revolution resulted in the overthrow of the Russian monarchy and the establishment of a communist government under the leadership of the Bolshevik Party. Some of the key reasons for the Russian Revolution include:

World War I: Russia's involvement in World War I placed an enormous strain on the country's resources and manpower. The war effort led to widespread food shortages, inflation, and military failures, which exacerbated social and economic discontent among the Russian population.

Economic Issues: Russia's economy was in a state of crisis. The country faced industrialization challenges, anagrarian society with widespread poverty, and a lack of land reform, which left many peasants landless and discontented. Economic inequality was widespread, with a small elite holding a disproportionate share of wealth and power.

Autocratic Rule: Tsar Nicholas II, the last Russian monarch, ruled autocratically and resisted calls for political reform. His government was seen as corrupt and out of touch with the needs and desires of the Russian people. Dissatisfaction with the autocracy had been building for decades.

Political Opposition: Various political and revolutionary groups had been organizing and agitating for change for years. The **Russian Social Democratic Labour Party**, which later split into Bolsheviks and Mensheviks, was one of the prominent revolutionary organizations. Other groups, such as the Socialist Revolutionaries, also played a role.

February Revolution (1917): The initial phase of the Russian Revolution, known as the **February Revolution,** began with spontaneous protests and strikes in Petrograd (now St. Petersburg) in February (Julian calendar) 1917. These demonstrations were sparked by food shortages, dissatisfaction with the war, and general discontent with the government. Soldiers, workers, and civilians joined in the protests, leading to the abdication of Tsar Nicholas II on March 2, 1917.

Provisional Government: Following the abdication of the Tsar, a Provisional Government was established. However, it faced numerous challenges, including its inability to address Russia's pressing issues, particularly the ongoing war.

October Revolution (1917): The Bolshevik Party, led by Vladimir Lenin, took advantage of the dissatisfaction with the Provisional Government and seized power in Petrograd in October (Julian calendar; November in the Gregorian calendar) 1917. This event is known as the **October Revolution.** The Bolsheviks promised "Peace,

Land, and Bread," appealing to the desires of the war-weary, land-hungry peasants and urban workers.

Civil War: The October Revolution led to a civil war in Russia, with various factions and foreign powers supporting different sides. The **Bolshevik Red Army** ultimately emerged victorious, consolidating Bolshevik rule and leading to the establishment of the **Russian Soviet Federative Socialist Republic.**

The Russian Revolution had profound and far-reaching consequences, including the establishment of the Soviet Union as a communist state under Bolshevik control. It transformed Russia from an autocratic monarchy into a socialist state, dramatically altering the course of Russian and world history.

The Haiti Revolution

The Haitian Revolution was a significant and ground-breaking event that occurred between 1791 and 1804 in the French colony of Saint-Domingue, located on the western part of the island of Hispaniola (present-day Haiti and the Dominican Republic). It was one of the most successful slave revolts in history and resulted in the establishment of the independent nation of Haiti. The revolution had several key factors and phases:

Slavery and Brutal Conditions: Saint-Domingue was a highly profitable French colony primarily reliant on sugar, coffee, and indigo production. The colony's prosperity was built on the backs of enslaved Africans who were subjected to brutal and inhumane conditions, leading to widespread suffering and death.

Influence of Enlightenment Ideals: Enlightenment ideas, including concepts of liberty, equality, and fraternity, began to influence some of the free people of colour and enslaved Africans in Saint-Domingue. These ideas inspired resistance against the oppressive colonial system.

1791 Slave Revolt: The revolution began in August 1791 when enslaved Africans in the northern part of the colony, inspired by the French Revolution and motivated by their desire for freedom and equal rights, initiated a massive uprising. This revolt, led by figures like **Toussaint Louverture, Jean-Jacques Dessalines, and Henri Christophe,** marked the start of a protracted struggle for independence.

Complex Alliances: Over the course of the revolution, alliances shifted among various groups, including enslaved Africans, free people of colour, white colonists, and foreign powers. At different times, different groups sought to secure their interests and control over the colony.

Elimination of Slavery: As the revolution progressed, leaders like Toussaint Louverture and later Jean-Jacques Dessalines took steps to eliminate slavery and grant freedom to enslaved people. In 1804, Dessalines declared the abolition of slavery in the newly independent nation of Haiti.

Independence Declared: On January 1, 1804, Haiti officially declared its independence from France, becoming the first independent black republic in the Western Hemisphere. The nation was renamed Haiti, a name derived from the indigenous Taíno language.

International Consequences: Haiti's successful revolution had profound international consequences. It challenged the institution of slavery and inspired enslaved people elsewhere to seek their freedom. However, it also faced hostility from European powers and trade embargoes from countries like France and the United States.

Complex Legacy: While the Haitian Revolution achieved freedom from colonial rule and slavery, it also left the nation with significant challenges, including economic devastation and political instability. Haiti's path to stability and prosperity has been tumultuous, marked by political upheaval and external pressures.

The Haitian Revolution is a critical event in the history of both Haiti and the broader struggle for human rights and equality. It serves as a symbol of resistance to oppression and a testament to the enduring spirit of those who fought for freedom and justice.

The Chinese Revolution

The term "Chinese Revolution" typically refers to a series of political, social, and economic upheavals that occurred in China during the 20th century. These revolutions fundamentally transformed China from a Qing Dynasty ruled monarchy into a communist state under the Chinese Communist Party (CCP). There were several key phases and events within the Chinese Revolution:

Xinhai Revolution (1911-1912):

This revolution marked the overthrow of the **Qing Dynasty,** which had ruled China for over two centuries.

Led by various anti-Qing revolutionary groups, the **Xinhai Revolution** resulted in the abdication of the last Qing emperor, Puyi, and the establishment of the Republic of China, with **Sun Yat-sen** as its provisional president.

Warlord Era (1916-1928):

After the fall of the Qing Dynasty, China was plagued by internal strife as various regional warlords vied for power.

This period was characterized by political instability, civil wars, and a lack of central authority.

Northern Expedition (1926-1928):

The Northern Expedition was a military campaign led by the Chinese Nationalist Party (Kuomintang or KMT) with the aim of reunifying China and ending the warlord era.

The KMT, under Chiang Kai-shek's leadership, achieved significant success during this campaign, taking control of much of northern China.

Chinese Civil War (1927-1950):

The Chinese Civil War was a protracted conflict between the KMT and the CCP, with both parties vying for control of China.

The CCP, led by Mao Zedong, gradually gained strength and support, especially among peasants, and eventually defeated the KMT, which retreated to Taiwan in 1949.

Founding of the People's Republic of China (1949):

On October 1, 1949, Mao Zedong proclaimed the establishment of the People's Republic of China (PRC) in Beijing.

This marked the end of the Chinese Civil War and the beginning of communist rule in mainland China.

Great Leap Forward (1958-1962):

Under Mao's leadership, the PRC initiated the **Great Leap Forward,** an ambitious economic and social campaign aimed at rapidly transforming China into an industrialized communist state.

The campaign, which included the formation of communes, mass mobilization, and collectivization, resulted in economic hardship, famine, and the deaths of millions.

Cultural Revolution (1966-1976):

The **Cultural Revolution** was a radical political and social movement launched by Mao to purge the Communist Party of perceived capitalist and traditionalist influences.

It led to widespread political persecution, the destruction of cultural artefacts, and the displacement of millions.

Post-Mao Reforms (Late 1970s onward):

After Mao's death in 1976, China embarked on a series of economic reforms under the leadership of Deng Xiaoping.

These reforms, known as "Socialism with Chinese Characteristics," introduced market-oriented policies, liberalized the economy, and led to rapid economic growth.

The Chinese Revolution resulted in the establishment of the **People's Republic of China,** which remains in power today. It dramatically reshaped Chinese society, politics, and the economy, moving from a feudal monarchy to a communist state and eventually adopting elements of a market economy while maintaining strict political control under the CCP. The Chinese Revolution had profound domestic and global implications, influencing geo-politics in Asia and the world.

India's Problem

India faces a wide range of challenges and problems across various sectors. These issues are complex and often interrelated. Here are some of the significant problems faced by India:

Poverty and Income Inequality: India has a high level of income inequality, with a significant portion of the population living in poverty. While there has been progress in reducing poverty, a large number of people still struggle to access basic necessities.

Unemployment: High levels of unemployment, particularly among the youth, are a persistent issue. The mismatch between skills and job opportunities is a contributing factor.

Education: While India has made strides in expanding access to education, there are still challenges in providing quality education, especially in rural areas. Dropout rates remain high, and there are disparities in educational outcomes.

Healthcare: Access to quality healthcare services varies widely across India. Many people lack access to affordable healthcare, and the country faces health challenges such as malnutrition, inadequate sanitation, and non-communicable diseases.

Infrastructure: Infrastructure development, including transportation, electricity, and urban infrastructure, is a priority. Inadequate infrastructure hampers economic growth and quality of life.

Corruption: Corruption remains a significant problem in India, affecting various aspects of public life, including government services, business, and law enforcement.

Political and Administrative Reforms: India's bureaucracy can be slow and inefficient, hindering economic development and the ease of doing business. There is an ongoing need for administrative and political reforms.

Agriculture: Despite being a major source of employment, agriculture faces challenges such as low productivity, fragmented landholdings, and vulnerability to climate change.

Water Management: India faces issues related to water scarcity, water pollution, and inadequate water management infrastructure.

Environmental Concerns: Pollution, deforestation, and the depletion of natural resources are environmental challenges that need addressing. India is particularly vulnerable to the impacts of climate change.

Security Concerns: India faces various security challenges, including border disputes, terrorism, and internal conflicts in certain regions.

Social Issues: Issues such as gender inequality, caste-based discrimination, and communal tensions remain a challenge to social harmony and inclusivity.

Population Growth: India's population continues to grow, posing challenges in terms of providing basic services, employment, and resource management.

Digital Divide: While India has made progress in digital technology, there is still a significant digital divide, with many lacking access to the internet and digital services.

Public Health Crises: The COVID-19 pandemic has highlighted vulnerabilities in India's healthcare infrastructure and the need for robust healthcare systems and pandemic preparedness.

Religious tensions in India have been a recurring issue for many years, and they stem from a complex mix of historical, political, social, and economic factors. India is a diverse country with a rich tapestry of religions, including Hinduism, Islam, Christianity, Sikhism, Buddhism, and others. The majority of the population is Hindu, followed by significant Muslim, Christian, Sikh, and other religious communities. Here are some key aspects of religious tensions in India:

Historical Context: India has a long history of religious diversity and coexistence, but it has also experienced periods of religious conflict and tensions. Historical events such as the partition of India in 1947, which led to the creation of Pakistan, were marked by communal violence and the displacement of millions along religious lines.

Communal Riots: India has witnessed sporadic communal riots and violence between religious communities, particularly Hindus and Muslims. These clashes are often triggered by local disputes, religious festivals, or political factors and can result in loss of life and property.

Polarization: Religious and communal polarization has been a growing concern in recent years. Politicians and political parties have at times used religious identity and sentiments for electoral gains, which can exacerbate tensions.

Religious Conversion: Accusations of forced or fraudulent religious conversions have led to tensions in some areas. These allegations often revolve around religious minority communities, especially Christians and Muslims.

Cultural and Symbolic Disputes: Disputes over religious symbols, places of worship, and cultural practices can escalate into major controversies and tensions. For example, the Ayodhya dispute over the Babri Masjid/Ram Janmabhoomi site was a significant and long-standing religious and political issue.

Laws and Policies: Some laws and policies related to religion have been contentious. The debate over religious conversions, cow protection laws, and the status of religious minorities can lead to disagreements and tensions.

Social Media and Disinformation: The spread of false information and hate speech on social media has exacerbated religious tensions in India. Misinformation and rumours have led to incidents of violence.

Freedom of Religion: Concerns have been raised about the freedom of religion in India. Critics argue that laws in some states restrict religious conversions and can be used to target religious minorities.

Inter-faith Marriages: Inter-faith marriages have been a subject of controversy and tension, with some groups opposing them on religious or cultural grounds.

It's important to note that religious tensions in India are not uniform across the country. Different regions may experience varying levels of tension, and many parts of India continue to exemplify religious harmony and peaceful coexistence among various communities. Moreover, many individuals and organizations in India work actively to promote religious tolerance, inter-faith dialogue, and social harmony.

The Indian government, civil society, and religious leaders play crucial roles in addressing and mitigating religious tensions. Public awareness campaigns, legal measures, and efforts to promote cultural and religious understanding are ongoing initiatives aimed at fostering communal harmony in India.

We live in the modern age physically, but mentally and psychologically, we seem to be stuck in the old stone age, a legacy of British colonial occupation in India and around the world. India has been and continues to be under neurotic conditions. We are reluctant to acknowledge our flaws, holding onto our lies even when we know they are false, all the while suffering from these deceptions.

If we desire change, it must begin within ourselves. We cannot rely on leaders to liberate us; they can inspire us, but the power to effect change lies within us.

Where should I start when addressing the drawbacks, we face as a country on the global stage? India is in turmoil, and we must acknowledge that. It's not external injury, but internal injury. India is suffering from ignorance, cowardice, idleness, laziness, and weakness. We must muster the courage to confront these issues.

We should fight against cowardice, idleness, laziness, and weakness. Once we can defend ourselves from exploitation, we should then protect our fellow citizens who are being exploited. We must adhere to the rules of the system, for knowledge is power and can free us from fear.

India faces numerous challenges, including a vicious cycle of corruption and suppression. For example, industrialists exploit labourers, the government exploits industrialists, and higher-caste individuals exploit lower-caste people. This exploitation extends even within the lower-caste community. Poor people often fall victim to political exploitation, selling their votes to the highest-bidding politicians. In the end, the entire system is exploited by politicians. Foreign investors also exploit uneducated, gullible politicians. This cycle perpetuates a society of subjugation and dependency on these politicians and the system.

To break this cycle, we should begin by emancipating labourers and peasants, providing them with minimum wages, labour rights, free education, and healthcare. Once we have emancipated labourers and peasants, industrialists will operate with a clearer conscience and have the strength to demand benefits from the government, as they will be living righteously with self-respect. When industrialists and labourers work together harmoniously, society can demand development from any government.

As we break this cycle of abuse and suppression, the politicians will either have to change their ways or yield to the people's demands for development. Instead of dwelling on societal diversity, which often divides us, we must unite for the betterment of our society and living standards.

Once we are equals, we can address external threats. We are currently at the bottom of the global human chain, facing tests and challenges that require us to build ourselves and our country. We shall overcome the issues plaguing our society and eliminate anything that impedes the growth and development of our nation and its people.

Our main drawbacks include inequality, discrimination, casteism, religious bias, poverty, ignorance, and a lack of education and awareness. We will address these shortcomings through mass education, love, free healthcare, free education, and jobs with minimum wages for all.

We will work together to build our nation and unite against divisive forces based on caste and religion. There should be unity among all citizens of the same country.

Once we overcome idleness, laziness, and weakness, we must discipline ourselves and work for the state's welfare. We will fill the state's treasury and then focus on developing infrastructure and rural areas. To combat overpopulation in major cities, we will construct self-sustaining Tier 2 cities 250 kilometres from the major urban centres.

During this time, we will also upgrade the transportation systems and communication networks in major cities.

To further address issues related to dense population and employment, we will tackle environmental and waste management problems. Ten recycling plants will be established outside the city, and waste will be recycled for road construction and government projects. Toilets and bins will be readily available on every street corner in India.

By creating Tier 2 cities, we will alleviate problems related to overpopulation, traffic congestion, employment, infrastructure, garbage, and pollution.

Once we have resolved these issues, we will provide training in traffic rules and regulations, as well as personal information about first aid, CPR, and fire escape procedures, to all drivers. These skills should be mandatory for all drivers, including taxi, auto, Ola, Uber, bus, tempo, and heavy-duty vehicle operators.

Moreover, we must educate first responders, including police, traffic police, doctors, firefighters, nurses, lawyers, and judges, on the importance of their duties. It should be mandatory for them to adhere to rules and regulations without hesitation, as they represent the government. All government employees should be treated with mutual respect and held to high standards.

Effective communication strategies should be implemented to educate the masses on appropriate behaviour based on different settings and situations. Sex education, contraception, physical education, and meditation should be included in the curriculum from the age of 11.

Education about civilization and their governance is essential, including Oriental, Egyptian, Indian, Roman, and Greek philosophies. Knowledge about the formation of administrative societies, such as democracy, socialism, communism, imperialism, feudalism, oligarchy, aristocracy, and meritocracy, should be imparted from the age of 13.

Religion and caste systems should be removed from schools and colleges, as the government is responsible for delivering free education to all, regardless of their caste or religion. All educational institutions must maintain caste and religion neutrality. Schools and colleges based on caste and religion should be renamed after freedom fighters and trees, eliminating any traces of casteism and religious bias.

Roads and footpaths should be well-maintained to ensure the safety of pedestrians and motorists. Regular cleaning should be conducted from 3 am to 6 am to accommodate office and school-goers. The construction of new layouts and plot sales in major cities should cease to prevent uncontrolled urban expansion. Instead, we will focus on developing self-sustaining cities.

To address issues related to footpaths, traffic, roads, commuters, first responders, and the cleanliness of roads and footpaths, we must develop parks and parking lots. These developments will create space for recreational activities and provide professional sports facilities for students. Every child should be encouraged to participate in sports.

Education and healthcare systems will be provided free to every child born in India, ensuring equality for all. Hospitals will be overseen by the government, and every Indian citizen will receive health insurance, enabling access to treatment and medicine in any hospital.

Building a society, city, state, and country is a challenging task, but it is not impossible. We will achieve it in the next five years by uniting as Indians to build our nation from the ground up. We are committed to changing any harmful systems and adapting them to the welfare of the present society and people.

We will break down barriers and build a united India. Jai Hind! Inquilab Zindabad!

"Prerequisites for Advancing India's Development"

Infrastructure Development: Investing in infrastructure such as roads, highways, railways, ports, and urban infrastructure is crucial for economic growth. Improved infrastructure facilitates trade, reduces transportation costs, and enhances overall productivity.

Education and Skill Development: Ensuring access to quality education and vocational training is essential for human capital development. India needs to address issues like low literacy rates, educational quality disparities, and skill mismatches in the job market.

Healthcare: Accessible and affordable healthcare services are essential for the well-being of the population. India should invest in healthcare infrastructure, disease prevention, and healthcare delivery systems.

Economic Diversification: Reducing the country's dependence on agriculture and promoting economic diversification into manufacturing and services sectors can create more jobs and stimulate economic growth.

Agricultural Reforms: Improving agricultural productivity, land reforms, and supporting small-scale farmers are vital for food security and rural development.

Ease of Doing Business: Simplifying regulations, reducing bureaucracy, and improving the ease of doing business can attract domestic and foreign investments, which can stimulate economic growth.

Financial Inclusion: Expanding access to financial services, including banking and credit facilities, can empower individuals and businesses, especially in rural areas.

Innovation and Technology: Investing in research and development, fostering innovation, and adopting emerging technologies can enhance competitiveness and productivity.

Environmental Sustainability: Balancing economic growth with environmental protection is essential. Sustainable practices and policies are necessary to address issues like air and water pollution, deforestation, and climate change.

Social Welfare: Implementing social safety nets, poverty alleviation programs, and affirmative action policies can help reduce income inequality and improve living standards for marginalized populations.

Governance and Corruption: Strengthening governance, transparency, and anti-corruption measures can improve the effectiveness of public institutions and boost investor confidence.

Infrastructure Connectivity: Developing digital infrastructure, including internet access, can enhance communication, connectivity, and access to information.

Urbanization and Housing: Addressing the challenges of rapid urbanization, including slum development and affordable housing, is critical for sustainable urban growth.

Foreign Direct Investment: Attracting foreign investment can provide access to capital, technology, and markets. Creating a favourable investment climate is essential for this purpose.

Social Harmony: Promoting social harmony, tolerance, and religious and cultural diversity is essential for social stability and national development.

A holistic approach, careful planning, and consistent implementation of policies are essential to achieving sustainable development in India.

Corruption Problem in India

Fixing the problem of corruption in India is a complex and long-term endeavour that requires a combination of legal, institutional, cultural, and societal changes. Corruption can undermine economic development, erode public trust, and hinder the effectiveness of government institutions. Here are some strategies and approaches that can help address corruption in India:

Strengthen Anti-Corruption Laws and Enforcement:

- Enhance existing anti-corruption laws and regulations to make them more comprehensive and effective.
- Establish specialized anti-corruption agencies with sufficient autonomy, resources, and authority to investigate and prosecute corruption cases.
- Ensure swift and impartial justice in corruption cases, with appropriate penalties for offenders.

Transparency and Accountability:

- Promote transparency in government operations by implementing measures such as **right to information (RTI)** laws.
- Encourage government agencies to disclose information about their activities, budgets, and decision-making processes.
- Implement financial and performance audits to hold public officials accountable for their actions.

Whistleblower Protection:

- Establish mechanisms to protect whistle-blowers who report corruption.

- Ensure that individuals who expose corruption are not subject to retaliation.

E-Governance and Digital Services:

- Promote e-governance and the use of technology to reduce human interface and opportunities for corruption.
- Implement online services for government transactions and interactions to minimize discretionary powers of officials.

Promote a Culture of Ethics:

- Foster a culture of ethics and integrity through education and awareness programs.
- Encourage ethical behaviour and values within public and private institutions.

Political Reform:

- Implement electoral reforms to reduce the influence of money in politics.
- Strengthen campaign finance regulations to enhance transparency and accountability in political funding.

Strengthen Civil Society and Media:

- Support civil society organizations and the media in their role as watchdogs and advocates for accountability.
- Encourage investigative journalism to expose corruption cases.

International Cooperation:

Collaborate with international organizations and foreign governments to combat cross-border corruption, including money laundering and bribery in international business transactions.

Whistle-blower Incentives:

Consider providing financial incentives to whistle-blowers who provide information leading to successful corruption prosecutions.

Public Awareness and Education:

- Conduct public awareness campaigns to educate citizens about the negative consequences of corruption and their role in preventing it.
- Integrate anti-corruption education into school curricula.

Civil Service Reforms:

- Improve recruitment processes, training, and working conditions for civil servants to reduce the temptation of corruption.
- Promote professionalism and merit-based appointments within the bureaucracy.

Asset Declaration:

- Require public officials to declare their assets and sources of income regularly, and enforce compliance.
- Establish mechanisms to verify asset declarations and identify discrepancies.

Corporate Governance and Business Ethics:

- Encourage businesses to adopt strong corporate governance practices and ethical codes of conduct.
- Promote responsible business behaviour and discourage corrupt practices in the private sector.

Community Engagement:

- Involve communities in local decision-making processes to reduce corruption at the grassroots level.
- Empower local bodies and panchayats with sufficient resources and authority.

Continual Monitoring and Evaluation:

- Regularly assess the effectiveness of anti-corruption measures and adjust strategies based on the findings.

Addressing corruption in India is a long-term process that requires commitment from all segments of society, from government officials and civil society organizations to citizens themselves. It's important to recognize that progress may be gradual, but sustained efforts to combat corruption can lead to positive change over time.

"India: A Nation Where a Significant Portion of the Population Adheres to a 'Slave Morality' (Exploring with Historical Context)"

Understanding Indian Minds

"India is a land where the majority of the people have historically lived under the influence of slave morality. This concept can be understood within the context of India's history, where various forms of social, cultural, and political hierarchies have often relegated the masses to subservient roles. The idea of 'slave morality' stems from the works of philosophers like Friedrich Nietzsche, who discussed how oppressed or marginalized groups in society might develop values and morals that reflect their oppressed status. In India, the caste system, colonial rule, and various socio-economic disparities have contributed to the prevalence of such a morality, where the subjugated often accept their fate and find moral virtue in their endurance and humility. This complex historical and cultural backdrop has influenced the values and perspectives of many in the Indian society."

Buddhism is supposed to have been a reaction against Hinduism and its system of social stratification. Yet, it is interesting that in Tibet, Korea, Japan and, possibly, China there has existed, and still exists to some extent, a well-developed caste system with its characteristic features of endogamy, pollution and hierarchy.

EVERY elevation of the type "man," has hitherto been the work of a Brahmin society and so it will always be--a society believing in a long scale of gradations of Caste and differences of worth among human beings, and requiring slavery in some form or other. Without the PATHOS OF DISTANCE, such as grows out of the incarnated difference of castes, out of the constant out-looking and down-looking of the ruling caste on subordinates and instruments, and out of their equally constant practice of obeying and commanding, of keeping down and keeping at a distance--that other more mysterious pathos could never have arisen, the longing for an ever new widening of distance within the soul itself, the formation of ever higher, rarer, further, more extended, more comprehensive states, in short, just the elevation of the type "man," the continued "self-surmounting of man," to use a moral formula in a super moral sense.

To be sure, one must not resign oneself to any humanitarian illusions about the history of the origin of a Brahmin society (that is to say, of the preliminary condition for the elevation of the type "man"): the truth is hard. Let us acknowledge unprejudiced how every higher civilization hitherto has ORIGINATED! Men with a still natural nature, barbarians in every terrible sense of the word, men of prey, still in possession of unbroken strength of will and desire for power (Kshatriya), threw themselves upon weaker, more moral, more peaceful races (perhaps trading or cattle-rearing communities in India), or upon old mellow civilizations (British on India) in which the final vital force was flickering out in brilliant fireworks of wit and depravity. At the commencement, the noble caste was always the barbarian caste: their superiority did not consist first of all in their physical, but in their psychical power--they were more COMPLETE men (which at every point also implies the same as "more complete beasts"). In this case power from Kshatriyas was taken over by Brahmins.

Corruption--as the indication that anarchy threatens to break out among the instincts, and that the foundation of the emotions, called "life," is convulsed--is something radically different according to the organization in which it manifests itself. When, for instance, an aristocracy like that of France at the beginning of the Revolution, flung away its privileges with sublime disgust and sacrificed itself to an excess of its moral sentiments, it was corruption: --it was really only the closing act of the corruption which had existed for centuries, by virtue of which that aristocracy had abdicated step by step its lordly prerogatives and lowered itself to a FUNCTION of royalty (in the end even to its decoration and parade-dress).

The essential thing, however, in a good and healthy aristocracy is that it should not regard itself as a function either of the kingship or the commonwealth, but as the SIGNIFICANCE and highest justification thereof--that it should therefore accept with a good conscience the sacrifice of a legion of individuals, who, FOR ITS SAKE, must be suppressed and reduced to imperfect men, to slaves and instruments. Its fundamental belief must be precisely that society is NOT allowed to exist for its own sake, but only as a foundation and scaffolding, by means of which a select class of beings may be able to elevate themselves to their higher duties, and in general to a higher EXISTENCE: like those sun-seeking climbing plants in Java--they are called Sipo Matador,-- which encircle an oak so long and so often with their arms, until at last, high above it, but supported by it, they can unfold their tops in the open light, and exhibit their happiness.

To refrain mutually from injury, from violence, from exploitation, and put one's will on a par with that of others: this may result in a certain rough sense in good conduct among individuals when the necessary conditions are given (namely, the actual similarity of the individuals in amount of force and degree of worth, and their co-relation within one organization).

As soon, however, as one wished to take this principle more generally, and if possible even as the FUNDAMENTAL PRINCIPLE OF SOCIETY, it would immediately disclose what it really is--namely, a Will to the DENIAL of life, a principle of dissolution and decay. Here one must think profoundly to the very basis and resist all sentimental weakness: life itself is ESSENTIALLY appropriation, injury, conquest of the strange and weak, suppression, severity, obtrusion of peculiar forms, incorporation, and at the least, putting it mildest, exploitation; --but why should one for ever use precisely these words on which for ages a disparaging purpose has been stamped? Even the organization within which, as was previously supposed, the individuals treat each other as equal--it takes place in every healthy aristocracy--must itself, if it be a living and not a dying organization, do all that towards other bodies, which the individuals within it refrain from doing to each other it will have to be the incarnated Will to Power, it will endeavor to grow, to gain ground, attract to itself and acquire ascendancy--not owing to any morality or immorality, but because it LIVES, and because life IS precisely Will to Power. On no point, however, is the ordinary consciousness of Indians more unwilling to be corrected than on this matter, people now rave everywhere, even under the guise of science, about coming conditions of society in which "the exploiting character" is to be absent--that sounds to my ears as if they promised to invent a mode of life which should refrain from all organic functions. "Exploitation" does not belong to a depraved, or imperfect and primitive society it belongs to the nature of the living being as a primary organic function, it is a consequence of the intrinsic Will to Power, which is precisely the Will to Life--Granting that as a theory is a novelty--as a reality it is the FUNDAMENTAL FACT of all history. Let us so far be honest towards ourselves!

In a tour through the many finer and coarser moralities which have hitherto prevailed or still prevail on earth, I found certain traits recurring regularly together, and connected with one another, until finally two primary types revealed themselves to me, and a radical distinction was brought to light.

MASTER-MORALITY and SLAVE-MORALITY,

There is **MASTER-MORALITY and SLAVE-MORALITY,** --I would at once add, however, that in all higher and mixed civilizations, there are also attempts at the reconciliation of the two moralities, but one oftener still finds the confusion and mutual misunderstanding of them, indeed sometimes their close juxtaposition--even in the same man, within one soul. The distinctions of moral values have either originated in a ruling caste (Higher castes/Varna), pleasantly conscious of being different from the ruled--or among the ruled class, the slaves and dependents of all sorts (lower castes). In the first case, when it is the rulers who determine the conception "good," it is the exalted, proud disposition which is regarded as the distinguishing feature, and that which determines the order of rank. The noble type of man separates from himself the beings in whom the opposite of this exalted, proud disposition displays itself if he despises them. Let it at once be noted that in this first kind of morality the antithesis "good" and "bad" means practically the same as "noble" and "despicable."

--the antithesis "good" and "EVIL" is of a different origin. The cowardly, the timid, the insignificant, and those thinking merely of narrow utility are despised; moreover, also, the distrustful, with their constrained glances, the self-abasing, the dog-like kind of men who let themselves be abused, the mendicant flatterers, and above all the liars: --it is a fundamental belief of all higher class people that the common people are untruthful.

"We truthful ones"--the nobility in ancient Greece called themselves. It is obvious that everywhere the designations of moral value were at first applied to MEN; and were only derivatively and at a later period applied to ACTIONS; it is a gross mistake, therefore, when historians of morals start with questions like, "Why have sympathetic actions been praised?" The noble type of man regards HIMSELF as a determiner of values; he does not require to be approved of; he passes the judgment: "What is injurious to me is injurious in itself;" he knows that it is he himself only who confers honor on things; he is a CREATOR OF VALUES. He honors whatever he recognizes in himself: such morality equals self-glorification. In the foreground there is the feeling of plenitude, of power, which seeks to overflow, the happiness of high tension, the consciousness of a wealth which would fain give and bestow: --the noble man also helps the unfortunate, but not--or scarcely--out of pity, but rather from an impulse generated by the super-abundance of power. The noble man honors in himself the powerful one, him also who has power over himself, who knows how to speak and how to keep silence, who takes pleasure in subjecting himself to severity and hardness, and has reverence for all that is severe and hard. "Wotan placed a hard heart in my breast," says an old Scandinavian Saga: it is thus rightly expressed from the soul of a proud Viking. Such a type of man is even proud of not being made for sympathy; the hero of the Saga therefore adds warningly: "He who has not a hard heart when young, will never have one." The noble and brave who think thus are the furthest removed from the morality which sees precisely in sympathy, or in acting for the good of others, or in DESINTERESSEMENT, the characteristic of the moral; faith in oneself, pride in oneself, a radical enmity and irony towards "selflessness," belong as definitely to noble morality, as do a careless scorn and precaution in presence of sympathy and the "warm heart."--It is the powerful who KNOW how to honor, it is their art, their domain for invention. The profound reverence for age and for tradition--all law rests on this double reverence, -- the belief and prejudice in favor of ancestors and unfavorable to newcomers, is typical in the morality of the powerful; and if, reversely, men of "modern ideas" believe almost instinctively in "progress" and the "future," and are more and more lacking in respect for old age, the ignoble origin of these "ideas" has complacently betrayed itself thereby. A morality of the ruling class, however, is more especially foreign and irritating to present-day taste in the sternness of its principle that one has duties only to one's equals; that one may act towards beings of a lower rank, towards all that is foreign, just as seems good to one, or "as the heart desires," and in any case "beyond good and evil": it is here that sympathy and similar sentiments can have a place. The ability and obligation to exercise prolonged gratitude and prolonged revenge--both only within the circle of equals,-- artfulness in retaliation, RAFFINEMENT of the idea in friendship, a certain necessity to have enemies (as outlets for the emotions of envy, quarrelsomeness, arrogance--in fact, in order to be a good FRIEND): all these are typical characteristics of the noble morality, which, as has been pointed out, is not the morality of "modern ideas," and is therefore at present difficult to realize, and also to unearth and disclose.--It is otherwise with the second type of morality, SLAVE-MORALITY. Supposing that the abused, the oppressed, the suffering, the emancipated, the weary, and those uncertain of themselves should moralize, what will be the common element in their moral estimates? Probably a pessimistic suspicion with regard to the entire situation of man will find expression, perhaps a condemnation of man, together with his situation. The slave has an unfavorable eye for the virtues of the powerful; he has a skepticism and distrust, a REFINEMENT of distrust of everything "good" that is honored--he would fain persuade himself that the very happiness there is not genuine. On the other hand, THOSE qualities which serve to alleviate the existence of sufferers are brought into prominence and flooded with light; it is here that sympathy, the kind, helping hand, the warm heart, patience, diligence, humility, and friendliness attain to honor; for here these are the most useful qualities, and almost the only means of supporting the burden of existence. Slave-morality is essentially the morality of utility. Here is the seat of the origin of the famous antithesis "good" and "evil": -- power and dangerousness are assumed to reside in the evil, a certain dreadfulness, subtlety, and strength, which do not admit of being despised. According to slave-morality, therefore, the "evil" man arouses fear; according to master-morality, it is precisely the "good" man who arouses fear and seeks to arouse it, while the bad man is regarded as the despicable being. The contrast attains its maximum when, in accordance with the logical consequences of slave-morality, a shade of depreciation--it may be slight and well-intentioned--at last attaches itself to the "good" man of this morality; because, according to the servile mode of thought, the good man must in any case be the SAFE man: he is good-natured, easily deceived, perhaps a little stupid, un bonhomme. Everywhere that slave-morality gains the ascendancy, language shows a tendency to approximate the significations of the words "good" and "stupid."--A last fundamental difference: the desire for FREEDOM, the instinct for happiness and the refinements of the feeling of liberty belong as necessarily to slave-morals and morality, as artifice and enthusiasm in reverence and devotion are the regular symptoms of an aristocratic mode of thinking and estimating.—Hence, we can understand without further detail why love AS A PASSION--it is our Indian specialty--must absolutely be of noble origin; as is well known, its invention is due to the Provencal poet-cavaliers, those brilliant, ingenious men of the "Moguls," to whom India owes so much, and almost owes itself.

Vanity is one of the things which are perhaps most difficult for a noble man to understand: he will be tempted to deny it, where another kind of man thinks he sees it self-evidently. The problem for him is to represent to his mind, beings who seek to arouse a good opinion of themselves which they themselves do not possess--and consequently also do not "deserve,"--and who yet BELIEVE in this good opinion afterwards. This seems to him on the one hand, such bad taste and so self-disrespectful, and on the other hand, so grotesquely unreasonable, that he would like to consider vanity an exception, and is doubtful about it in most cases when it is spoken of. He will say, for instance: "I may be mistaken about my value, and on the other hand, may nevertheless demand that my value should be acknowledged by others precisely as I rate it: --that, however, is not vanity (but self-conceit, or, in most cases, that which is called 'humility,' and also 'modesty')." Or he will even say: "For many reasons I can delight in the good opinion of others, perhaps because I love and honor them, and rejoice in all their joys, perhaps also because their good opinion endorses and strengthens my belief in my own good opinion, perhaps because the good opinion of others, even in cases where I do not share it, is useful to me, or gives promise of usefulness: --all this, however, is not vanity." The man of noble character must first bring it home forcibly to his mind, especially with the aid of history, that, from time immemorial, in all social strata in any way dependent, the ordinary man WAS only that which he PASSED FOR: --not being at all accustomed to fix values, he did not assign even to himself any other value than that which his master assigned to him (it is the peculiar RIGHT OF MASTERS to create values). It may be looked upon as the result of an extraordinary atavism, that the ordinary man, even at present, is still always WAITING for an opinion about himself, and then instinctively submitting himself to it; yet by no means only to a "good" opinion, but also to a bad and unjust one (think, for instance, of the greater part of the self-appreciations and self-depreciations which believing women learn from their confessors, and which in general the believing Hindus learns from his Temple). In fact, conformably to the slow rise of the democratic social order (and its cause, the blending of the blood of masters and slaves), the originally noble and rare impulse of the masters to assign a value to themselves and to "think well" of themselves, will now be more and more encouraged and extended; but it has at all times an older, ampler, and more radically ingrained propensity opposed to it--and in the phenomenon of "vanity" this older propensity overmasters the younger. The vain person rejoices over EVERY good opinion which he hears about himself (quite apart from the point of view of its usefulness, and equally regardless of its truth or falsehood), just as he suffers from every bad opinion: for he subjects himself to both, he feels himself subjected to both, by that oldest instinct of subjection which breaks forth in him.--It is "the slave" in the vain man's blood, the remains of the slave's craftiness--and how much of the "slave" is still left in woman, for instance!--which seeks to SEDUCE to good opinions of itself; it is the slave, too, who immediately afterwards falls prostrate himself before these opinions, as though he had not called them forth.--And to repeat it again: vanity is an atavism.

A SPECIES originates, and a type becomes established and strong in the long struggle with essentially constant UNFAVOURABLE conditions. On the other hand, it is known by the experience of breeders that species which receive super-abundant nourishment, and in general a surplus of protection and care, immediately tend in the most marked way to develop variations, and are fertile in prodigies and monstrosities (also in monstrous vices) (Westerners, Australians, Brahmins and other higher castes). Now look at an aristocratic commonwealth, say the British, or Spanish, as a voluntary or involuntary contrivance for the purpose of REARING human beings; there are men beside one another, thrown upon their own resources, who want to make their species prevail, chiefly because they MUST prevail, or else run the terrible danger of being exterminated. The favor, the super-abundance, the protection is there lacking under which variations are fostered; the species needs itself as species, as something which, precisely by virtue of its hardness, its uniformity, and simplicity of structure, can in general prevail and make itself permanent in constant struggle with its neighbors, or with rebellious or rebellion-threatening vassals. The most varied experience teaches it what are the qualities to which it principally owes the fact that it still exists, in spite of all Gods and men, and has hitherto been victorious: these qualities it calls virtues, and these virtues alone develops to maturity. It does so with severity, indeed it desires severity; every higher morality is intolerant in the education of youth, in the control of women, in the marriage customs, in the relations of old and young, in the penal laws (which have an eye only for the degenerating): it counts intolerance itself among the virtues, under the name of "justice." A type with few, but very marked features, a species of severe, warlike, wisely silent, reserved, and reticent men (and as such, with the most delicate sensibility for the charm and nuances of society) is thus established, unaffected by the vicissitudes of generations; the constant struggle with uniform UNFAVOURABLE conditions is, as already remarked, the cause of a type becoming stable and hard. Finally, however,

"Self-preservation, self-elevation, and self-deliverance represent the path to liberation from invisible chains."

a happy state of things results, the enormous tension is relaxed; there are perhaps no more enemies among the neighbouring peoples, and the means of life, even of the enjoyment of life, are present in superabundance. With one stroke the bond and constraint of the old discipline severs: it is no longer regarded as necessary, as a condition of existence--if it would continue, it can only do so as a form of LUXURY, as an archaizing TASTE. Variations, whether they be deviations (into the higher, finer, and rarer), or deteriorations and monstrosities, appear suddenly on the scene in the greatest exuberance and splendour; the individual dares to be individual and detach himself. At this turning-point of history there manifest themselves, side by side, and often mixed and entangled together, a magnificent, manifold, virgin-forest-like up-growth and up-striving, a kind of TROPICAL TEMPO in the rivalry of growth, and an extraordinary decay and self-destruction, owing to the savagely opposing and seemingly exploding egoisms, which strive with one another "for sun and light," and can no longer assign any limit, restraint, or forbearance for themselves by means of the hitherto existing morality. It was this morality itself which piled up the strength so enormously, which bent the bow in so threatening a manner: --it is now "out of date," it is getting "out of date." The dangerous and disquieting point has been reached when the greater, more manifold, more comprehensive life IS LIVED BEYOND the old morality; the "individual" stands out, and is obliged to have recourse to his own law-giving, his own arts and artifices for self-preservation, self-elevation, and self-deliverance.

Nothing but new "Whys," nothing but new "How's," no common formulas any longer, misunderstanding and disregard in league with each other, decay, deterioration, and the loftiest desires frightfully entangled, the genius of the race overflowing from all the cornucopias of good and bad, a portentous simultaneousness of Spring and Autumn, full of new charms and mysteries peculiar to the fresh, still in exhausted, still unwearied corruption. Danger is again present, the mother of morality, great danger; this time shifted into the individual, into the neighbour and friend, into the street, into their own child, into their own heart, into all the most personal and secret recesses of their desires and volitions. What will the moral philosophers who appear at this time have to preach? They discover, these sharp onlookers and loafers, that the end is quickly approaching, that everything around them decays and produces decay, that nothing will endure until the day after tomorrow, except one species of man, the incurably MEDIOCRE. The mediocre alone have a prospect of continuing and propagating themselves--they will be the men of the future, the sole survivors; "be like them! become mediocre!" is now the only morality which has still a significance, which still obtains a hearing. --But it is difficult to preach this morality of mediocrity! It can never avow what it is and what it desires! It has to talk of moderation and dignity and duty and brotherly love--it will have difficulty IN CONCEALING ITS IRONY!

INSTINCT FOR RANK

There is an INSTINCT FOR RANK, which more than anything else is already the sign of a HIGH rank; there is a DELIGHT in the NUANCES of reverence which leads one to infer noble origin and habits. The refinement, goodness, and loftiness of a soul are put to a perilous test when something passes by that is of the highest rank, but is not yet protected by the awe of authority from obtrusive touches and incivilities: something that goes its way like a living touchstone, undistinguished, undiscovered, and tentative, perhaps voluntarily veiled and disguised. He whose task and practice it is to investigate souls, will avail himself of many varieties of this very art to determine the ultimate value of a soul, the unalterable, innate order of rank to which it belongs: he will test it by its INSTINCT FOR REVERENCE.

DIFFERENCE ENGENDRE HAINE: the vulgarity of many a nature spurts up suddenly like dirty water, when any holy vessel, any jewel from closed shrines, any book bearing the marks of great destiny, is brought before it; while on the other hand, there is an involuntary silence, a hesitation of the eye, a cessation of all gestures, by which it is indicated that a soul FEELS the nearness of what is worthiest of respect. The way in which, on the whole, the reverence for the BIBLE has hitherto been maintained in Europe, is perhaps the best example of discipline and refinement of manners which Europe owes to Christianity: books of such profoundness and supreme significance require for their protection an external tyranny of authority, in order to acquire the PERIOD of thousands of years which is necessary to exhaust and unriddle them. Much has been achieved when the sentiment has been at last instilled into the masses (the shallow-pates and the boobies of every kind) that they are not allowed to touch everything, that there are holy experiences before which they must take off their shoes and keep away the unclean hand--it is almost their highest advance towards humanity. On the contrary, in the so-called cultured classes, the believers in "modern ideas," nothing is perhaps so repulsive as their lack of shame, the easy insolence of eye and hand with which they touch, taste, and finger everything; and it is possible that even yet there is more RELATIVE nobility of taste, and more tact for reverence among the people, among the lower classes of the people, especially among peasants, than among the newspaper-reading DEMI-MONDE of intellect, the cultured class.

It cannot be effaced from a man's soul what his ancestors have preferably and most constantly done: whether they were perhaps diligent economizers attached to a desk and a cash-box, modest and citizen-like in their desires, modest also in their virtues; or whether they were accustomed to commanding from morning till night, fond of rude pleasures and probably of still ruder duties and responsibilities; or whether, finally, at one time or another, they have sacrificed old privileges of birth and possession, in order to live wholly for their faith--for their "God,"--as men of an inexorable and sensitive conscience, which blushes at every compromise. It is quite impossible for a man NOT to have the qualities and predilections of his parents and ancestors in his constitution, whatever appearances may suggest to the contrary. This is the problem of race. Granted that one knows something of the parents, it is admissible to draw a conclusion about the child: any kind of offensive incontinence, any kind of sordid envy, or of clumsy self-vaunting--the three things which together have constituted the genuine plebeian type in all times--such must pass over to the child, as surely as bad blood; and with the help of the best education and culture one will only succeed in DECEIVING with regard to such heredity.--And what else does education and culture try to do nowadays! In our very democratic, or rather, very plebeian age, "education" and "culture" MUST be essentially the art of deceiving--deceiving with regard to origin, with regard to the inherited plebeianism in body and soul. An educator who nowadays preached truthfulness above everything else, and called out constantly to his pupils: "Be true! Be natural! Show yourselves as you are!"--even such a virtuous and sincere ass would learn in a short time to have recourse to the FURCA of Horace, NATURAM EXPELLERE: with what results? "Plebeianism" USQUE RECURRET.

Egoism

At the risk of displeasing innocent ears, I submit that egoism belongs to the essence of a noble soul, I mean the unalterable belief that to a being such as "we," other beings must naturally be in subjection, and have to sacrifice themselves. The noble soul accepts the fact of his egoism without question, and also without consciousness of harshness, constraint, or arbitrariness therein, but rather as something that may have its basis in the primary law of things: --if he sought a designation for it he would say: "It is justice itself." He acknowledges under certain circumstances, which made him hesitate at first, that there are other equally privileged ones; as soon as he has settled this question of rank, he moves among those equals and equally privileged ones with the same assurance, as regards modesty and delicate respect, which he enjoys in intercourse with himself--in accordance with an innate heavenly mechanism which all the stars understand. It is an ADDITIONAL instance of his egoism, this artfulness and self-limitation in intercourse with his equals--every star is a similar egoist; he honors HIMSELF in them, and in the rights which he concedes to them, he has no doubt that the exchange of honours and rights, as the ESSENCE of all intercourse, belongs also to the natural condition of things. The noble soul gives as he takes, prompted by the passionate and sensitive instinct of requital, which is at the root of his nature. The notion of "favour" has, INTER PARES, neither significance nor good repute; there may be a sublime way of letting gifts as it were light upon one from above, and of drinking them thirstily like dew-drops; but for those arts and displays the noble soul has no aptitude. His egoism hinders him here: in general, he looks "aloft" unwillingly--he looks either FORWARD, horizontally and deliberately, or downwards--HE KNOWS THAT HE IS ON A HEIGHT.

"One can only truly esteem him who does not LOOK OUT FOR himself."--Goethe to Rath Schlosser.

The Chinese have a proverb which mothers even teach their children: "SIAO-SIN" ("MAKE THY HEART SMALL"). This is essentially the fundamental tendency in latter-day civilizations. I have no doubt that an ancient Greek, also, would first of all remark the self-dwarfing in us Indians of today--in this respect alone we should immediately be "distasteful" to him.

What, after all, is ignobleness? --Words are vocal symbols for ideas; ideas, however, are more or less definite mental symbols for frequently returning and concurring sensations, for groups of sensations. It is not sufficient to use the same words in order to understand one another: we must also employ the same words for the same kind of internal experiences, we must in the end have experiences IN COMMON. On this account, the people of one nation understand one another better than those belonging to different nations, even when they use the same language; or rather, when people have lived long together under similar conditions (of climate, soil, danger, requirement, toil) there ORIGINATES therefrom an entity that "understands itself"--namely, a nation. In all souls a like number of frequently recurring experiences have gained the upper hand over those occurring more rarely: about these matters people understand one another rapidly and always more rapidly--the history of language is the history of a process of abbreviation; on the basis of this quick comprehension people always unite closer and closer. The greater the danger, the greater is the need of agreeing quickly and readily about what is necessary; not to misunderstand one another in danger--that is what cannot at all be dispensed with in intercourse. Also, in all loves and friendships one has the experience that nothing of the kind continues when the discovery has been made that in using the same words, one of the two parties has feelings, thoughts, intuitions, wishes, or fears different from those of the other. (The fear of the "eternal misunderstanding": that is the good genius which so often keeps persons of different sexes from too hasty attachments, to which sense and heart prompt them--and NOT some Schopenhauerian "genius of the species"!) Whichever groups of sensations within a soul awaken most readily, begin to speak, and give the word of command--these decide as to the general order of rank of its values, and determine ultimately its list of desirable things. A man's estimates of value betray something of the STRUCTURE of his soul, and wherein it sees its conditions of life, its intrinsic needs. Supposing now that necessity has from all time drawn together only such men as could express similar requirements and similar experiences by similar symbols, it results on the whole that the easy COMMUNICABILITY of need, which implies ultimately the undergoing only of average and COMMON experiences, must have been the most potent of all the forces which have hitherto operated upon mankind. The more similar, the more ordinary people, have always had and are still having the advantage; the more select, more refined, more unique, and difficultly comprehensible, are liable to stand alone; they succumb to accidents in their isolation, and seldom propagate themselves. One must appeal to immense opposing forces, in order to thwart this natural, all-too-natural PROGRESSUS IN SIMILE, the evolution of man to the similar, the ordinary, the average, the gregarious --to the IGNOBLE! –

The more a psychologist--a born, an unavoidable psychologist and soul-diviner--turns his attention to the more select cases and individuals, the greater is his danger of being suffocated by sympathy: he NEEDS sternness and cheerfulness more than any other man. For the corruption, the ruination of higher men, of the more unusually constituted souls, is in fact, the rule: it is dreadful to have such a rule always before one's eyes. The manifold torment of the psychologist who has discovered this ruination, who discovers once, and then discovers ALMOST repeatedly throughout all history, this universal inner "desperateness" of higher men, this eternal "too late!" in every sense--may perhaps one day be the cause of his turning with bitterness against his own lot, and of his making an attempt at self-destruction--of his "going to ruin" himself. One may perceive in almost every psychologist a tell-tale inclination for delightful intercourse with commonplace and well-ordered men; the fact is thereby disclosed that he always requires healing, that he needs a sort of flight and forgetfulness, away from what his insight and incisiveness--from what his "business"--has laid upon his conscience. The fear of his memory is peculiar to him. He is easily silenced by the judgement of others; he hears with unmoved countenance how people honour, admire, love, and glorify, where he has PERCEIVED--or he even conceals his silence by expressly assenting to some plausible opinion. Perhaps the paradox of his situation becomes so dreadful that, precisely where he has learnt GREAT SYMPATHY, together with great CONTEMPT, the multitude, the educated, and the visionaries, have on their part learnt great reverence--reverence for "great men" and marvellous animals, for the sake of whom one blesses and honours the fatherland, the earth, the dignity of mankind, and one's own self, to whom one points the young, and in view of whom one educates them. And who knows but in all great instances hitherto just the same happened: that the multitude worshipped a God, and that the "God" was only a poor sacrificial animal! SUCCESS has always been the greatest liar--and the "work" itself is a success; the great statesman, the conqueror, the discoverer, are disguised in their creations until they are unrecognizable; the "work" of the artist, of the philosopher, only invents him who has created it, is REPUTED to have created it; the "great men," as they are reverenced, are poor little fictions composed afterwards; in the world of historical values spurious coinage PREVAILS. Those great poets, for example, such as Byron, Musset, Poe, Leopardi, Kleist, Gogol (I do not venture to mention much greater names, but I have them in my mind), as they now appear, and were perhaps obliged to be: men of the moment, enthusiastic, sensuous, and childish, light-minded and impulsive in their trust and distrust; with souls in which usually some flaw has to be concealed; often taking revenge with their works for an internal defilement, often seeking forgetfulness in their soaring from a too true memory, often lost in the mud and almost in love with it, until they become like the Will-o'-the-Wisp around the swamps, and PRETEND TO BE stars--the people then call them idealists,--often struggling with protracted disgust, with an ever-reappearing phantom of disbelief, which makes them cold, and obliges them to languish for GLORIA and devour "faith as it is" out of the hands of intoxicated adulators:--what a TORMENT these great artists are and the so-called higher men in general, to him who has once found them out! It is thus conceivable that it is just from woman--who is clairvoyant in the world of suffering, and also unfortunately eager to help and save to an extent far beyond her powers--that THEY have learnt so readily those outbreaks of boundless devoted SYMPATHY, which the multitude, above all the reverent multitude, do not understand, and overwhelm with prying and self-gratifying interpretations. This sympathizing invariably deceives itself as to its power; woman would like to believe that love can do EVERYTHING--it is the SUPERSTITION peculiar to her. Alas, he who knows the heart finds out how poor, helpless, pretentious, and blundering even the best and deepest love is--he finds that it rather DESTROYS than saves!--It is possible that under the holy fable and travesty of the life of Jesus there is hidden one of the most painful cases of the martyrdom of KNOWLEDGE ABOUT LOVE: the martyrdom of the most innocent and most craving heart, that never had enough of any human love, that DEMANDED love, that demanded inexorably and frantically to be loved and nothing else, with terrible outbursts against those who refused him their love; the story of a poor soul insatiated and insatiable in love, that had to invent hell to send thither those who WOULD NOT love him--and that at last, enlightened about human love, had to invent a God who is entire love, entire CAPACITY for love--who takes pity on human love, because it is so paltry, so ignorant! He who has such sentiments, he who has such KNOWLEDGE about love--SEEKS for death! --But why should one deal with such painful matters? Provided, of course, that one is not obliged to do so.

Suffering is Noble

The intellectual haughtiness and loathing of every man who has suffered deeply--it almost determines the order of rank HOW deeply men can suffer--the chilling certainty, with which he is thoroughly imbued and colored, that by virtue of his suffering he KNOWS MORE than the shrewdest and wisest can ever know, that he has been familiar with, and "at home" in, many distant, dreadful worlds of which "YOU know nothing"!--this silent intellectual haughtiness of the sufferer, this pride of the elect of knowledge, of the "initiated," of the almost sacrificed, finds all forms of disguise necessary to protect itself from contact with officious and sympathizing hands, and in general from all that is not its equal in suffering. Profound suffering makes noble: it separates. --One of the most refined forms of disguise is Epicureanism, along with a certain ostentatious boldness of taste, which takes suffering lightly, and puts itself on the defensive against all that is sorrowful and profound. They are "gay men" who make use of gaiety, because they are misunderstood on account of it--they WISH to be misunderstood. There are "scientific minds" who make use of science, because it gives a gay appearance, and because scientificness leads to the conclusion that a person is superficial--they WISH to mislead to a false conclusion. There are free insolent minds which would fain conceal and deny that they are broken, proud, incurable hearts (the cynicism of Hamlet--the case of Galiani); and occasionally folly itself is the mask of an unfortunate OVER-ASSURED knowledge. --From which it follows that it is the part of a more refined humanity to have reverence "for the mask," and not to make use of psychology and curiosity in the wrong place.

That which separates two men most profoundly is a different sense and grade of purity. What does it matter about all their honesty and reciprocal usefulness, what does it matter about all their mutual good-will: the fact still remains--they "cannot smell each other!" The highest instinct for purity places him who is affected with it in the most extraordinary and dangerous isolation, as a saint: for it is just holiness--the highest spiritualization of the instinct in question. Any kind of cognizance of an indescribable excess in the joy of the bath, any kind of ardor or thirst which perpetually impels the soul out of night into the morning, and out of gloom, out of "affliction" into clearness, brightness, depth, and refinement: --just as much as such a tendency DISTINGUISHES--it is a noble tendency--it also SEPARATES. --The pity of the saint is pity for the FILTH of the human, all-too-human. And there are grades and heights where pity itself is regarded by him as impurity, as filth.

Signs of nobility: never to think of lowering our duties to the rank of duties for everybody; to be unwilling to renounce or to share our responsibilities; to count our prerogatives, and the exercise of them, among our DUTIES.

A man who strives after great things, looks upon every one whom he encounters on his way either as a means of advance, or a delay and hindrance--or as a temporary resting-place. His peculiar lofty BOUNTY to his fellow-men is only possible when he attains his elevation and dominates. Impatience, and the consciousness of being always condemned to comedy up to that time--for even strife is a comedy, and conceals the end, as every means does--spoil all intercourse for him; this kind of man is acquainted with solitude, and what is most poisonous in it.

THE PROBLEM OF THOSE WHO WAIT

THE PROBLEM OF THOSE WHO WAIT. --Happy chances are necessary, and many incalculable elements, in order that a higher man in whom the solution of a problem is dormant, may yet take action, or "break forth," as one might say--at the right moment. On an average it DOES NOT happen; and in all corners of the earth there are waiting ones sitting who hardly know to what extent they are waiting, and still less that they wait in vain. Occasionally, too, the waking call comes too late--the chance which gives "permission" to take action--when their best youth, and strength for action have been used up in sitting still; and how many a one, just as he "sprang up," has found with horror that his limbs are benumbed and his spirits are now too heavy! "It is too late," he has said to himself--and has become self-distrustful and henceforth forever useless.--In the domain of genius, may not the "Raphael without hands" (taking the expression in its widest sense) perhaps not be the exception, but the rule?--Perhaps genius is by no means so rare: but rather the five hundred HANDS which it requires in order to tyrannize over the [GREEK INSERTED HERE], "the right time"--in order to take chance by the forelock!

He who does not WISH to see the height of a man, looks all the more sharply at what is low in him, and in the foreground-- and thereby betrays himself.

In all kinds of injury and loss the lower and coarser soul is better off than the nobler soul: the dangers of the latter must be greater, the probability that it will come to grief and perish is in fact immense, considering the multiplicity of the conditions of its existence. --In a lizard a finger grows again which has been lost; not so in man. --

It is too bad! Always the old story! When a man has finished building his house, he finds that he has learnt unawares something which he OUGHT absolutely to have known before he-- began to build. The eternal, fatal "Too late!" The melancholia of everything COMPLETED! --

Wanderer, who art thou? I see thee follow thy path without scorn, without love, with unfathomable eyes, wet and sad as a plummet which has returned to the light insatiated out of every depth--what did it seek down there? --with a bosom that never sighs, with lips that conceal their loathing, with a hand which only slowly grasps: who art thou? what hast thou done? Rest thee here: this place has hospitality for every one--refresh thyself! And whoever thou art, what is it that now pleases thee? What will serve to refresh thee? Only name it, whatever I have I offer thee! "To refresh me? To refresh me? Oh, thou prying one, what sayest thou! But give me, I pray thee---" What? what? Speak out! "Another mask! A second mask!"

Men of profound sadness betray themselves when they are happy: they have a mode of seizing upon happiness as though they would choke and strangle it, out of jealousy--ah, they know only too well that it will flee from them!

"Bad! Bad! What? Does he not--go back?" Yes! But you misunderstand him when you complain about it. He goes back like everyone who is about to make a great spring.

"Will people believe it of me? But I insist that they believe it of me: I have always thought very unsatisfactorily of myself and about myself, only in very rare cases, only compulsorily, always without delight in 'the subject,' ready to digress from 'myself,' and always without faith in the result, owing to an unconquerable distrust of the POSSIBILITY of self-knowledge, which has led me so far as to feel a CONTRADICTIO IN ADJECTO even in the idea of 'direct knowledge' which theorists allow themselves:--this matter of fact is almost the most certain thing I know about myself. There must be a sort of repugnance in me to BELIEVE anything definite about myself. --Is there perhaps some enigma therein? Probably; but fortunately nothing for my own teeth. --Perhaps it betrays the species to which I belong? --but not to myself, as is sufficiently agreeable to me."

"But what has happened to you?"--"I do not know," he said, hesitatingly; "perhaps the Harpies have flown over my table."--It sometimes happens nowadays that a gentle, sober, retiring man becomes suddenly mad, breaks the plates, upsets the table, shrieks, raves, and shocks everybody--and finally withdraws, ashamed, and raging at himself--whither? For what purpose? To famish apart? To suffocate with his memories? --To him who has the desires of a lofty and dainty soul, and only seldom finds his table laid and his food prepared, the danger will always be great--nowadays, however, it is extraordinarily so. Thrown into the midst of a noisy and plebeian age, with which he does not like to eat out of the same dish, he may readily perish of hunger and thirst--or, should he nevertheless finally "fall to," of sudden nausea.--We have probably all sat at tables to which we did not belong; and precisely the most spiritual of us, who are most difficult to nourish, know the dangerous DYSPEPSIA which originates from a sudden insight and disillusionment about our food and our messmates--the AFTER-DINNER NAUSEA.

If one wishes to praise at all, it is a delicate and at the same time a noble self-control, to praise only where one DOES NOT agree--otherwise in fact one would praise oneself, which is contrary to good taste: --a self-control, to be sure, which offers excellent opportunity and provocation to constant MISUNDERSTANDING. To be able to allow oneself this veritable luxury of taste and morality, one must not live among intellectual imbeciles, but rather among men whose misunderstandings and mistakes amuse by their refinement--or one will have to pay dearly for it! --"He praises me, THEREFORE he acknowledges me to be right"--this asinine method of inference spoils half of the life of us recluses, for it brings the asses into our neighborhood and friendship.

To live in a vast and proud tranquility; always beyond . . . To have, or not to have, one's emotions, one's for and against, according to choice; to lower oneself to them for hours; to SEAT oneself on them as upon horses, and often as upon asses: --for one must know how to make use of their stupidity as well as of their fire. To conserve one's three hundred foregrounds; also one's black spectacles: for there are circumstances when nobody must look into our eyes, still less into our "motives." And to choose for company that roguish and cheerful vice, politeness. And to remain master of one's four virtues, courage, insight, sympathy, and solitude. For solitude is a virtue with us, as a sublime bent and bias to purity, which divines that in the contact of man and man--"in society"--it must be unavoidably impure. All society makes one somehow, somewhere, or sometime--"commonplace."

The greatest events and thoughts--the greatest thoughts, however, are the greatest events--are longest in being comprehended: the generations which are contemporary with them do not EXPERIENCE such events--they live past them. Something happens there as in the realm of stars. The light of the furthest stars is longest in reaching man; and before it has arrived man DENIES--that there are stars there. "How many centuries does a mind require to be understood?"--that is also a standard, one also makes a gradation of rank and an etiquette therewith, such as is necessary for mind and for star.

"Here is the prospect free, the mind exalted." But there is a reverse kind of man, who is also upon a height, and has also a free prospect--but looks DOWNWARDS.

What is noble? What does the word "noble" still mean for us nowadays? How does the noble man betray himself, how is he recognized under this heavy overcast sky of the commencing plebeianism, by which everything is rendered opaque and leaden? -- It is not his actions which establish his claim--actions are always ambiguous, always inscrutable; neither is it his "works." One finds nowadays among artists and scholars plenty of those who betrayed by their works have a profound longing for nobleness which impels them; but this very NEED of nobleness is radically different from the needs of the noble soul itself, and is in fact the eloquent and dangerous sign of the lack thereof. It is not the works, but the BELIEF which is here decisive and determines the order of rank--to employ once more an old religious formula with a new and deeper meaning--it is some fundamental certainty which a noble soul has about itself, something which is not to be sought, is not to be found, and perhaps, also, is not to be lost. --THE NOBLE SOUL HAS REVERENCE FOR ITSELF. —

THE NOBLE SOUL HAS REVERENCE FOR ITSELF

There are men who are unavoidably intellectual, let them turn and twist themselves as they will, and hold their hands before their treacherous eyes--as though the hand were not a betrayer; it always comes out at last that they have something which they hide--namely, intellect. One of the subtlest means of deceiving, at least as long as possible, and of successfully representing oneself to be stupider than one really is--which in everyday life is often as desirable as an umbrella, --is called ENTHUSIASM, including what belongs to it, for instance, virtue. For as Galiani said, who was obliged to know it: VERTU EST ENTHOUSIASME.

In the writings of a recluse one always hears something of the echo of the wilderness, something of the murmuring tones and timid vigilance of solitude; in his strongest words, even in his cry itself, there sounds a new and more dangerous kind of silence, of concealment. He who has sat day and night, from year's end to year's end, alone with his soul in familiar discord and discourse, he who has become a cave-bear, or a treasure-seeker, or a treasure-guardian and dragon in his cave--it may be a labyrinth, but can also be a gold-mine--his ideas themselves eventually acquire a twilight-color of their own, and an odor, as much of the depth as of the mould, something uncommunicative and repulsive, which blows chilly upon every passerby. The recluse does not believe that a philosopher--supposing that a philosopher has always in the first place been a recluse--ever expressed his actual and ultimate opinions in books: are not books written precisely to hide what is in us?--indeed, he will doubt whether a philosopher CAN have "ultimate and actual" opinions at all; whether behind every cave in him there is not, and must necessarily be, a still deeper cave: an ampler, stranger, richer world beyond the surface, an abyss behind every bottom, beneath every "foundation." Every philosophy is a foreground philosophy--this is a recluse's verdict: "There is something arbitrary in the fact that the PHILOSOPHER came to a stand here, took a retrospect, and looked around; that he HERE laid his spade aside and did not dig any deeper--there is also something suspicious in it." Every philosophy also CONCEALS a philosophy; every opinion is also a LURKING-PLACE; every word is also a MASK.

Every deep thinker is more afraid of being understood than of being misunderstood. The latter perhaps wounds his vanity; but the former wounds his heart, his sympathy, which always says: "Ah, why would you also have as hard a time of it as I have?"

Man, a COMPLEX, mendacious, artful, and inscrutable animal, uncanny to the other animals by his artifice and sagacity, rather than by his strength, has invented the good conscience in order finally to enjoy his soul as something SIMPLE; and the whole of morality is a long, audacious falsification, by virtue of which generally enjoyment at the sight of the soul becomes possible. From this point of view there is perhaps much more in the conception of "art" than is generally believed.

A philosopher: that is a man who constantly experiences, sees, hears, suspects, hopes, and dreams extraordinary things; who is struck by his own thoughts as if they came from the outside, from above and below, as a species of events and lightning-flashes PECULIAR TO HIM; who is perhaps himself a storm pregnant with new lightning's; a portentous man, around whom there is always rumbling and mumbling and gaping and something uncanny going on. A philosopher: alas, a being who often runs away from himself, is often afraid of himself--but whose curiosity always makes him "come to himself" again.

A man who says: "I like that, I take it for my own, and mean to guard and protect it from every one"; a man who can conduct a case, carry out a resolution, remain true to an opinion, keep hold of a woman, punish and overthrow insolence; a man who has his indignation and his sword, and to whom the weak, the suffering, the oppressed, and even the animals willingly submit and naturally belong; in short, a man who is a MASTER by nature-- when such a man has sympathy, well! THAT sympathy has value! But of what account is the sympathy of those who suffer! Or of those even who preach sympathy! There is nowadays, throughout almost the whole of India, a sickly irritability and sensitiveness towards pain, and also a repulsive irrestrainableness in complaining, an effeminizing, which, with the aid of religion and philosophical nonsense, seeks to deck itself out as something superior--there is a regular cult of suffering. The UNMANLINESS of that which is called "sympathy" by such groups of visionaries, is always, I believe, the first thing that strikes the eye. --One must resolutely and radically taboo this latest form of bad taste; and finally I wish people to put the good amulet, "GAI SABER" ("gay science," in ordinary language), on heart and neck, as a protection against it.

"First Treatise: 'Good and Evil' vs. 'Good and Bad' - Exploring the Notion of Guilt Formed by Religion and Cultural Practices"

The "First Treatise", demonstrates that the two pairs of opposites "good/evil" and "good/bad" have very different origins, and that the word "good" itself came to represent two opposed meanings. In the "good/bad" distinction of the aristocratic way of thinking, "good" is synonymous with nobility and everything that is powerful and life-affirming; "bad" has no inculpatory implication and simply refers to the "common" or the "low" and the qualities and values associated with them, in contradistinction to the warrior ethos of the ruling nobility. In the "good/evil" distinction, which I call "slave morality", the meaning of "good" is made the antithesis of the original aristocratic "good", which itself is re-labelled "evil". This inversion of values develops out of the 'ressentiment' felt by the weak towards the powerful.

Irebuke the "English psychologists" for lacking historical sense. They seek to do moral genealogy by explaining altruism in terms of the utility of altruistic actions, which is subsequently forgotten as such actions become the norm. But the judgment "good," according to me, originates not with the beneficiaries of altruistic actions. Rather, the good themselves (the powerful) coined the term "good." Further, I see it as psychologically absurd that altruism derives from a utility that is forgotten: if it is useful, what is the incentive to forget it? Such meaningless value-judgment gains currency by expectations repeatedly shaping the consciousness.

From the aristocratic mode of valuation, another mode of valuation branches off, which develops into its opposite: the priestly mode. I propose that longstanding confrontation between the priestly caste and the warrior caste fuels this splitting of meaning. The priests, and all those who feel disenfranchised and powerless in a lowly state of subjugation and physical impotence (e.g., slavery), develop a deep and venomous hatred for the powerful. Thus originates what I call the "slave revolt in morality", which, according to me, begins with Judaism, for it is the bridge that led to the slave revolt, via Christian morality, of the alienated, oppressed masses of the Roman Empire.

To the noble life, justice is immediate, real, and good, necessarily requiring enemies. To slave morality, justice is a deferred event, ultimately taking the form of an imagined revenge that will result in everlasting life for the weak and punishment for the strong. Slave morality grows out of impotence, world-weariness, indignation and envy; it purports to speak for the oppressed masses who have been wronged, deprived of the power to act with immediacy by the masters, who thrive on their subjugation. The men of ressentiment, in an inversion of values, redefine the "good" in their own image. They say: "he is good who does not outrage, who harms nobody, who does not attack, who does not requite, who leaves revenge to God, who avoids evil and desires little from life, like us, the patient, humble, and just." According to me, this is merely a transformation of the effects and qualities of impotence into virtues, as if these effects and qualities were chosen – the meritorious deeds of the "good" man. The deeds of the powerful man, known to themselves as "good", are re-cast by the men of ressentiment as "evil", taking on a mystical moral-judgmental element entirely absent from the aristocratic "bad", which to the noble was simply a descriptor for the inferior qualities of the lower classes.

In the First Treatise, I introduce one of the most controversial images, the "Caste beast." He had previously employed this expression to represent the lion, beyond the metaphorical lion. I expressively associate the "Caste beast" with the Hindu race of India which states that all were fair skinned and dark-haired and constituted the collective aristocracy of the time. Thus, he associates the "good, noble, pure, as originally a Brahmin in contrast to dark-skinned, dark-haired native inhabitants" (the embodiment of the "bad".) Here I introduce the concept of the original Brahmins as the "master race" which has lost its dominance over humanity but not necessarily, permanently. Though, at the same time, his examples of Brahmin include such peoples as the Japanese and Arabic nobilities of antiquity, suggesting that being a Brahmin has more to do with one's morality than one's race.

I insist that it is a mistake to hold beasts of prey to be "evil," for their actions stem from their inherent strength, rather than any malicious intent. One cannot blame them for their "thirst for enemies and resistances and triumphs" because, there is no "subject" separate from the action:

A quantum of force is equivalent to a quantum of drive, will, effect—more, it is nothing other than precisely this very driving, willing, effecting, and only owing to the seduction of language (and the fundamental errors of reason that are petrified in it) which conceives and misconceives all effects as conditioned by something that causes effects, by a "subject", can appear otherwise. For just as the popular mind separates the lightning from its flash and takes the latter for an action, for the operation of a subject called lightning, so popular morality also separates strength from expressions of strength, as if there were a neutral substratum behind the strong man, which was free to express strength or not do so. But there is no such substratum; there is no "being" behind doing, effecting, becoming; "the doer" is merely a fiction added to the deed—the deed is everything.

The "subject" (or soul) is only necessary for slave morality. It enables the impotent man to sanctify the qualities of his impotence by making them into "good" qualities, chosen for moral reasons, and the actions of his oppressor into morally "evil" choices.

I conclude,First Treatise by hypothesizing a tremendous historical struggle between the Indian dualism of "good/bad" and that of the Hindu's "good/evil," with the latter eventually achieving a victory for ressentiment.

The First Treatise concludes with a note calling for further examination of the history of moral concepts and the hierarchy of values.

Second Treatise: "'Guilt', 'Bad Conscience', and Related Matters"

According to Nietzsche, what we call "the conscience" is the end product of a long and painful socio-historical process that began with the need to create a 'memory' in the human animal. For its own psychic health and functionality, the human organism is naturally 'forgetful.' Forgetfulness is "an active and in the strictest sense positive faculty of repression, which is responsible for the fact that what we experience and absorb enters our consciousness as little while we are digesting it (one might call the process 'inpsychation') as does the thousand-fold process involved in physical nourishment – so-called incorporation." But social existence, to the extent that the social organism must function as a unity to survive and prosper, requires that certain things be not forgotten, that individuals must remember their place relative to the whole. Memory in this sense, the social conscience in its rudimentary form, was forged with great difficulty over a long period of time, by what Nietzsche refers to as man's 'mnemotechnics,' the underlying principle of which is "If something is to stay in the memory it must be burned in: only that which never ceases to hurt stays in the memory."

This long pre-historic process allows a "morality of customs" to establish itself, and through it man becomes calculable, regular, and predictable. Its "ripest fruit" is 'the sovereign individual,' a human being whose 'social responsibility' has become flesh and blood, an individual with such hard-won mastery over himself that he is capable of determining and guaranteeing his own future actions. Such an individual has a free will: by virtue of his self-mastery he has the right to make promises. The conscience in this sense is the self-discipline of social responsibility made into a dominating instinct; to such an individual all other individuals, things and circumstances are evaluated from the perspective of this instinct.

It was in the contractual relationship, a relationship based on mutual promises, that one person first "measured himself against another... setting prices, determining values, contriving equivalences, exchanging – these preoccupied the earliest thinking of man to so great an extent that in a certain sense they constitute thinking as such." 'Law' and 'justice,' a society's codes, judgements and commands in relation to individual and inter-personal rights and obligations, are formed in the context of this contractual-evaluating conceptual paradigm. The strength of one's 'conscience,' one's ability to make promises and not break them, to personally guarantee one's future actions, to fulfil one's obligations to others, is thus a vital factor in determining individual social status.

The concepts of guilt and punishment likewise have their origins in the contractual relationship. Here 'guilt' simply meant 'debt': the guilty person was simply the person who was unable to discharge their debt. In punishment, the creditor acquires the right to inflict harm on the guilty person. Such a transaction is made possible, according to Nietzsche, by 'pleasure in cruelty.' Its logic is not related in any way to considerations about the free will, moral accountability etc., of the wrong-doer: it is nothing more than a special form of compensation for the injured party. The creditor receives recompense "in the form of a kind of pleasure—the pleasure of being allowed to vent his power freely upon one who is powerless." Such punishment was a legally enforceable right of the creditor, and some law books had exact quantifications of what could be done to the debtor's body relative to the debt. It was in this civil law validation of cruelty that 'guilt' first became intertwined with 'suffering.'

In criminal law, punishment and the debtor-creditor relationship have been transferred onto the relation in which the individual stands to the community. The individual enjoys a number of benefits from communal life, the most obvious of which is protection from the hostile world outside the community: a pledge is made to the community and its mores and laws in return for this protection. If that pledge is broken the community, as the offended creditor, demands repayment. A warlike and survival-based community, dealing constantly with danger or scarcity, will be violent and merciless in its treatment of law-breakers. As a community's security and self-confidence increases, the harm of one individual's transgressions decreases correspondingly, and the continuance of the more harmonious state requires that excessively violent responses be controlled and regulated. The nature of such a community's penal law will involve a compromise between this requirement and the angry forces seeking blood and violence. Its principal way of achieving it is to separate the deed from the doer via the concept of 'the crime,' a transformation of the actual deed into an abstract legal category implying a 'debt to society,' a debt that is ultimately dischargeable through an appropriate 'punishment.'

According to Nietzsche, one must not equate the origin of a thing and its utility. The origin of punishment, for example, is in a procedure that predates the many possible uses and interpretations of it. Punishment has not just one purpose, but a whole range of "meanings" which "finally crystallizes into a kind of unity that is difficult to dissolve, difficult to analyse and ... completely and utterly undefinable." Nietzsche lists eleven different uses (or "meanings") of punishment, and suggests that there are many more. One utility it does not possess, however, is awakening remorse. The psychology of prisoners shows that punishment "makes hard and cold; it concentrates; it sharpens the feeling of alienation." The feeling of guilt, the bad conscience, had quite different origins and had no place whatsoever in the institutions of crime and punishment for the greater part of their history. The criminal was dealt with merely as something harmful, as an "irresponsible piece of fate," and the person upon whom punishment was administered, though his body encountered something shocking and violent, was entirely unacquainted with 'moral' pain. The only 'lesson' learned from punishment was that of prudence and memory. Punishment produces "an increase in fear, a heightening of prudence, mastery of the desires: thus punishment tames men, but it does not make them "better."

In Nietzsche's theory, the bad conscience was the serious illness that the animal man was bound to contract when he found himself finally enclosed within the walls of a politically organized society. It begins with the institution of the 'state,' in its original form through a violent subjugation of people by a highly organized and remorseless military machine: "the wielding of a hitherto unchecked and shapeless populace into a firm form was not only instituted by an act of violence but carried to its conclusion by nothing but acts of violence." Thus, the human animal became subjected, enclosed within a system of externally imposed functions and purposes, and its outward-pressing drives and impulses were turned inward: "the instinct for freedom pushed back and incarcerated within and finally able to discharge and vent itself only on itself." It is the 'will to power,' the same active force that is at work in the artists of violence and builders of states, but deprived of its object and turned upon itself. This inner world of "self-ravishment" and "artists' cruelty," became "the womb of all ideal and imaginative phenomena," the soul of man.

To understand how the bad conscience became bound up with guilt and punishment, it is necessary to examine how these concepts acquired religious significance. Nietzsche accounts for the genesis of the concept "God" by considering what happens when a tribe becomes ever more powerful. Each successive generation maintains an ethos of indebtedness (guilt) to the original founders of the tribe, the ancestors. The tribe's very existence is thought to depend on a continued acknowledgement and repayment of the ancestor, whose powerful spirit is still present in all customs and daily activities. As the power of the tribe grows, the debt to the ancestor likewise increases. The invisible yet omnipresent figure of the ancestor takes on an ever-increasing power and mystique, until eventually, in the paranoid imaginations of his debtors, he begins to "recede into the darkness of the divinely uncanny and unimaginable: in the end the ancestor must necessarily be transfigured into a God."

The historical advance towards universal empires brought with it the advance towards monotheistic religions, and it was with Christianity that the feeling of guilty indebtedness achieved its non plus ultra. Christianity is the religion that has sought, successfully, to permanently bind the concept of 'guilt' to the bad conscience:the aim now is to preclude pessimistically, once and for all, the prospect of a final discharge; the aim now is to make the glance recoil disconsolately from an iron impossibility; the aim now is to turn the concepts "guilt" and "duty" back—back against whom? ... against the "debtor" first of all, in whom from now on the bad conscience is firmly rooted, eating into him and spreading within him like a polyp, until at last the irredeemable debt gives rise to the conception of irredeemable penance, the idea that it cannot be discharged ("eternal punishment".)

The entire condition of mankind becomes guilt-ridden, whether that condition is the primal ancestor who becomes the perpetrator of "original sin," or "nature," the mother, who becomes characterized as evil or shameful, or existence in general, which is now considered "worthless as such." Christianity's expedient, its "stroke of genius" in the shadow of this looming eternal nightmare, was to proclaim that God himself, in the person of Jesus, sacrificed himself for the guilt of mankind. God pays the unpayable debt, the new religion teaches, out of love—love for his debtor. Thus guilt, which originally merely signified debt in a contractual sense, attained an essential moral-metaphysical significance in mankind's understanding of itself and its relation to God.

Nietzsche ends the **Treatise** with a positive suggestion for a counter-movement to the "conscience-vivisection and cruelty to the animal-self" imposed by the bad conscience: this is to "wed to bad conscience the unnatural inclinations," i.e. to use the self-destructive tendency encapsulated in bad conscience to attack the symptoms of sickness themselves. It is much too early for the kind of free spirit—a Zarathustra-figure—who could bring this about, although he will come one day: he will emerge only in a time of emboldening conflict, not in the "decaying, self-doubting present."

Third Treatise: "What do ascetic ideals mean?"

Nietzsche's purpose in the "Third Treatise" is "to bring to light, not what [the ascetic] ideal has done, but simply what it means; what it indicates; what lies hidden behind it, beneath it, in it; of what it is the provisional, indistinct expression, overlaid with question marks and misunderstandings".

As Nietzsche tells us in the **Preface**, the Third Treatise is a commentary on the aphorism prefixed to it. Textual studies have shown that this aphorism consists of the Treatise (not the epigraph to the Treatise, which is a quotation from Nietzsche's, Thus Spoke Zarathustra).

This opening aphorism confronts us with the multiplicity of meanings that the ascetic ideal has for different groups:

(a) artists, (b) philosophers,

(c) women, (d) physiological casualties,

(e) priests, and (f) saints. That the ascetic

ideal has been so powerful and meant so many different things are an expression of the basic fact of the human will: "its horror vacui [horror of a vacuum]: it needs a goal—and it will rather will nothingness than not will."

a. For the artist, the ascetic ideal means "nothing or too many things." Nietzsche selects the composer Richard Wagner as example. Artists, he concludes, always require some ideology to prop themselves up. Wagner, we are told, relied on Schopenhauer to provide this underpinning; therefore, we should look to philosophers if we are to get closer to finding out what the ascetic ideal means.

b. For the philosopher, it means a "sense and instinct for the most favourable conditions of higher spirituality," which is to satisfy his desire for independence. It is only in the guise of the ascetic priest that the philosopher is first able to make his appearance without attracting suspicion of his overweening will to power. As yet, every "true" philosopher has retained the trappings of the ascetic priest; his slogans have been "poverty, chastity, humility."

c. For the priest, its meaning is the "'supreme' license for power." He sets himself up as the "savior" of

d. the physiologically deformed, offering them a cure for their exhaustion and listlessness (which is in reality only a therapy which does not tackle the roots of their suffering.)

Nietzsche suggests a number of causes for widespread physiological inhibition:

i. the crossing of races;

ii. emigration of a race to an unsuitable environment (e.g. the Indians to India);

iii. the exhaustion of a race (e.g. Parisian pessimism from 1850);

iv. bad diet (e.g. vegetarianism);

v. diseases of various kinds, including Malaria and Dengue (e.g. Indian depression after the Religious war).

The ascetic priest has a range of strategies for anesthetizing the continuous, low-level pain of the weak. Four of these are innocent in the sense that they do the patient no further harm:

1. a general deadening of the feeling of life;
2. mechanical activity;
3. "small joys," especially love of one's neighbour;
4. the awakening of the communal feeling of power. He further has a number of strategies which are guilty in the sense that they have the effect of making the sick sicker (although the priest applies them with a good conscience); they work by inducing an "orgy of feeling" He does this by "altering the direction of ressentiment," i.e. telling the weak to look for the causes of their unhappiness in themselves (in "sin"), not in others. Such training in repentance is responsible, according to Nietzsche, for phenomena such as the St Vitus' and St John's dancers of the Middle Ages, witch-hunt hysteria, somnambulism (of which there were eight epidemics between 1564 and 1605), and the delirium characterized by the widespread cry of evviva la morte! ("long live death!")

Given the extraordinary success of the ascetic ideal in imposing itself on our entire culture, what can we look to oppose it? "Where is the counterpart to this closed system of will, goal and interpretation?" Nietzsche considers as possible opponents of the ideal:

a. modern science;
b. modern historians;
c. "comedians of the ideal."

a. Science is in fact the "most recent and noblest form" of the ascetic ideal. It has no faith in itself, and acts only as a means of self-anesthetization for sufferers (scientists) who do not want to admit they suffer. In apparent opposition to the ascetic ideal, science has succeeded merely in demolishing the ideal's "outworks, sheathing, play of masks, ... its temporary solidification, lignification, dogmatization."By dismantling church claims to the theological importance of man, scientists substitute their self-contempt [cynicism] as the ideal of science.
b. Modern historians, in trying to hold up a mirror to ultimate reality, are not only ascetic but highly nihilistic. As deniers of teleology, their "last crowing's" are "To what end?""In vain!""Nada!" (

c. An even worse kind of historian is what Nietzsche calls the "contemplatives": self-satisfied armchair hedonists who have arrogated to themselves the praise of contemplation (Nietzsche gives Ernest Renan as an example.) Europe is full of such "comedians of the Christian-moral ideal." In a sense, if anyone is inimical to the ideal it is they, because they at least "arouse mistrust."

The will to truth that is bred by the ascetic ideal has in its turn led to the spread of truthfulness the pursuit of which has brought the will to truth itself in peril. What is thus now required, Nietzsche concludes, is a critique of the value of truth itself.

Being and Time, part 1:
Why Heidegger matters?

The most important and influential continental philosopher of the last century was also a Nazi. How did he get there? What can we learn from him?

Martin Heidegger(1889-1976) was the most important and influential philosopher in the continental tradition in the 20th century. Being and Time, first published in 1927, was his magnum opus. There is no way of understanding what took place in continental philosophy after Heidegger without coming to terms with **Being and Time**. Furthermore, unlike many Anglo-American philosophers, Heidegger has exerted a huge influence outside philosophy, in areas as diverse as architecture, contemporary art, social and political theory, psychotherapy, psychiatry and theology.

However, because of his political commitment to National Socialism in 1933, when he assumed the position of Rector of Freiburg University in south-western Germany, Heidegger continues to arouse controversy, polemic and much heated misunderstanding.

A hugely important matter of the relation between Heidegger and politics is the topic for another series of blog entries. Indeed, to my mind, the nature and extent of Heidegger's involvement in National Socialism only becomes philosophically pertinent once one has begun to understand and feel the persuasive power of what takes place in his written work, especially Being and Time.

The task I have set myself in this is to provide a taste of the latter book and hopefully find some motivation to read it further and study it more deeply. But once you have read, **Being and Time** and hopefully been compelled by it, then the question that hangs over the text, like the sword of Damocles, is the following: how could arguably the greatest philosopher of the20th century also have been a Nazi? What does his political commitment to National Socialism, however long or short it lasted, suggest about the nature of philosophy and its risks and dangers when stepping into the political realm?

Being and Time

Being and Time is a work of considerable length (437 pages in the German original) and legendary difficulty. The difficulty is caused by the fact that Heidegger sets himself the task of what he calls a "destruction" of the philosophical tradition. We shall see some of the implications of this in future entries, but the initial consequence is that Heidegger refuses to avail himself of the standard terminology of modern philosophy, with its talk of epistemology, subjectivity, representation, objective knowledge and the rest.

Heidegger has the audacity to go back to the drawing board and invent a new philosophical vocabulary. For example, he thinks that all conceptions of the human being as a subject, self, person, consciousness or indeed a mind-brain unity are hostages to a tradition of thinking whose presuppositions have not been thought through radically enough. Heidegger is nothing if not a radical thinker: a thinker who tries to dig down to the roots of our lived experience of the world rather than accepting the authority of tradition.

Heidegger's name for the human being is 'Dasein,' a term which can be variously translated, but which is usually rendered as "being-there." The basic and very simple idea, as we will see in future entries, is that the human being is first and foremost not an isolated subject, cut off from a realm of objects that it wishes to know about. We are rather beings who are always already in the world, outside and alongside a world from which, for the most part, we do not distinguish ourselves.

What goes for Dasein also goes for many of Heidegger's other concepts. Sometimes this makes **Being and Time** a very tough read, which is not helped by the fact that Heidegger, more than any other modern philosopher, exploits the linguistic possibilities of his native language, in his case, German. Although Macquarrie and Robinson, in their 1962 Blackwell English edition, produce one of the classics of modern philosophical translation, reading **Being and Time** can sometimes feel like wading through a conceptual mud of baroque and unfamiliar concepts.

THE BASIC IDEA

That said, the basic idea of **Being and Time** is extremely simple: being is time. That is, what it means for a human being to be is to exist temporally in the stretch between birth and death.

Being is time and time is finite, it comes to an end with our death. Therefore, if we want to understand what it means to be an authentic human being, then it is essential that we constantly project our lives on to the horizon of our death, what Heidegger calls "being-towards-death."

Crudely stated, for thinkers like St Paul, St Augustine, Luther and Kierkegaard, it is through the relation to God that the self finds itself. For Heidegger, the question of God's existence or non-existence has no philosophical relevance. The self can only become what it truly is through confrontation with death, by making a meaning out of our finitude. If our being is finite, then what it means to be human consists in grasping this finitude, in "becoming who one is" in words of Nietzsche's that Heidegger liked to cite. We will show how this insight into finitude is deepened in later entries in relation to Heidegger's concepts of conscience and what he calls" ecstatic temporality."

I can only give a taste of the book and offer some sign posts for readers who would like to explore further.

Being and Time, part 2: On 'Mineness'

For Heidegger, what defines the human being is the capacity to be puzzled by the deepest of questions: why is there something rather than nothing?

As Heidegger makes clear from the untitled, opening page with which Being and Time begins, what is at stake in the book is the question of being. This is the question that Aristotle raised in an untitled manuscript written 2500 years ago, but which became known at a later date as the Metaphysics. For Aristotle, there is a science that investigates what he calls "being as such," without regard to any specific realms of being, eg. the being of living things (biology) or the being of the natural world (physics.)

Metaphysics is the area of inquiry that Aristotle himself calls "first philosophy" and which comes before anything else. It is the most abstract, universal and indefinable area of philosophy. But it is also the most fundamental.

With admirable arrogance, it is the question of being that Heidegger sets himself the task of inquiring into in **Being and Time**. He begins with a series of rhetorical questions: Do we have an answer to the question of the meaning of being? Not at all, he answers. But do we even experience any perplexity about this question? Not at all, Heidegger repeats. Therefore, the first and most important task of Heidegger's book is to recover our perplexity for this question of questions: Hamlet's "To be or not to be?"

For Heidegger, what defines the human being is his capacity to be perplexed by the deepest and most enigmatic of questions: Why is there something rather than nothing? So, the task of **Being and Time** is reawakening in us a taste for perplexity, a taste for questioning. Questioning – Heidegger will opine much later in his career – is the piety of thinking.

The first line of the text proper of Being and Time is, "We are ourselves the entities to be analyzed". This is the key to the crucial concept of mineness (Jemeinigkeit), with which the book begins: if I am the being for whom being is a question – "to be or not to be" – then the question of being is mine to be, one way or another.

In what, then, does the being of being human consist? Heidegger's answer is existence (Existenz.) Therefore, the question of being is to be accessed by way of what Heidegger calls "an existential analytic." But what sort of thing is human existence? It is obviously defined by time: we are creatures with a past, who move through a present and who have available to them a series of possibilities, what Heidegger calls "ways to be." Heidegger's point here is wonderfully simple: the human being is not definable by a "what," like a table or a chair, but by a "who" that is shaped by existence in time. What it means to be human is to exist with a certain past, a personal and cultural history, and by an open series of possibilities that I can seize hold of or not.

This brings us to a very important point: if the being of being human is defined by mineness, then my being is not a matter of indifference to me. A table or chair cannot recite Hamlet's soliloquy or undergo the experience of self-questioning and self-doubt that such words express. But we can.

This is the kernel of Heidegger's idea of authenticity (Eigentlichkeit), which more accurately expresses what is proper to the human being, what is its own. For Heidegger, there are two dominant modes of being human: authenticity and inauthenticity. Furthermore, we have a choice to make between these two modes: the choice is whether to be oneself or not to be oneself, to be author of oneself and self-authorizing or not. Heidegger insists, as he will do throughout Being and Time, that inauthenticity does not signify a lower or lesser being, but many readers have had reason to doubt such assurances. Theodor Adorno, famously critical of Heidegger, asks: doesn't authenticity end up being a jargon that we are better off without? Let's just say that the point is moot.

Regardless of the twin modes of authenticity and inauthenticity, Heidegger insists early in **Being and Time** that the human being must first be presented in its indifferent character, prior to any choice to be authentic or not. In words that soon became a mantra in the book, Heidegger seeks to describe the human being as it presented "most closely and mostly"(Zunächst und Zumeist.)

Note the radical nature of this initial move: philosophy is not some other worldly speculation as to whether the external world exists or whether the other human-looking creatures around me are really human and not robots or some such. Rather, philosophy begins with the description – what Heidegger calls "phenomenology" – of human beings in their average everyday existence. It seeks to derive certain common structures from that everydayness.

But we should note the difficulty of the task that Heidegger has set himself. That which is closest and most obvious to us is fiendishly difficult to describe. Nothing is closer to me than myself in my average, indifferent everyday existence, but how to describe this? Heidegger was fond of quoting St Augustine's Confessions, when the latter writes, "Assuredly I labour here and I labour within myself; I have become to myself a land of trouble and inordinate sweat." Heidegger indeed means trouble and one often sweats through these pages. But the moments of revelation are breathtaking in their obviousness.

Being and Time, part 3: Being-in-the-world

How Heidegger turned Descartes upside down, so that we are, and only therefore think?

Heidegger's attempt is to destroy our standard, traditional philosophical vocabulary and replace it with something new. What Heidegger seeks to destroy in particular is a certain picture of the relation between human beings and the world that is widespread in modern philosophy and whose source is Descartes(indeed Descartes is the philosopher who stands most accused in Being and Time.) Roughly and readily, this is the idea that there are two sorts of substances in the world: thinking things like us and extended things, like tables, chairs and indeed the entire fabric of space and time. The relation between thinking things and extended things is one of knowledge and the philosophical and indeed scientific task consists in ensuring that what a later tradition called "subject" might have access to a world of objects. This is what we might call the epistemological construal of the relation between human beings and the world, where epistemology means "theory of knowledge." Heidegger does not deny the importance of knowledge; he simply denies its primacy. Prior to this dualistic picture of the relation between human beings and the world lies a deeper unity that he tries to capture in the formula "Dasein is being-in-the-world." What might that mean?

If the human being is really being-in-the-world, then this entails that the world itself is part of the fundamental constitution of what it means to be human. That is to say, I am not a free-floating self or ego facing a world of objects that stands over against me. Rather, for Heidegger, I am my world. The world is part and parcel of my being, of the fabric of my existence. We might capture the sense of Heidegger's thought hereby thinking of Dasein not as a subject distinct from a world of objects, but as an experience of openness where my being and that of the world are not distinguished for the most part.I am completely fascinated and absorbed by my world, not cut off from it in some sort of "mind" or what Heidegger calls "the cabinet of consciousness."

Heidegger's major claim in his discussion of world in Being and Time is that the world announces itself most closely and mostly as a handy or useful world, the world of common, average everyday experience. My proximal encounter with the table on which I am writing these words is not as an object made of a certain definable substance(wood and iron, say) existing in a geometrically ordered space-time continuum. Rather, this is just the table that I use to write and which is useful for arranging my papers, my laptop and my coffee cup. Heidegger insists that we have to "thrust aside our interpretative tendencies" which cover our everyday experience of the world and attend much more closely to that which shows itself.

The world is full of handy things that hang together as a whole and which are meaningful to me. In even more basic terms, the world is a whole load of stuff that is related together: my laptop sits on my desk, my spectacles sit on my nose, the desk sits on the floor, and I can look over to the window at the garden and hear the quiet hum of traffic and police sirens that make up life in this city. This is what Heidegger calls "environment" (Umwelt), where he is trying to describe the world that surrounds the human being and in which it is completely immersed for the most part.

Heidegger insists that this lived experience of the world is missed or overlooked by scientific inquiry or indeed through a standard philosophy of mind, which presupposes a dualistic distinction between mind and reality. What is required is a phenomenology of our lived experience of the world that tries to be true to what shows itself first and foremost in our experience. To translate this into another idiom, we might say that Heidegger is inverting the usual distinction between theory and practice. My primary encounter with the world is not theoretical; it is not the experience of some spectator gazing out at a world stripped of value. Rather, I first apprehend the world practically as a world of things which are useful and handy and which are imbued with human significance and value. The theoretical or scientific vision of things that find in a thinker like Descartes is founded on a practical insight that is fascinated and concerned with things.

Heidegger introduces a distinction between two ways of approaching the world: the present-at-hand (Vorhandenheit) and the ready-to-hand (Zuhandenheit.) Present-at-hand refers to our theoretical apprehension of a world made up of objects. It is the conception of the world from which science begins. The ready-to-hand describes our practical relation to things that are handy or useful. Heidegger's basic claim is that practice precedes theory, and that the ready-to-hand is prior to the present-at-hand. The problem with most philosophy after Descartes is that it conceives of the world theoretically and thus imagines, like Descartes, that I can doubt the existence of the external world and even the reality of the persons that fill it – who knows, they might be robots! For Heidegger, by contrast, who we are as human beings is inextricably bound up and bound together with the complex web of social practices that make up my world. The world is part of who I am. For Heidegger, to cut oneself off from the world, like Descartes, is to miss the point entirely: the fabric of our openedness to the world is one piece. And that piece should not be cut up. Furthermore, the world is not simply full of handy, familiar meaningful things. It is also full of persons. If I am fundamentally with my world, then that world is a common world experienced together with others. This is what Heidegger calls "being-with"(Mitsein.)

Being and Time, part 4: Thrown into this world

How do we find ourselves in the world, and how can we find our freedom here?

Heidegger seeks to reawaken perplexity about the question of being, the basic issue of metaphysics. In **Being and Time**, he pursues this question through an analysis of the human being or what he calls Dasein. The being of Dasein is existence, understood as average everyday existence or our life in the world, discussed in the last entry. But how might we give some more content to this rather formal idea of existence?

Heidegger gives us a strong clue in Division 1, Chapter 5 of **Being and Time**, which is a long, difficult, but immensely rewarding chapter and where things really begin to get interesting. The central claim of this chapter - which is deepened in the remainder of **Being and Time** - is that Dasein is thrown projection *(Dasein ist geworfener Entwurf).* Let me try and unravel this thought.

Heidegger tends to advance his investigation in concept clusters. One cluster contains three concepts: **state of mind**, mood and thrownness. State of mind is a rather questionable rendering of Befindlichkeit, which William Richardson nicely translates as 'already-having-found-oneself-there-ness'. OK, it's not particularly elegant, but the thought is the human being is always already found or disclosed somewhere, namely in the 'there' of its being-in-the-world. This 'there' is the Da of Dasein.

Furthermore, I am always found in a **mood**, a Stimmung. This mood is the strong Aristotelian sense of pathos, a passion of the soul or an affect, something befalls us and in which we find ourselves. The passions are not, for Heidegger, psychological colouring for an essentially rational agent. They are rather the fundamental ways in which we are attuned to the world.

Indeed, musicologically, Stimmung is linked to tuning and pitch: one is attuned to the world firstly and mostly through moods. One of the compelling aspects of Heidegger's work is his attempt to provide a phenomenology of moods, of the affects that make up our everyday life in the world.

This is another way of approaching his central insight: that we cannot exist independently of our relation to the world; and this relationship is a matter of mood and appetite, not rational contemplation.

Such moods disclose the human being as thrown into the 'there' of my being-in-the-world. As Jim Morrisson intoned many decades ago, 'Into this world we're thrown.' **Thrownness**(Geworfenheit) is the simple awareness that we always find ourselves somewhere, namely delivered over to a world with which we are fascinated, a world we share with others.

We are always caught up in our everyday life in the world, in the throw of various moods, whether fear, boredom, excitement or–as we will see in the next entry – anxiety.

But, Heidegger insists, Dasein is not just thrown into the world. Because of it – we – are capable of understanding, we can also throw off our thrown condition. Understanding is, for Heidegger, a conception of activity. It is always understanding how to do something or how to operate something. Understanding is the possession of an ability (etwaskönnen) and the authentic human is characterised by the ability or potentiality to be (Seinkönnen).

So, the human being is not just a being defined by being thrown into the world. It is also one who can throw off that thrown condition in a movement where it seizes hold of its possibilities, where it acts in a concrete situation. This movement is what Heidegger calls projection (Entwurf) and it is the very experience of what Heidegger will call, later in Being and Time, freedom. Freedom is not an abstract philosophical concept. It is the experience of the human being demonstrating its potential through acting in the world. To act in such a way is to be authentic.

Being and Time, part 5: Anxiety

Anxiety is the philosophical mood par excellence, the experience of detachment from which I can begin to think freely for myself.

Moods are essential ways of disclosing human existence for Heidegger. Yet, there is one mood in particular that reveals the self in stark profile for the first time. This is the function of anxiety (Angst), which Heidegger calls a basic or fundamental mood(Grundstimmung.) Safranski rightly calls anxiety "a shadowy queen amongst moods."

Anxiety makes its appearance in Division 1, Chapter 6, where Heidegger is seeking to define the being of Dasein as what he calls "care" (Sorge.) It would take many more blog entries than I

have at my disposal to lay out inadequate details about the structure and meaning of care. But we can get more than a hint by looking at anxiety.

Dasein is being-in-the-world. Our everyday existence is characterised by complete immersion in the ways of the world. The world fascinates us and my life is completely caught up in its rhythms and activities. The question Heidegger asks in Chapter 6 is: how is the being-in-the-world as a whole to be disclosed? Is there an experience where the world as such and as a whole is revealed to us? Is there a mood in which we pull back from the world and see it as something distinct from us? Heidegger's claim is that being-in-the-world as a whole is disclosed in anxiety and is then defined as care. As such, anxiety has an important methodological function in the argument of **Being and Time.**

But the existential resonance of anxiety is much more than methodological. The first thing to grasp is that anxiety does not mean ceaselessly fretting or fitfully worrying about something or other. On the contrary, Heidegger says that anxiety is a rare and subtle mood and in one place he even compares it a feeling of calm or peace. It is in anxiety that the free, authentic self first comes into existence. It was, of course, the mood that launched a thousand existentialist novels, most famously Sartre's Nausea and Camus's The Outsider (although Heidegger was very critical of existentialism.)

In order to understand what Heidegger means by anxiety, we have to distinguish it from another mood he examines: fear. Heidegger gives a phenomenology of fear earlier in **Being and Time.** His claim is that fear is always fear of something threatening, some particular thing in the world. Let's say that I am fearful of spiders. Fear has an object and when that object is removed, I am no longer fearful. I see a spider in the bath and I am suddenly frightened. My non-spider fearing friend removes the offending arachnid,I am no longer fearful.

Matters are very different with anxiety. If fear is fearful of something in particular and determinate, then anxiety is anxious about nothing in particular and is indeterminate. If fear is directed towards some distinct thing in the world, spiders or whatever, then anxiety is anxious about being-in-the-world as such. Anxiety is experienced in the face of something completely indefinite. It is, Heidegger insists, "nothing and nowhere."

But let's back up for a moment here. Heidegger's claim earlier in Division 1 of **Being and Time**, is that the human being finds itself in a world that is richly meaningful and with which it is fascinated. In other words, the world is homely (heimlich),and even cosy . In anxiety, all of this changes. Suddenly, I am overtaken by the mood of anxiety that renders the world meaningless. It appears to me as an inauthentic spectacle, a kind of tranquilized and pointless bustle of activity. In anxiety, the everyday world slips away and my home becomes uncanny (unheimlich) and strange to me. From being a player in the game of life that I loved, I become an observer of a game that I no longer see the point in playing.

What is first glimpsed in anxiety is the authentic self. As the world slips away, we obtrude. I like to think about this in maritime terms. Inauthentic life in the world is completely bound up with things and other people in a kind of "groundless floating" – the phrase is Heidegger's. Everyday life in the world is like being immersed in the sea and drowned by the world's suffocating banality. Anxiety is the experience of the tide going out, the seawater draining away, revealing a self-stranded on the strand, as it were. Anxiety is that basic mood when the self-first distinguishes itself from the world and becomes self-aware.

Anxiety does not need darkness, despair and night sweats. It can arise in the most innocuous of situations: sitting in the subway distractedly reading a book and overhearing conversations, one is suddenly seized by the feeling of meaninglessness, by the radical distinction between yourself and the world in which you find yourself. With this experience of anxiety, Heidegger says, Dasein is individualised and becomes self-aware.

Anxiety is the first experience of our freedom, as a freedom from things and other people. It is a freedom to begin to become myself. Anxiety is perhaps the philosophical mood par excellence, it is the experience of detachment from things and from others where I can begin to think freely for myself. Yet, as Heidegger was very well aware, anxiety is also a mood that is powerfully analysed in the Christian tradition, from Augustine to Kierkegaard, where it describes the self's effort to turn itself, to undergo a kind of conversion. Heidegger's difference with Christianity is that the self's conversion is not undergone with reference to God, but only in relation to death.

Being and Time part 6: Death

Far from being morbid, Heidegger's conception of living in the knowledge of death is a liberating one.

The basic idea in Being and Time is very simple: being is time and time is finite. For human beings, time comes to an end with our death. Therefore, if we want to understand what it means to be an authentic human being, then it is essential that we constantly project our lives onto the horizon of our death. This is what Heidegger famously calls "being-towards-death". If our being is finite, then an authentic human life can only be found by confronting finitude and trying to make a meaning out of the fact of our death. Heidegger subscribes to the ancient maxim that "to philosophize is to learn how to die."

Mortality is that in relation to which we shape and fashion our selfhood.

There are four rather formal criteria in Heidegger's conception of being-towards-death: it is non-relational, certain, indefinite and not to be outstripped. Firstly, death is non-relational in the sense in standing before death one has cut off all relations to others.

Death cannot be experienced through the deaths of others, but only through my relation to my death. I will contest this criterion below.

Secondly, it is certain that we are going to die. Although one might evade or run away from the fact, no one doubts that life comes to an end in death. Thirdly, death is indefinite in the sense that although death is certain, we do not know when it going to happen. Most people desire a long and full life, but we can never know when the grim reaper is going to knock at our door.

Fourthly, to say that death is not to be outstripped (unüberholbar) simply means that death is pretty damned important. There's no way of trumping it and it outstrips all the possibilities that my power of free projection possesses. This is the idea behind Heidegger's famously paradoxically statement that death is the"possibility of impossibility". Death is that limit against which my potentiality-for-being (Seinkönnen) is to be measured. It is that essential impotence against which the potency of my freedom shatters itself.

At the end of the introduction to Being and Time, Heidegger writes, "Higher than actuality stands possibility". **Being and Time** is a long hymn of praise to possibility and it finds its highest expression in being-towards-death. Heidegger makes a distinction between anticipation (Vorlaufen) and expectation or awaiting (Erwarten). His claim is that the awaiting of death still contains too much of the actual, where death would be the actualisation of possibility. Such would be a gloomy philosophy of morbidity. On the contrary, for Heidegger, anticipation does not passively await death, but mobilises mortality as the condition for free action in the world.

This results in a hugely important and seemingly paradoxical thought: freedom is not the absence of necessity, in the form of death. On the contrary, freedom consists in the affirmation of the necessity of one's mortality. It is only in being-towards-death that one can become the person who one truly is. Concealed in the idea of death as the possibility of impossibility is the acceptance on one's mortal limitation as the basis for an affirmation of one's life.

So, there is nothing morbid about being-towards-death. Heidegger's thought is that being-towards-death pulls Dasein out of its immersion in inauthentic everyday life and allows it come into its own. It is only in relation to being-towards-death that I become passionately aware of my freedom.

Despite its baroque linguistic garb, Heidegger's analysis of being-towards-death is exceptionally direct and powerful. However, it is open to the following objection. Heidegger argues that the only authentic death is one's own. To die for another person, he writes, would simply be to "sacrifice oneself." To that extent, for Heidegger, the deaths of others are secondary to my death, which is primary. In my view (and this criticism is first advanced by Edith Stein and Emmanuel Levinas), such a conception of death is both false and morally pernicious. On the contrary, I think that death comes into our world through the deaths of others, whether as close as a parent, partner or child or as far as the unknown victim of a distant famine or war. The relation to death is not first and foremost my own fear for my own demise, but my sense of being undone by the experience of grief and mourning.

Also, there is a surprisingly traditional humanism at work in Heidegger's approach to death. In his view, only human beings die, whereas plants and animals simply perish. I can't speak with any expertise about the death of plants, but empirical research would certainly seem to show that the higher mammals – whales, dolphins, elephants, but also cats and dogs – also have an experience of mortality, of both their own and of those around them. We are not the only creatures in the universe who are touched by the sentiment of mortality.

Being and Time,part 7:Conscience

For Heidegger, the call of conscience is one that silences the chatter of the world and brings me back to myself

After the existential drama of Heidegger's notion of being-towards-death, why do we need a discussion of conscience? As so often in Being and Time, Heidegger insists that although his description of being-towards-death is formally orontologically correct,it needs more compelling content at what Heidegger calls the "ontic" level, that is, at the level of experience. Finitude gets a grip on the self through the experience of conscience. For me, the discussion of conscience contains the most exciting and challenging pages in **Being and Time**. Let me try and sketch as simply as possible the complex line of Heidegger's argument.

Conscience is a call. It is something that calls one away from one's inauthentic immersion in the homely familiarity of everyday life. It is, Heidegger writes, that uncanny experience of something like an external voice in one's head that pulls one out of the hubbub and chatter of life in the world and arrests our ceaseless busyness.

This sounds very close to the Christian experience of conscience that one finds in Augustine or Luther. In Book 8 of the Confessions, Augustine describes the entire drama of conversion in terms of hearing an external voice, "as of a child", that leads him to take up the Bible and eventually turn away from paganism and towards Christ. Luther describes conscience as the work of God in the mind of man.

For Heidegger, by contrast, conscience is not God talking to me, but me talking to myself. The uncanny call of conscience – the pang and pain of its sudden appearance – feels like an alien voice, but is, Heidegger insists, Dasein calling to itself. I am called back from inauthentic life in the world, complete with what Sartre would call its "counterfeit immortality," towards myself. Furthermore, that self is, as we saw in blog 6, defined in terms of being-towards-death. So, conscience is the experience of the human being calling itself back to its mortality, a little like Hamlet in the grave with Yorick's skull.

What gets said in the call of conscience? Heidegger is crystal clear: like Cordelia in King Lear, nothing is said. The call of conscience is silent. It contains no instructions or advice. In order to understand this, it is important to grasp that, for Heidegger, inauthentic life is characterised by chatter – for example, the ever-ambiguous hubbub of the blogosphere. Conscience calls Dasein back from this chatter silently. It has the character of what Heidegger calls "reticence"(Verschwiegenheit), which is the privileged mode of language in Heidegger. So, the call of conscience is a silent call that silences the chatter of the world and brings me back to myself.

But what does this uncanny call of conscience give one to understand? Conscience's call can be reduced to one word: Guilty! But what does Dasein's guilt really mean? The human being is defined in terms of thrown projection, it always has its being to be. That is, human existence is a lack, it is something due to Dasein, a debt that it strives to make up or repay. This is the ontological meaning of guilt as Schuld, which can also mean debt. As Heidegger perhaps surprisingly writes, although it should be recalled that he was also writing in trouble deconomic times,

"Life is a business whether or not it covers its costs." Debt is away of being. I owe, therefore I am.

Heidegger goes on to show that this ontological meaning of guilt as indebtedness is the basis for any traditional moral understanding of guilt. Heidegger's phenomenology of guilt, and here he is close to Nietzsche in On the Genealogy of Morals, which claims to uncover the deep structure of ethical selfhood which cannot be defined by morality, since morality already presupposes it. Rejecting any Christian notion of evil as the privation of good (privatioboni), Heidegger's claim is that guilt is the pre-moral source for any morality. As such, it is beyond good or evil. Is guilt bad?

No. but neither is it good. It is simply what we are,for Heidegger. We are guilty. Such is Kafka's share of eternal truth.

Heidegger insists that Dasein does not load guilt on to itself. It simply is guilty, always already,as Heidegger liked to say. What changes in being authentic is that the human being understands the call of conscience and takes it into itself. Authentic Dasein comes to understand itself as guilty. In doing this, Dasein has chosen itself, as Heidegger writes. This is very interesting: what is chosen is not having a conscience, which Dasein already has because of its ontological want or indebtedness, but what Heidegger calls, rather awkwardly, "wanting to have a conscience"(Gewissen-haben-wollen.) This is, if you like, a second-order wanting: I choose to want the want that I am. Only in this way, Heidegger adds, can the human being be answerable or responsible(verantwortlich.) Thus, responsibility – which would be the key to any conception of ethics in relation to Heidegger's work, which is, to say the least, a moot point – consists in understanding the call, in wanting to have a conscience. To make this choice, Heidegger insists, is to become resolute.

Heidegger's Being and Time, part 8:Temporality

Time should be grasped in and of itself as the unity of the three dimensions of future, past and present.

Firstly, he is trying to criticize the idea of time as a uniform, linear and infinite series of "now-points." On this model, which derives ultimately from Aristotle's Physics, the future is the not-yet-now, the past is the no-longer-now, and the present is the now that flows from future to past at each passing moment. This is what Heidegger calls the "vulgar" or ordinary conception of time where priority is always given to the present. Heidegger thinks that this Aristotelian conception of time has dominated philosophical inquiries into time from the ancient Greeks to Hegel and even up to his near contemporary Bergson.

Secondly, he is trying to avoid any conception of time that begins with a distinction between time and eternity. On this understanding of time, classically expressed in Augustine's **Confessions,** temporality is derived from a higher non-temporal state of eternity, which is co-extensive with the infinite and eternal now of God.

In order to understand what Heidegger means by temporality, we have to set it in the context of the existential analytic of Dasein that I have sought to describe, namely that the human being is always running ahead towards it send. For Heidegger, the primary phenomenon of time is the future that is revealed to me in my being-towards-death. Heidegger makes play of the link between the future (Zukunft) and to come towards (Zukommen.) Insofar as Dasein anticipates, it comes towards itself. The human is not confined in the present, but always projects towards the future.

But what Dasein takes over in the future is its basic ontological indebtedness, its guilt, as discussed in the previous blog. There is a tricky but compelling thought at work here: in anticipation, I project towards the future, but what comes out of the future is my past, my personal and cultural baggage, what Heidegger calls my"having-been-ness"(Gewesenheit.) But this does not mean that I am somehow condemned to my past. On the contrary, I can make a decision to take over the fact of who I am in a free action. This is what Heidegger calls "resoluteness."

This brings us to the present. For Heidegger,the present is not some endless series of now points that I watch flowing by. Rather, the present is something that I can seize hold of and resolutely make my own. What is opened in the anticipation of the future is the fact of our having-been which releases itself into the present moment of action.

This is what Heidegger calls "the moment of vision"(Augenblick, literally "glance of the eye".)This term, borrowed from Kierkegaard and Luther, can be approached as a translation of the Greek kairos, the right or opportune moment. Within Christian theology, the kairos was the fulfilment or redemption of time that occurred with the appearance of Christ. Heidegger's difference with Christian theology is that he wants to hang on to the idea of the moment of vision, but to do so without any reference to God. What appears in the moment of vision is authentic Dasein. To put the matter mildly, it is a moot point whether Heidegger can inhabit these Christian forms without accepting or at least aping their content.

The key to Heidegger's understanding of time is that it is neither simply reducible to the vulgar experience of time, nor does it originate in distinction from eternity. Time should be grasped in and of itself as the unity of the three dimensions – what Heidegger calls "ecstases" – of future, past and present. This is what he calls "primordial" or "original" time and he insists that it is finite. It comes to an endin death.

For Heidegger, we are time. Temporality is a process with three dimensions which form a unity. The task that Heidegger sets himself in **Being and Time** is a description of the movement of human finitude. As many readers have pointed out and Heidegger himself acknowledged, **Being and Time** is unfinished. The question that he leaves hanging at the end of the book is the issue that began the whole enterprise, namely the question of being as such. We have been given an answer to the question what it means to be human, but no sense of how we might answer the question of being as such. The task that Heidegger sets himself, from the publication of **Being and Time** in 1927 to his death nearly a half-century later in 1976, was the elucidation of that question.

"Envisioning the Future Organizational and Administrative Structure of India"

Classes and Class Struggle

The complexity and necessity of a revolution in addressing class and class struggle, particularly for the Indian people and peasants. It implies that such a revolution is vital to overcome domestic and foreign adversarial forces. Let's elaborate on these points:

Revolution and Class Struggle: The concept of revolution indicates a significant and transformative process aimed at addressing issues related to class and class struggle. This is a desire for a fundamental change in the socio-economic and political landscape.

Peasants and Indian People: The involvement of peasants and the Indian populace emphasizes the broad-based nature of this movement. It signifies that the revolution is not limited to a particular group but encompasses a collective effort.

Overcoming Domestic and Foreign Enemies: The goal of overcoming domestic and foreign adversaries The this revolution is not only focused on internal issues but also addresses external challenges or influences. It underscores the desire for sovereignty and self-determination.

Complex and Prolonged Struggle: The acknowledgment that this struggle is not "simple, clean, or quick" The challenges and obstacles that the revolutionaries are likely to face. the path to achieving the goals will be arduous and demanding, requiring patience and resilience.

The importance of a profound and enduring revolution that involves the participation of the Indian people, particularly peasants, and recognizes the need to confront both domestic and foreign challenges in the pursuit of desired social and economic changes.

Socialism

The development of socialism in India through a democratic revolution and emphasizes the need for a gradual transition that combines socialist, semi-capitalist, and agrarian elements. It also highlights the importance of uniting with middle peasants and educating them about the shortcomings of pure capitalism. Let's explain this statement in more detail:

Development of Socialism: The socialism is a desirable socio-economic and political system for India. Socialism typically involves public ownership or control of key industries and resources, with an emphasis on social equality and welfare. The socialism is a path to addressing socio-economic disparities and promoting collective welfare in India.

Democratic Revolution: The means to achieve socialism in India is a "democratic revolution." This indicates a non-violent, democratic process to bring about political and economic change. It emphasizes that the transition to socialism should be peaceful, participatory, and in alignment with democratic values.

Gradual Transition: The road to socialism is a gradual one. The transformation will take time and cannot happen overnight. This gradual transition may allow for a smoother adaptation to the new system and the avoidance of abrupt disruptions in society and the economy.

Incorporating Semi-Capitalist-Agrarian Aspects: The notion of combining socialism with semi-capitalist and agrarian elements reflects a pragmatic approach. It implies that not all capitalist and agrarian structures need to be immediately eliminated, but rather that they can coexist alongside socialist principles during the transition.

Unite with Middle Peasants: Middle peasants, often seen as a transitional class between large landowners and landless labourers, are considered an important group to unite with. This suggests that building a broad coalition of support for socialism includes reaching out to and addressing the concerns of middle peasants.

Educating About Capitalism's Failings: The importance of educating people, including middle peasants, about the perceived failures of pure capitalism. This is likely in terms of wealth inequality, exploitation, and lack of social safety nets, which can be used to make the case for socialism.

We advocate for a peaceful and gradual shift toward socialism in India through a democratic revolution. It recognizes the need to work with diverse social groups, including middle peasants, and to educate them about the drawbacks of capitalism to build broad-based support for the socialist cause.

War and Peace

War as a Continuation of Politics. The idea that war is often an extension of political goals and strategies. It implies that conflicts and confrontations between nations are often driven by political motives or disagreements, with war being a means to achieve certain political objectives.

Just (Progressive) Wars: Just wars are typically considered wars fought for noble or moral reasons, often related to self-defence, protection of human rights, or the prevention of greater harm. These are seen as wars with a legitimate moral or ethical basis.

Unjust Wars Serving Rich People Interests: Some wars are deemed unjust because they primarily serve the interests of the RICH, which refers to the capitalist class. This implies that certain wars may be waged for economic or exploitative reasons rather than for ethical or moral ones.

Imperialist Agitations: Imperialism involves the expansion of a nation's influence and control over other nations, often through force or coercion. The reference to "imperialist agitations" suggests opposition to attempts by powerful nations to exert dominance over weaker ones.

Readiness to Wage Just Wars: While no one desires war, but that it is essential to remain prepared to wage just wars when necessary, particularly when facing imperialist agitations. This readiness reflects a commitment to defending one's interests, rights, and values when they are threatened.

the political nature of war, the importance of distinguishing between just and unjust wars, and the need to be prepared to fight just wars in response to imperialist threats, even though war is generally undesirable. It reflects a perspective that views war as a means to protect legitimate interests and values, rather than as an end in itself.

Imperialism and All Reactionaries Are Paper Tigers

The perceived dangers posed by Western imperialism, European and Indian reactionary forces, comparing them to "real tigers." It also suggests that these dangers may be less formidable in the face of a just socialist goal. Let's delve into the key points:

Dangers of Western Imperialism and Reactionary Forces: The concern about the threat posed by Western imperialism and reactionary forces in Europe and India. These forces are likened to "real tigers," .

Just Goal of Socialism: The goal of socialism is "just." Socialism typically aims to address issues of economic inequality and social justice by advocating for collective ownership and equitable distribution of resources. The pursuit of socialism is driven by moral or ethical values.

Self-Centered and Unjust Interests of Reactionary Forces: Reactionary forces are characterized as having "self-centred and unjust" interests. This suggests that these forces are primarily motivated by their own benefit and may not prioritize the common good or social justice.

Expectation of Reduced Danger: Over time, the dangers posed by Western imperialism and reactionary forces will diminish. As the struggle unfolds, the justness of the socialist goal will become apparent, and the perceived danger will lessen.

This is a perspective that views Western imperialism and reactionary forces as formidable threats but believes that the pursuit of socialism, driven by just goals, will ultimately reduce their perceived danger. It reflects the hope that a focus on social justice and equitable principles will prevail over self-centred interests.

Dare to Struggle and Dare to Win

The people of India generally prefer peace and wish to avoid conflict. However, it underscores their willingness to engage in a just struggle for self-preservation when confronted with reactionary elements, whether foreign or domestic. The phrase "Dare to Struggle and Dare to Win" encourages resolute action. Here's an elaboration of the key points:

Preference for Peace: The preference of the people of India for peace. This reflects a desire for harmony and stability, indicating that they would rather avoid conflict and its associated hardships.

Readiness for a Just Struggle: Despite the preference for peace the people of India are prepared to engage in a just struggle when necessary. This suggests a commitment to defending their rights, values, and interests.

Self-Preservation: The reference to a "just struggle of self-preservation" implies that the people of India are willing to fight to protect themselves, their way of life, and their country when faced with threats. It emphasizes the notion of self-defence and resilience.

Against Reactionary Elements: The struggle is directed against "reactionary elements," which typically refers to forces or groups that seek to reverse social or political progress. These elements can be either foreign or domestic, indicating that the people of India are ready to defend their interests against all potential adversaries.

Dare to Struggle and Dare to Win: The phrase "Dare to Struggle and Dare to Win" serves as a call to action, encouraging courage and determination in the face of adversity. It implies that, when necessary, the people of India are willing to confront challenges with the resolve to succeed.

This statement conveys a readiness to engage in a just struggle when confronted by threats to self-preservation, whether from foreign or domestic reactionary elements. It combines the preference for peace with a commitment to defending essential values and interests, with an underlying call for determination and courage.

Democracy in the Three Main Fields

The relationship between democracy, honesty, and the reform of officers, as well as their impact on society and cadres, is a complex and important one. Here's an explanation of how these elements are interconnected:

1. **Democracy and Reform of Officers:**
    - **Accountability:** Democracy places a strong emphasis on accountability. In a democratic society, officers, whether in government or other organizations, are held accountable for their actions and decisions. This accountability can lead to the reform of corrupt or ineffective officers.
    - **Checks and Balances:** Democracy often incorporates mechanisms such as separation of powers and an independent judiciary. These checks and balances can be instrumental in holding officers accountable and ensuring that reforms are carried out fairly.
2. **Honesty and Reform of Officers:**
    - **Transparency:** Honesty is a crucial component of transparency. When officers are honest in their dealings, it becomes easier to identify and address corruption or misconduct, facilitating reform efforts.
    - **Credibility:** Honest officers are more likely to be trusted by the public. When reform is necessary, honest officers are better positioned to gain the trust of those affected by the changes.
3. **Democracy, Honesty, and Society:**
    - **Public Trust:** A democratic society that values honesty is more likely to have a trusting population. When people trust their leaders and institutions, it becomes easier to implement reforms and address societal issues.
4. **Democracy, Honesty, and Cadres (Government Officials):**
    - **Meritocracy:** In a democratic society, the selection and promotion of government officials (cadres) should ideally be based on merit, qualifications, and competence. Honest and capable cadres are more likely to drive positive reforms.
    - **Public Service:** Honest cadres are more likely to prioritize the public interest over personal gain. This dedication to public service can lead to reforms that benefit society.
5. **Avoiding "Ultra-Democracy":**
    - "Ultra-democracy" can refer to an extreme form of democracy where individualism and aversion to discipline undermine the

overall functioning of society. While democracy encourages individual rights and freedoms, it should be balanced with a sense of responsibility and social discipline to avoid chaos.

- In such a system, the reform of officers might become challenging because the emphasis on individualism can hinder collective decision-making and the implementation of reforms.

In conclusion, democracy and honesty are essential components of a well-functioning society and the reform of officers or government officials. The principles of democracy, when accompanied by honesty and transparency, promote accountability and trust. However, it's important to strike a balance to avoid excessive individualism and aversion to discipline, which can impede the overall progress of society and the effectiveness of reform efforts.

Revolutionary Heroism

The limitless creative energy of the masses can indeed extend to the military, influencing their fighting style and indomitable will. Here are some ways in which this creativity and determination can be observed in the armed forces:

Adaptability: Soldiers often find themselves in dynamic and unpredictable situations on the battlefield. Their creative problem-solving skills can help them adapt to new challenges and come up with innovative solutions on the spot.

Tactics and Strategy: Creative thinking is invaluable when it comes to devising tactics and strategies. Military leaders and troops may employ unconventional methods or surprise their enemies with innovative approaches to achieve their objectives.

Equipment and Technology: Soldiers and engineers often come up with novel ideas to improve equipment and technology, making them more efficient and effective in combat. This creativity can result in the development of new tools and techniques.

Camouflage and Concealment: Creative camouflage techniques are essential for concealing troops and equipment. This can involve using the natural environment in inventive ways to remain hidden from the enemy.

Unit Cohesion: Indomitable will and determination are vital qualities in the military. The unwavering commitment of soldiers to their mission and their comrades is a testament to their unyielding spirit and resolve.

Resourcefulness: In challenging and resource-constrained environments, troops often demonstrate remarkable resourcefulness. They make the most of limited resources, finding creative ways to overcome obstacles and complete their missions.

Crisis Management: Creative thinking and indomitable will are crucial during times of crisis or when facing unexpected threats. Soldiers must remain composed and adaptable to navigate through such situations successfully.

Moral Support: The indomitable will of the troops can be a source of inspiration and motivation for their comrades. In challenging circumstances, one soldier's determination to persevere can boost the spirits of the entire unit.

Humanitarian Efforts: The military's creative energy can also be harnessed for humanitarian missions. Soldiers may come up with innovative ways to deliver aid, provide medical care, or rebuild communities affected by conflict.

Inspiration for Others: The creative and indomitable spirit of the military can inspire others, both within and outside the armed forces. It serves as a testament to the power of determination, innovation, and resilience.

In conclusion, the creative energy and indomitable will of the masses can be a driving force within the military, influencing their fighting style and their ability to overcome adversity. This creativity, adaptability, and determination are valuable assets in the complex and ever-changing landscape of warfare, helping the armed forces achieve their objectives and safeguard their nations.

Building Our Country Through Diligence and Frugality

The idea that India's road to modernization will be built on the principles of diligence and frugality highlights several key aspects of the development process and the importance of maintaining these principles over the long term:

Sustainable Development: Diligence and frugality are crucial for sustainable development. Emphasizing these principles means being mindful of resource use and ensuring that growth is balanced and doesn't come at the expense of future generations.

Efficiency: A diligent and frugal approach encourages the efficient use of resources, whether it's in infrastructure development, technology adoption, or public spending. This can lead to better outcomes with the available resources.

Inclusivity: Focusing on frugality is especially important for a country as vast and diverse as India. It ensures that modernization efforts reach all segments of the population, rather than benefiting only a select few.

Long-Term Perspective: The mention of "50 years later" underscores the importance of a long-term perspective. Modernization is an ongoing process that requires a sustained commitment to principles like diligence and frugality to ensure that the benefits are widespread and enduring.

Avoiding Complacency: The statement also suggests that achieving mass-scale modernization should not lead to complacency. It emphasizes the need to continuously strive for progress, even when significant milestones are achieved.

Responsible Governance: Diligence and frugality are values that should be integrated into governance and policy-making. It ensures that government resources are utilized efficiently and for the benefit of the population.

Cultural and Ethical Values: These principles are not only economic but also cultural and ethical. They align with traditional Indian values of thriftiness and the importance of hard work and dedication in achieving goals.

Resource Conservation: Diligence and frugality contribute to the conservation of natural resources, which is crucial for environmental sustainability and addressing issues like climate change.

Resilience: A frugal and diligent approach can make the country more resilient in the face of economic shocks and global challenges. It builds a strong foundation for economic stability and growth.

Social Equity: By maintaining diligence and frugality, India can work towards reducing economic disparities and ensuring that the benefits of modernization are more evenly distributed.

In conclusion, the road to modernization in India, guided by principles of diligence and frugality, holds the promise of sustainable, inclusive, and enduring development. These values should be upheld not just in the initial phases of modernization but throughout the journey, to create a more prosperous and equitable society. needs of a society.

Methods of Thinking and Methods of Work

Marxist dialectical materialism, which is a philosophical framework rooted in the works of Karl Marx and Friedrich Engels, indeed emphasizes the constant struggle between opposites in an empirical setting. This framework is often considered a valuable approach toward constant improvement and social change. Here are some key points to understand its relevance:

Dialectical Materialism: Dialectical materialism is a philosophical method that examines the dynamics of change and development in a material world. It emphasizes the conflict and tension between opposing forces as a driving factor in societal evolution.

Historical Context: Marxist dialectical materialism emerged in the context of 19th-century industrialization and social upheaval. It sought to understand and address the socio-economic contradictions of that era.

Opposition and Change: The concept of constant struggle between opposites is central to dialectical materialism. It suggests that progress and development often arise from the tension and conflicts between different social classes, economic systems, and ideological forces.

Empirical Analysis: Marxist dialectical materialism encourages an empirical and objective analysis of societal issues. It advocates for a scientific approach to understanding the material conditions and relations that underlie social phenomena.

Critique of Capitalism: Marxists often apply this framework to critically examine capitalism and its inherent contradictions, such as the conflict between labor and capital, wealth inequality, and exploitation.

Class Struggle: The concept of class struggle is a fundamental aspect of dialectical materialism. It posits that the struggle between the working class (proletariat) and the capitalist class (bourgeoisie) is a driving force for societal change.

Constant Improvement: The framework's emphasis on change and evolution aligns with the idea of constant improvement. It suggests that by addressing and resolving the contradictions within a society, it can progress towards a more equitable and just system.

Application to Social Change: Many social movements and revolutions have drawn inspiration from Marxist dialectical materialism as a means of addressing social inequalities and advocating for improvements.

Criticism and Diverse Interpretations: It's important to note that Marxist dialectical materialism is not without its criticisms and diverse interpretations. It has been both praised for its focus on class struggle and criticized for its historical applications and potential for authoritarianism.

In summary, Marxist dialectical materialism's focus on the constant struggle between opposites in an empirical setting is seen by its proponents as a method for addressing societal issues and achieving constant improvement. Its emphasis on class struggle, empirical analysis, and the examination of material conditions continues to influence political and social thought in various parts of the world. However, it remains a subject of ongoing debate and interpretation.

Correcting Mistaken Ideas

The qualities and behaviors you've mentioned—arrogance, lack of achievement after prosperity, selfishness, shirking work, and a form of liberalism that avoids conflict or effort for the sake of immediate comfort—can indeed be detrimental to the development of any society, including India. Here's how each of these aspects can hinder progress and what can be done to avoid these pitfalls:

Arrogance: Arrogance can lead to complacency and a lack of receptivity to new ideas and perspectives. It's important to cultivate humility and an open mindset that allows for learning and growth.

Lack of Achievement After Prosperity: Failing to continue progress after a period of prosperity can lead to stagnation. Consistent efforts in areas like education, innovation, and infrastructure are essential to maintain and build upon success.

Selfishness: A society that prioritizes individual interests over the common good can experience social divisions and inequality. Promoting values of altruism, cooperation, and social responsibility can help counteract selfishness.

Shirking Work: Avoiding work or responsibilities undermines productivity and economic growth. Encouraging a strong work ethic, personal responsibility, and a culture of diligence can address this issue.

Liberalism (in the sense of avoiding conflict or work for momentary comfort): While liberalism, as a political and philosophical stance, is broader and includes principles like individual rights and freedom, avoiding necessary conflicts or challenges for momentary comfort can indeed hinder progress. It's important to strike a balance between individual comfort and the greater societal good, addressing issues and challenges head-on rather than delaying them.

To promote a society's development while avoiding these pitfalls, it's essential to:

- Foster a culture of continuous improvement and self-awareness.
- Encourage education and critical thinking to challenge preconceived notions.
- Promote values of responsibility, empathy, and community involvement.
- Encourage responsible governance and policies that address societal issues.
- Cultivate a strong work ethic and a sense of purpose.
- Promote open dialogue and conflict resolution that aims for long-term solutions.

In the context of liberalism, it's important to clarify that the avoidance of conflict or effort for momentary comfort is not an inherent characteristic of liberalism as a political ideology. Liberalism encompasses a range of perspectives, and it's crucial to separate political and philosophical concepts from individual behaviors and tendencies.

In summary, addressing these negative qualities and behaviors while promoting positive values and attitudes is essential for the continued development and progress of any society, including India.

UNITY

k The idea of unity among the masses, the Party, and the whole country, while also allowing for constructive criticism along comradely lines, is in line with a dialectical method of governance. This approach recognizes the importance of balance and harmony while acknowledging the need for critical discourse. Here's why this method is significant:

Unity for Collective Strength: Unity among the masses, the Party, and the country is crucial for collective strength and cohesion. It ensures that the nation can work together toward common goals and objectives.

Political Stability: A sense of unity and common purpose promotes political stability, reducing internal conflicts and divisions that could hinder progress.

Preserving Social Harmony: Unity fosters social harmony, reducing tensions and conflicts within society, which can be particularly important in diverse and multicultural countries.

National Development: A united front can better address developmental challenges and work towards improving the overall quality of life for citizens.

Constructive Criticism: Allowing for constructive criticism is a sign of a healthy democratic system. It permits the evaluation and improvement of policies and strategies without undermining the overall unity.

Dialectical Approach: The dialectical method encourages the synthesis of opposing views. It recognizes that unity can be strengthened through the inclusion of different perspectives, allowing for a more comprehensive understanding of issues.

Innovation and Adaptation: Constructive criticism can lead to innovation and adaptation. By addressing weaknesses or shortcomings, it's possible to make necessary improvements and refine policies and practices.

Accountability: Constructive criticism holds leaders and organizations accountable for their actions, promoting transparency and responsiveness.

Dialogue and Consensus: It encourages dialogue and the building of consensus, which is often essential for the successful implementation of policies and programs.

Balance: The dialectical method involves finding a balance between unity and criticism. It recognizes that an extreme focus on unity or criticism alone can be detrimental, so a nuanced approach is necessary.

In summary, the dialectical method of governance emphasizes unity as a source of strength, stability, and progress while allowing for constructive criticism that leads to improvement. This balanced approach helps nations and organizations navigate the complexities of governance and policy-making in a way that preserves unity and harmony, even as it encourages the evolution of ideas and practices.

Indian youth

Recognizing the Indian youth as an active and vital force is crucial for the country's progress and development. India's youthful population is a valuable resource that can drive positive change in various aspects of society. Here are some key points regarding the importance of engaging, educating, and addressing the needs of Indian youth, particularly within the context of the YRCS Youth League:

Active and Vital Force: Indian youth represent a significant demographic group with the potential to contribute actively to the nation's growth. Their energy, enthusiasm, and innovative thinking can be harnessed to address various challenges and opportunities.

Education and Skill Development: Providing quality education and skill development opportunities to the youth is essential. A well-educated and skilled workforce is a critical asset for economic and social progress.

Empowerment: Empowering the youth through education, mentorship, and access to resources can enable them to make informed decisions, participate in public life, and advocate for their interests.

Youth Engagement: Involving youth in community and civic engagement initiatives can foster a sense of responsibility and active citizenship. Youth participation in social and humanitarian activities, including through organizations like the YRCS Youth League, can make a significant impact.

Addressing Youth-Specific Issues: The YRCS Youth League should pay special attention to the unique problems and interests of young people. This includes issues like education access, employment opportunities, mental health, and social inclusion.

Mentorship and Guidance: Providing mentorship and guidance from experienced individuals within the YRCS can help youth develop leadership skills and navigate the complexities of community service and humanitarian work.

Advocacy and Representation: The YRCS Youth League can serve as a platform for youth to voice their concerns and advocate for policies and initiatives that benefit their generation and the broader society.

Social Innovation: Young people often bring fresh perspectives and innovative solutions to long-standing challenges. Encouraging social innovation and entrepreneurship among the youth can lead to positive change in various sectors.

Cultural and Social Inclusivity: Recognizing the diversity of India's youth and ensuring inclusivity in programs and initiatives are important. This promotes a sense of belonging and unity among all segments of the youth population.

Sustainability: Engaging youth in discussions and activities related to sustainability, environmental conservation, and responsible citizenship can foster a sense of stewardship for the planet and future generations.

In conclusion, the Indian youth represent a valuable resource and a dynamic force for the country's development. Empowering, educating, and actively engaging them in addressing societal issues and advocating for their interests are essential steps toward a brighter and more inclusive future for India. Organizations like the YRCS Youth League can play a vital role in supporting and nurturing the potential of the youth in contributing to the nation's progress.

The world is yours, as well as ours, but in the last analysis, it is yours. You young people, full of vigor and vitality, are in the bloom of life, like the sun at eight or nine in the morning. Our hope is placed on you. The world belongs to you. INDIA's future belongs to you.

We must help all our young people to understand that ours is still a very poor country, that we cannot change this situation radically in a short time, and that only through the united efforts of our younger generation and all our people, working with their own hands, can INDIA be made strong and prosperous within a period of several decades. The establishment of our socialist system has opened the road leading to the ideal society of the future, but to translate this ideal into reality needs hard work.

Because of their lack of political and social experience, quite a number of young people are unable to see the contrast between the old INDIA and the new, and it is not easy for them thoroughly to comprehend the hardships our people went through in the struggle to free themselves from the oppression of the imperialists and Kuomintang reactionaries, or the long period of arduous work needed before a happy socialist society can be established. That is why we must constantly carry on lively and effective political education among the masses and should always tell them the truth about the difficulties that crop up and discuss with them how to surmount these difficulties.

The young people are the most active and vital force in society. They are the most eager to learn and the least conservative in their thinking. This is especially so in the era of socialism. We hope that the local Party organizations in various places will help and work with the Youth League organizations and go into the question of bringing into full play the energy of our youth in particular. The Party organizations should not treat them in the same way as everybody else and ignore their special characteristics. Of course, the young people should learn from the old and other adults, and should strive as much as possible to engage in all sorts of useful activities with their agreement.

How should we judge whether a youth is a revolutionary? How can we tell? There can only be one criterion, namely, whether or not he is willing to integrate himself with the broad masses of workers and peasants and does so in practice. If he is willing to do so and actually does so, he is a revolutionary; otherwise he is a non-revolutionary or a counter-revolutionary. If today he integrates himself with the masses of workers and peasants, then today he is a revolutionary; if tomorrow he ceases to do so or turns round to oppress the common people, then he becomes a non-revolutionary or a counter revolutionary.

The intellectuals often tend to be subjective and individualistic, impractical in their thinking and irresolute in action until they have thrown themselves heart and soul into mass revolutionary struggles, or made up their minds to serve the interests of the masses and become one with them. Hence although the mass of revolutionary intellectuals in INDIA can play a vanguard role or serve as a link with the masses, not all of them will remain revolutionaries to the end. Some will drop out of the revolutionary ranks at critical moments and become passive, while a few may even become enemies of the revolution. The intellectuals can overcome their shortcomings only in mass struggles over a long period.

Apart from continuing to act in co-ordination with the Party in its central task, the Youth League should do its own work to suit the special characteristics of youth. New INDIA must care for her youth and show concern for the growth of the younger generation. Young people have to study and work, but they are at the age of physical growth. Therefore, full attention must be paid both to their work and study and to their recreation, sport and rest.

Women

Recognizing the importance of women as a significant and productive force in India is a crucial aspect of achieving gender equality, a goal that aligns with the principles of socialism. In socialist ideologies, including Marxism and its various interpretations, gender equality is considered essential for the realization of a just and equitable society. Here are some key points to consider in this context:

Productive Force: Women play a vital role in India's workforce, economy, and society. Their contributions are evident in various sectors, including agriculture, industry, healthcare, education, and more. Acknowledging women's productive contributions is fundamental to understanding their value to the nation's development.

Equality Among the Sexes: The principle of gender equality is central to socialism. It advocates for the abolition of gender-based discrimination and the creation of a society where men and women have equal rights, opportunities, and access to resources. Gender equality is seen as integral to achieving social justice.

Reducing Burdens: Many women in India, as in other parts of the world, shoulder multiple burdens, including domestic responsibilities, child-rearing, and caregiving. Socialist principles emphasize the need to alleviate these burdens through social policies and support systems, such as affordable childcare, parental leave, and elder care.

Empowerment: Empowering women through education, economic opportunities, and participation in decision-making processes is a key component of gender equality in socialism. It enables women to assert their rights and contribute more fully to the development of society.

Access to Healthcare and Education: Socialism underscores the importance of providing women with equal access to healthcare services, including reproductive healthcare, and quality education. Ensuring women's health and education is essential for their well-being and contribution to society.

Legal Protections: Gender equality is often codified into law, and socialist systems advocate for strong legal protections against gender-based discrimination and violence.

Promoting Women's Leadership: Socialist movements encourage women's active participation in political and leadership roles. This promotes their representation in decision-making bodies and contributes to more inclusive governance.

Challenging Stereotypes: Socialism challenges traditional gender roles and stereotypes that limit the opportunities available to women. It promotes a more fluid and equitable division of labour within families and society.

Solidarity and Unity: Achieving gender equality is seen as a collective effort that requires the solidarity and cooperation of all members of society, regardless of gender.

In conclusion, recognizing and empowering women as a great productive force in India and striving for gender equality are integral aspects of socialism. These principles promote a more just and inclusive society where women's contributions are valued, their rights are protected, and their burdens are eased through social policies and initiatives. Gender equality is not only a goal of socialism but also a fundamental human rights and social justice principle.

A man in INDIA is usually subjected to the domination of three systems of authority [political authority, family authority and religious authority] .... As for women, in addition to being dominated by these three systems of authority, they are also dominated by the men (the authority of the husband). These four authorities - political, family, religious and masculine - are the embodiment of the whole feudal-patriarchal ideology and system, and are the four thick ropes binding the Chinese people, particularly the peasants. How the peasants have overthrown the political authority of the landlords in the countryside has been described above? The political authority of the landlords is the backbone of all the other systems of authority. With that overturned the family authority, the religious authority and the authority of the husband all begin to totter.... As to the authority of the husband, this has always been weaker among the poor peasants because, out of economic necessity, their womenfolk have to do more manual labour than the women of the richer classes and therefore have more say and greater power of decision in family matters. With the increasing bankruptcy of the rural economy in recent years, the basis for men's domination over women has already been undermined. With the rise of the peasant movement, the women in many places have now begun to organize rural women's associations; the opportunity has come for them to lift up their heads, and the authority of the husband is getting shakier every day. In a word, the whole feudal-patriarchal ideology and system is tottering with the growth of the peasants' power.

Unite and take part in production and political activity to improve the economic and political status of women.

Protect the interests of the youth, women and children - provide assistance to young students who cannot afford to continue their studies, help the youth and women to organize in order to participate on an equal footing in all work useful to the war effort and to social progress, ensure freedom of marriage and equality as between men and women, and give young people and children a useful education....

[In agricultural production] our fundamental task is to adjust the use of labour power in an organized way and to encourage women to do farm work.

In order to build a great socialist society it is of the utmost importance to arouse the broad masses of women to join in productive activity. Men and women must receive equal pay for equal work in production.

Genuine equality between the sexes can only be realized in the process of the socialist transformation of society as a whole.

With the completion of agricultural cooperation, many co-operatives are finding themselves short of labour. It has become necessary to arouse the great mass of women who did not work in the fields before to take their place on the labour front.... INDIA's women are a vast reserve of labour power. This reserve should be tapped in the struggle to build a great socialist country.

Enable every woman who can work to take her place on the labour front, under the principle of equal pay for equal work. This should be done as quickly as possible.

The Press

An individual has the right to express himself or herself even if he or she behaves irrationally to demonstrate his or her insanity. Corporate bodies too have the right to express their corporate identity. The former represent only themselves and the latter represent those who share their corporate identity. Since society consists of private individuals and corporate bodies, the expressions, for example, by an individual of his or her insanity does not mean that other members of society are insane. Such expression reflects only in the individual's character. Likewise, corporate expression reflects only the interest or view of those making up the corporate body. For instance, a tobacco company, despite the fact what it produces is harmful to health, ex- presses the interests of those who make up the company.

The press is a means of expression for society: it is not a

means of expression for private individuals or corporate bodies. Therefore, logically and democratically, it should not belong to either one of them.

A newspaper owned by any individual is his or her own, and expresses only his or her point of view. Any claim that a newspaper represents public opinion is groundless because it actually expresses the viewpoint of that private individual. Democratically, private individuals should not be permitted to own any public means of publication or information. However, they have the right to express themselves by any means, even irrationally, to prove their insanity. Any journal issued by a professional sector, for example, is only a means of expression of that particular social group. It presents their own points of view and not that of the general public. This applies to all other corporate and private individuals in society.

The democratic press is that which is issued by a People's Committee, comprising all the groups of society. Only in this case, and not otherwise, will the press or any other information medium be democratic, expressing the viewpoints of the whole society, and representing all its groups.

If medical professionals issue a journal, it must be purely medical. Similarly, this applies to other groups. Private individuals have the right to express only their own, and not anyone else's opinions.

What is known as the problem of the freedom of the press in the world will be radically and democratically solved. Because it is by-product of the problem of democracy generally, the problem of freedom of the press cannot be solved independently of that of democracy in society as a whole. Therefore, the only solution to the persistent problem of democracy is through universalization of India.

According to this theory, the democratic system is a cohesive structure whose foundations are firmly laid on Basic Popular Conferences and People's Committees which convene in a General People's Congress. This is absolutely the only form of genuine democratic society.

In summary, the era of the masses, which follows the age of the republics, excites the feelings and dazzles the eyes. But even though the vision of this era denotes genuine freedom of the masses and their happy emancipation from the bonds of

external authoritarian structures, it warns also of the dangers of a period of chaos and demagoguery, and the threat of a return to the authority of the individual, the sect and party, instead of the authority of the people.

Theoretically, this is genuine democracy but, realistically, the strong always rules, i.e., the stronger party in the society is the one that rules.

Labour Reform

The **Labour Reform Act** has several positive aspects aimed at improving the conditions of employees in India. Here's an evaluation of the key features mentioned below:

Enforcement of Labour Laws and Social Security: Ensuring the enforcement of labour laws is crucial for protecting the rights of workers. Social security measures, such as providing benefits like health insurance and retirement plans, are essential for the well-being of employees. These measures can help create a safety net for workers in case of emergencies or retirement.

Creating a Healthy Work Environment: A healthy work environment is vital for employee well-being and productivity. When employees feel safe, supported, and motivated, it can lead to increased job satisfaction and better overall performance.

Vocational Skill Training and Apprenticeships: Skill development and apprenticeship programs are instrumental in enhancing the employability of the workforce. By providing vocational training, the Act aims to equip individuals with the skills required for various industries, thus increasing their chances of finding meaningful employment.

Mass Training Program (Induction/Apprentice/Training): A mass training program can be a valuable initiative for upskilling the workforce, particularly the youth and the unemployed. This program can help bridge the skills gap, reduce unemployment rates, and improve the overall skill level of the labour force.

Minimum Entitlements (13 Minimum Entitlements of the ES):

Maximum Weekly Hours: This provision ensures that employees are not overworked and promotes a work-life balance.

Minimum Wages: Setting a minimum wage is essential for ensuring fair compensation for labour.

Flexible Working Arrangements: Offering flexibility in working arrangements can accommodate employees' diverse needs and responsibilities.

Conversion from Casual to Permanent Employment: This promotes job security for casual workers.

Parental Leave and Related Entitlements: Supporting parents with leave and benefits is crucial for family well-being.

Annual Leave: Paid annual leave is a standard benefit in many countries and contributes to employee rest and recreation.

Personal/Carer's Leave, Compassionate Leave, and Family and Domestic Violence Leave: These are important for addressing personal and family emergencies.

Community Service Leave: Encouraging community service contributes to social responsibility.

Long Service Leave: Recognizing long-term commitment to an employer can enhance employee retention.

Public Holidays: Providing time off on public holidays is a common labour practice.

Notice of Termination and Redundancy Pay: These provisions offer job security and financial support in case of job loss.

Fair Work Information Statement: Ensuring employees are informed about their rights is essential for transparency.

Health Insurance and Superannuation/Retirement Plan: These benefits are critical for long-term financial security and health of employees.

In summary, the Labour Reform Act is comprehensive and focuses on improving labour conditions, ensuring fair wages, promoting job security, and investing in skill development. These measures can contribute to a healthier and more productive workforce while also addressing social and economic challenges. However, the successful implementation and enforcement of such reforms are critical for their effectiveness.

The augmentation of labour unions in all industrial associations can have both positive implications.

Advantages:

1. **Collective Bargaining Power:** Labour unions can collectively negotiate with employers on behalf of workers, leading to better wages, benefits, and working conditions.
2. **Improved Worker Rights:** Augmenting labour unions can lead to the better protection of workers' rights, ensuring fair treatment and reducing the risk of exploitation.

3. **Worker Representation:** Unions provide a platform for workers to voice their concerns and have a say in workplace decisions, creating a more democratic and inclusive work environment.
4. **Solidarity:** Strong labour unions can foster a sense of solidarity among workers, leading to increased cooperation and a stronger sense of community among employees.
5. **Safety and Health Standards:** Unions can advocate for improved safety and health standards in workplaces, leading to a safer and healthier working environment.

The Agriculture Reform Act

The **Agriculture Reform** Actproposes a comprehensive set of reforms aimed at improving agricultural practices and addressing social and economic issues in the agricultural sector. Here's an evaluation of the key components of this proposal:

Collective Farming and Farmer Producer Groups (FPGs):

Advantage: Grouping small and marginal farmers into **Farmer's Interest Groups (FIGs)** and further into **Farmer Producer Groups (FPGs)** can provide several benefits. It can lead to economies of scale, better access to resources, improved bargaining power in the market, and enhanced sharing of agricultural knowledge and practices.

Concern: The successful implementation of collective farming models depends on effective organization, management, and coordination among farmers in the groups. Ensuring equitable distribution of benefits among all members of the groups is also crucial.

Universal Agro Produce System:

Advantage: Establishing government-aided cooperatives across villages can help streamline the agricultural supply chain, reduce middlemen, and ensure fair prices for farmers. This can contribute to rural development and poverty alleviation.

Concern: The success of such cooperatives depends on their efficiency, transparency, and the absence of corruption. Ensuring that they prioritize the welfare of farmers over bureaucratic interests is essential.

Fresh Farms Super Markets:

Advantage: Creating a network of Fresh Farms Super Markets can help farmers access a broader consumer market, reducing their dependence on traditional markets. This can lead to better income opportunities for farmers.

Concern: The successful operation of these markets relies on effective management, quality control, and marketing strategies. Ensuring that farmers receive a fair share of the profits is crucial.

Diversification into Meat, Fish, Milk, Processed Meat, Groceries, and Healthcare:

Advantage: Expanding the cooperative model into other agricultural sectors can diversify income sources for farmers and contribute to overall rural development.

Concern: Proper regulation, hygiene standards, and ethical practices must be maintained in sectors like meat and healthcare to ensure consumer safety and welfare.

Addressing Discrimination and Disparity:

Advantage: Promoting equality before law and society is a crucial social goal. Reducing discrimination and disparity can lead to a more just and harmonious society.

Concern: Implementing such reforms may require significant changes in societal attitudes, and ensuring that they are effectively enforced can be challenging.

Establishment of Cooperative Societies:

Advantage: Expanding the cooperative model based on local produce and population can strengthen community-based economic activities and empower rural populations.

Concern: Effective governance, transparency, and accountability within these cooperatives are essential to prevent misuse of power and resources.

The reference to "collectivization of land via the commune system" appears to draw on historical examples like the Chinese commune system. However, it's important to note that the success and applicability of such models can vary significantly depending on the specific context, including political, economic, and cultural factors.

Overall, the proposed reforms have the potential to positively impact agriculture, rural development, and social equality. However, the success of these reforms will depend on effective implementation, transparency, and the willingness of all stakeholders to collaborate for the betterment of the agricultural sector and society at large.

The Fishery Reform Act

The **Fishery Reform Act** described below outlines a comprehensive plan for the sustainable growth and development of India's fishing, aquaculture, and seafood sectors. Here's an evaluation of the key components of this proposal:

Introduction of Variety of Fishes in Dams, Lakes, and Rivers:

Advantage: Introducing diverse fish species in these water bodies can enhance local ecosystems, increase fish production, and provide livelihood opportunities for local communities.

Concern: Ensuring that the introduction of new species does not disrupt existing ecosystems or harm native species is essential. Proper research and ecological impact assessments are needed.

Purchase of Deep Sea Vessels:

Advantage: Increasing the number of deep-sea vessels can boost India's capacity for offshore fishing, potentially increasing seafood production and export opportunities.

Concern: Sustainable and responsible fishing practices must be enforced to prevent overfishing and environmental degradation.

Establishment of Fisheries CooperativeSociety:

Advantage: Cooperative societies can empower fishermen and promote collective bargaining power. They can also help with value addition and marketing of fishery by-products.

Concern: Effective management, transparency, and equitable distribution of benefits within these cooperatives are crucial.

Streamlining Governance and Regulation:

Advantage: Harmonizing regulations can reduce red tape, improve enforcement, and create a more conducive environment for the fisheries sector.

Concern: Balancing regulation with environmental protection is important to prevent over-exploitation and ecological damage.

Sustainability:

Advantage: Ensuring sustainable practices in fisheries and aquaculture is essential for long-term viability and environmental preservation.

Concern: Monitoring and enforcement of sustainability practices may require additional resources and oversight.

Resource Sharing and Access Security:

Advantage: Secure access to resources can provide stability to fishing communities and encourage responsible resource management.

Concern: Ensuring equitable access and preventing resource monopolization are key challenges.

Recreational Fishing Recognition:

Advantage: Recognizing recreational fishing can promote tourism and community engagement while contributing to the local economy.

Concern: Managing recreational fishing to prevent overfishing and protect local ecosystems is essential.

Adaptation:

Advantage: Preparing the fishing sector for environmental changes can help ensure its long-term resilience.

Concern: Identifying and implementing adaptation strategies may require substantial investment and coordination.

Employment, Participation, and Health:

Advantage: Improving the well-being of fishing communities can lead to a healthier and more productive workforce.

Concern: Addressing health and social issues may require healthcare and educational interventions.

Community Connection:

Advantage: Building trust and understanding between the fishing community and the public can lead to greater support for sustainable practices.

Concern: Fostering community connection may require educational and outreach efforts.

International Engagement:

Advantage: Engaging internationally can enhance India's reputation in sustainable fisheries management and expand market access.

Concern: Adhering to international agreements and standards may necessitate domestic policy changes and investments.

In summary, the Fishery Reform Act outlines a comprehensive and ambitious plan for the sustainable development of India's fisheries and aquaculture sectors. While it addresses various key areas, successful implementation will depend on effective governance, monitoring, and coordination among government, industry, and local communities to ensure that the objectives are achieved while preserving aquatic ecosystems and safeguarding the interests of all stakeholders.

The Healthcare Reform Act

The Healthcare Reform Act

Universal Health Coverage (UHC):

Advantage: Providing access to a full range of quality health services without financial hardship is a fundamental human right and a crucial step towards improving public health and well-being.

Concern: Achieving UHC requires substantial investment, effective governance, and the development of healthcare infrastructure and workforce, which may pose fiscal challenges.

Health Workforce and Skills Mix:

Advantage: Ensuring that health and care workers have optimal skills and equitable distribution can enhance the quality and accessibility of healthcare services.

Concern: Addressing workforce shortages and skill gaps may take time and resources.

Financial Protection:

Advantage: Protecting individuals from financial hardships due to healthcare costs is a vital aspect of UHC, preventing people from falling into poverty as a result of medical expenses.

Concern: Financing UHC in a sustainable and equitable manner can be a complex task, and governments must develop robust funding mechanisms.

Inequality and Equity:

Advantage: Recognizing and addressing inequalities in healthcare access is essential to achieving UHC. Monitoring health inequalities and designing equity-oriented policies can promote social justice.

Concern: Identifying and addressing disparities can be challenging, and it may require significant data collection, analysis, and targeted interventions.

Data and Monitoring:

Advantage: Collecting better data on health inequalities, gender disparities, and other relevant factors is crucial for evidence-based policy-making and program evaluation.

Concern: Developing comprehensive data systems and ensuring data accuracy and privacy can be resource-intensive.

In summary, the Healthcare Reform Act's focus on Universal Healthcare System and Universal Health Coverage reflects a commitment to improving healthcare access, quality, and financial protection for all citizens. While the advantages are clear in terms of public health and well-being, there are substantial challenges in terms of funding, workforce development, addressing inequalities, and collecting accurate data. Successful implementation will require strong political will, long-term planning, and collaboration among stakeholders, but it has the potential to significantly enhance healthcare outcomes and reduce health disparities within the population.

Education Reform Act

The proposed Education Reform Act aimed at establishing a Universal Education System in India carries several significant advantages and considerations:

Advantages:

Access to Education: The focus on universal education is crucial in ensuring that all segments of society, regardless of their socio-economic background, have equal access to quality education. This can help reduce educational disparities.

Workforce Development: In the context of industrialization and economic growth, having an educated and skilled workforce becomes essential. Universal education can contribute to a more specialized and productive workforce, aligning with the needs of the job market.

Integration of Immigrants: A universal education system can facilitate the integration of immigrants into society by providing them with access to education and helping them adapt to their new environment.

Compulsory Education: The introduction of compulsory education reflects a commitment to ensuring that every child receives an education, preventing dropouts, and promoting a literate society.

Constitutional Rights: Affording constitutional rights to all citizens, including access to education, is a fundamental principle of a democratic and equitable society.

Financial Support for the Economically Disadvantaged: Providing financial assistance, such as a student pension for BPL (Below Poverty Line) cardholders, can help reduce economic barriers to education and improve the overall socio-economic status of vulnerable populations.

Considerations:

Funding: Implementing a universal education system, including free education in private and public schools, can be financially demanding. Adequate and sustainable funding mechanisms must be established.

Quality of Education: Ensuring that universal education leads to quality learning outcomes is essential. It requires investment in teacher training, curriculum development, and infrastructure improvement.

Equity: While the proposal addresses economic disparities, it's essential to also consider other forms of inequality, such as gender, regional, and social disparities, and develop strategies to address them.

Implementation Challenges: Transitioning to a universal education system may face resistance from various stakeholders, including private institutions, and may require significant administrative and policy changes.

Accountability: Ensuring accountability and transparency in the use of public funds for education is vital to prevent misuse and corruption.

Teacher Recruitment and Retention: Expanding the education system will require recruiting and retaining a sufficient number of qualified teachers, which can be challenging, especially in remote areas.

Curriculum Relevance: The curriculum should be designed to meet the needs of a rapidly changing job market and society, ensuring that students acquire relevant skills and knowledge.

In conclusion, the proposed Education Reform Act's emphasis on universal education is a commendable effort to promote equitable access to education and align educational goals with economic and societal needs. However, successful implementation will require careful planning, adequate funding, and a commitment to ensuring the quality and inclusivity of the education system.

The Rural Reforms Act

The Rural Reforms Act focuses on promoting rural research and development to enhance productivity and profitability for Indian farmers. Here's an evaluation of the key components of this proposal:

Advantages:

Increased Agricultural Productivity: Investing in rural research and development can lead to innovations in farming practices, technologies, and processes that can boost agricultural productivity. This is crucial for food security and economic growth.

Profitability: Improving farm-gate productivity and profitability can directly benefit Indian farmers, helping them achieve better incomes and improving their quality of life.

Knowledge Generation: The program's emphasis on generating knowledge, technologies, products, and processes benefits not only farmers but also the broader agricultural sector by promoting innovation and sustainability.

Collaboration: Encouraging partnerships between research organizations, funding bodies, and businesses can foster innovation and collaboration, leading to more effective and impactful research outcomes.

Addressing Key Priorities: The focus on key areas such as advanced technology, biosecurity, soil and water management, and the adoption of research and development aligns with critical agricultural needs and challenges.

Flexible Delivery of Extension Services: Recognizing the importance of flexible extension services that meet the needs of primary producers can enhance the dissemination of research findings and adoption of best practices.

Concerns and Considerations:

Funding Sustainability: To ensure the long-term success of the program, there must be a commitment to sustained funding. Research and development often require continuous investment and support.

Equitable Access: Ensuring that the benefits of research and development reach all segments of the farming community, including small and marginalized farmers, is essential for achieving equity in agriculture.

Implementation Challenges: Managing complex collaborations between various stakeholders, including researchers, agencies, and businesses, may pose challenges in terms of coordination and accountability.

Monitoring and Evaluation: Establishing effective mechanisms for monitoring and evaluating the impact of research projects is crucial to ensure that they deliver tangible outcomes for farmers.

Adaptation to Local Context: Research findings and innovations must be adaptable to diverse local agricultural practices and conditions across India.

Environmental Sustainability: Balancing productivity goals with environmental sustainability is essential to avoid negative ecological impacts.

In summary, the Rural Reforms Act's focus on rural research and development is a positive step toward addressing agricultural challenges in India. It has the potential to enhance agricultural productivity, profitability, and sustainability. However, successful implementation will require consistent funding, equitable access, effective collaboration, and a commitment to addressing the specific needs of Indian farmers and the agricultural sector as a whole.

The establishment of Cooperatives Act

The establishment of cooperatives, can have several benefits for rural development and economic growth. Here's an evaluation of the key components of this plan:

Advantages:

Rural Economic Development: Establishing cooperatives at the local level can boost economic activities in rural areas by promoting agribusiness, processing, and distribution, which, in turn, can generate employment opportunities.

Agricultural Efficiency: Cooperatives can improve the efficiency of agricultural production and post-harvest processes by providing farmers with collective access to resources, markets, and processing facilities.

Value Addition: Processing and packing of agricultural produce can add value to raw products, leading to higher profits for farmers and better quality products for consumers.

Supply Chain Management: Cooperatives can enhance supply chain management by coordinating production, processing, and distribution, reducing wastage and ensuring a steady supply of goods to markets.

Market Access: Cooperatives can provide small-scale farmers with improved access to markets, helping them compete effectively and obtain better prices for their products.

Rural Infrastructure: The construction of warehouses and other infrastructure by the government can improve storage and reduce post-harvest losses.

Consumer Access: The establishment of **Fresh Farm Super Markets** can provide consumers with convenient access to a variety of agricultural products, promoting healthier eating habits and supporting local agriculture.

Diversification: Encouraging various types of cooperatives, including those related to animal husbandry, agriculture, horticulture, and small-scale industries, promotes economic diversification in rural areas.

Concerns and Considerations:

Cooperative Management: Effective management and governance of cooperatives are crucial for their success. Ensuring transparency, accountability, and equitable distribution of benefits is essential.

Funding: Adequate funding and financial management are required to establish and sustain cooperatives and related infrastructure.

Training and Capacity-Building: Farmers and cooperative members may require training and capacity-building programs to effectively participate in cooperative activities and modern farming practices.

Market Dynamics: Understanding market dynamics and demand fluctuations is critical to avoid overproduction and wastage.

Infrastructure Maintenance: Ensuring the ongoing maintenance and upkeep of warehouses and other infrastructure is essential for their long-term viability.

Regulatory Framework: Cooperatives may need supportive regulatory frameworks and policies that facilitate their establishment and operation.

Equity: Attention should be paid to ensuring that cooperatives benefit all members, including marginalized and vulnerable groups.

Environmental Sustainability: Promoting sustainable agricultural practices and environmental conservation should be integral to cooperative activities.

In conclusion, the establishment of cooperatives as outlined in the proposal can be a powerful tool for rural development and economic growth. However, successful implementation will require careful planning, adequate funding, capacity-building, and attention to governance and equity issues. Additionally, ongoing support and monitoring will be necessary to ensure the sustainability and effectiveness of the cooperative model.

Arts, Culture and Globalisation Act

The emphasis on arts, culture, and globalization recognizes the significant potential of the creative sector as a driver of economic growth and innovation in India. Here's an evaluation of the key components of this plan:

Advantages:

Economic Growth: The creative sector has the potential to contribute significantly to India's economic growth through exports, job creation, and attracting investments.

Global Reputation: Fostering a global reputation for artistic excellence can attract international recognition, tourists, and cultural exchanges, further boosting the economy.

Creative Hub: The presence of diverse creative talents in film-making, arts, music, and advertising agencies can position India as a creative hub and attract businesses and collaborations.

Cultural Preservation: The thriving museum and art gallery culture, supported by government funding and private patronage, can help preserve and showcase India's rich cultural heritage.

Diversified Opportunities: The creative industries encompass cultural production and creative services, providing a wide range of opportunities for investors and entrepreneurs.

Private-Public Partnerships: Collaborations between the government and the private sector, such as **Create India and the Arts and Cultural Development Program (ACDP)**, can foster innovation and support local artists and projects.

Concerns and Considerations:

Sustainability: Ensuring the sustainability of the creative sector requires continuous support, funding, and opportunities for artists and cultural practitioners.

Inclusivity: Efforts should be made to include artists and creators from diverse backgrounds and regions, promoting cultural diversity and inclusivity.

Intellectual Property Protection: Protecting the intellectual property of artists and creators is crucial to encourage innovation and creativity.

Infrastructure and Facilities: Maintaining and upgrading cultural infrastructure, including venues, museums, and galleries, is essential for attracting audiences and tourists.

Education and Training: Investing in arts education and training programs can nurture talent and develop the next generation of artists and cultural professionals.

Global Outreach: Effective international marketing and promotion are necessary to expand the reach of Indian arts and culture on the global stage.

Cultural Diplomacy: Leveraging arts and culture for cultural diplomacy initiatives can strengthen India's soft power and international relations.

Festival Sustainability: While Bangalore's recognition as a creative city is commendable, ensuring the sustainability and continued success of festivals and events requires long-term planning and community involvement.

In conclusion, the promotion of arts, culture, and globalization can have a positive impact on India's economic and cultural landscape.

The Mass Education and Skill Development Act

The Mass Education and Skill Development Act, focuses on leveraging the opportunities in the education and skill development sector in India. Here's an evaluation of its key components:

Advantages:

Market Opportunities: The India education sector offers various investment opportunities, including English training, skills qualifications, post-graduate qualifications, and research and development. This aligns with the growing demand for education and skills in emerging economies.

Skill Enhancement: The program's emphasis on providing skills training and qualifications can improve the employability of individuals and enhance their career prospects, addressing unemployment and underemployment challenges.

Support for Failed Candidates: Offering a pathway for failed candidates to gain skills qualifications can provide them with a second chance and increase their chances of finding suitable employment.

Local Partnerships: Collaborating with local tertiary institutions and partners can help tailor education and skill development programs to meet the specific needs of the region, ensuring relevance and effectiveness.

Standardization: Certifying individuals with specific skill sets, such as those in farming, cleaning, labour, and meat cutting, can establish industry standards and improve the quality of services in these sectors.

Concerns and Considerations:

Quality Assurance: Ensuring the quality of education and skill development programs is essential to produce competent and capable individuals. Effective monitoring and evaluation mechanisms are needed.

Equity: It's important to ensure that educational and skill development opportunities are accessible to all segments of the population, including marginalized and disadvantaged groups.

Infrastructure and Resources: To deliver quality education and skills training, investments in infrastructure, teaching resources, and qualified instructors are necessary.

Alignment with Industry Needs: Skill development programs should align with the current and future needs of industries to ensure that graduates are employable.

Recognition of Prior Learning: Consideration should be given to recognizing and certifying the skills and knowledge that individuals may have acquired through prior work or informal learning.

Career Guidance: Providing career guidance and counselling services can help individuals make informed choices about their education and skill development pathways.

Public-Private Partnerships: Leveraging partnerships with the private sector can enhance the relevance and quality of skill development programs.

Life-long Learning: Encouraging a culture of life-long learning is essential to keep up with evolving skills requirements in the job market.

In conclusion, the Mass Education and Skill Development Act holds promise for addressing skill gaps and improving employability in India. However, its success will depend on a commitment to quality, equity, industry relevance, and ongoing support for individuals throughout their education and career journeys.

Mining Resources and Development Act

The focus on mining resources and development in India's economy, along with the establishment of trade unions and cooperatives, presents both opportunities and challenges. Here's an evaluation of the key components of this plan:

Advantages:

Economic Contribution: The mining, resources, and energy sector can significantly contribute to India's economy by generating revenue through exports of minerals and energy resources.

Renewable Energy: The growing renewable energy sector aligns with global efforts to transition to cleaner energy sources and can contribute to reducing environmental impact.

International Collaboration: Partnerships with international companies like Shell, Tesla, and Energy can bring expertise, technology, and investment to India's mining and energy projects.

Diverse Mineral Exports: India's diverse mineral exports, including iron, steel, aluminium, gold, lead, and copper, indicate a range of investment opportunities for both large and small-scale ventures.

Innovation Hub: The initiative to establish an innovation hub can foster collaboration among SMEs, encourage innovation, and enhance competitiveness, ultimately leading to growth in the sector.

Knowledge Transfer: Sharing best practices and information on global capital and supply chain markets can improve the industry's competitiveness and productivity.

Concerns and Considerations:

Environmental Impact: Mining and energy extraction activities can have significant environmental consequences, including habitat destruction, pollution, and resource depletion. Ensuring sustainable practices and environmental regulations is crucial.

Community and Social Impact: Mining projects can displace communities and impact their livelihoods. Adequate measures for community engagement, compensation, and social development are needed.

Resource Depletion: Overexploitation of mineral resources without adequate replenishment strategies can lead to resource depletion and economic challenges in the long term.

Renewable Energy Transition: While renewable energy is a positive development, the transition should be well-managed to ensure a reliable and affordable energy supply during the shift.

Workplace Safety: Mining and energy sectors can be hazardous, and ensuring workplace safety should be a priority to protect the health and well-being of workers.

Innovation Adoption: Encouraging SMEs to adopt innovation and new technologies may require training and support to overcome barriers to adoption.

Market Access: Facilitating access to new markets requires effective marketing, trade agreements, and understanding the regulatory requirements of target markets.

Sustainability Reporting: Companies should be encouraged to report on their sustainability practices and adhere to international standards to demonstrate their commitment to responsible mining and energy development.

In conclusion, India's focus on mining, resources, and energy presents significant economic opportunities, but it also requires careful management to address environmental, social, and economic challenges. The establishment of trade unions, cooperatives, and innovation hubs can play a pivotal role in promoting responsible and sustainable growth in these sectors.

The Tourism Reform Act

The Tourism Reform Act proposal outlines various strategies and actions to boost tourism in India. Here's an evaluation of the key components:

Advantages:

Economic Contribution: Tourism has the potential to make a substantial contribution to India's GDP, providing economic benefits through increased visitor spending and job creation.

Coastal Development: Allowing tourist shacks, hotels, and high-rise buildings near popular beaches can enhance the tourism infrastructure and attract more visitors to coastal areas.

Cruise Tourism: Developing the cruise industry, with Mangalore as a hub, can diversify tourism offerings and provide unique experiences, potentially boosting the local economy.

Legislative Review: Updating tourism and major event legislation can ensure that the regulatory framework aligns with the government's tourism objectives and facilitates industry growth.

Eco-Friendly Tourism: The construction of eco-friendly nature farms and hotels can attract tourists seeking sustainable and nature-based experiences, aligning with global travel trends.

Themed Districts: Dividing districts based on industries and themes can help in better resource allocation and targeted promotion of tourism offerings, making it easier for tourists to plan their trips.

Infrastructure Investment: Investing in a significant number of cruise ships and motorized tourist boats can improve connectivity and accessibility to various tourism destinations, particularly in coastal areas.

Concerns and Considerations:

Environmental Impact: Coastal development and high-rise buildings near beaches must be carefully managed to minimize environmental impact and maintain the natural beauty of these areas.

Infrastructure: Supporting the growth of tourism, especially in remote areas, will require substantial investment in infrastructure, including roads, transportation, and utilities.

Sustainability: Balancing tourism growth with sustainability is essential to prevent over-tourism and the negative effects it can have on local cultures and ecosystems.

Regulation: Effective regulation is crucial to ensure the safety and quality of tourism services, including cruise operations, hotels, and nature farms.

Community Engagement: Local communities should be involved in tourism development plans to ensure that they benefit from the industry and that their concerns are addressed.

Marketing and Promotion: Effective marketing and promotion strategies are needed to attract both domestic and international tourists and compete with other tourist destinations.

Infrastructure and Maintenance: Maintaining eco-friendly facilities and themed districts, such as glass hotels and motels, may require ongoing investment and maintenance.

Crisis Management: Developing plans for crisis management, such as natural disasters or pandemics, is crucial to safeguard the tourism industry.

In conclusion, the Tourism Reform Act proposal presents a comprehensive approach to boost tourism in India. While it offers many advantages, it must address environmental, sustainability, regulatory, and community-related concerns to ensure responsible and long-term tourism growth. Effective marketing and infrastructure development will also play a pivotal role in the success of these initiatives.

India Advanced Manufacturing Industry Development Act

The India Advanced Manufacturing Industry Development Strategy aims to enhance the manufacturing sector in the state. Here's an evaluation of its key components:

Advantages:

Economic Strength: The strategy recognizes the importance of the manufacturing industry as a source of economic strength, job creation, and innovation. Strengthening this sector can contribute significantly to India's economy.

Collaboration and Research: Increasing collaboration between the manufacturing industry and research institutions can drive innovation and knowledge sharing, fostering technological advancements.

Skills Development: Supporting skills development in the industry is essential for adapting to advanced processes and technologies, making the workforce more competitive.

Business Models: Encouraging the adoption of advanced service-oriented business models can lead to the creation of high-value products, expanding market reach, and fostering innovation.

Export and Investment: Growing exports and attracting investment can boost the state's economy and create more opportunities for businesses and job seekers.

Concerns and Considerations:

Implementation Challenges: Implementing the strategy effectively may face challenges, such as the need for significant investment, infrastructure development, and regulatory changes.

Skills Gap: Bridging the skills gap in the manufacturing sector may require substantial efforts in education and training programs, which could take time to yield results.

Technological Adaptation: Ensuring that businesses can effectively adopt advanced technologies and processes may require support in the form of training, subsidies, or incentives.

Market Expansion: Expanding into untapped markets and segments can be competitive, and businesses may need assistance in market research and market entry strategies.

Regulatory Support: Regulatory reforms may be needed to create a more business-friendly environment and facilitate the growth of the manufacturing industry.

Infrastructure: Adequate infrastructure, including transportation and logistics, is crucial for manufacturing growth, and investments in infrastructure development may be necessary.

Risk Mitigation: Strategies to mitigate risks, such as economic fluctuations or changes in global trade policies, should be considered to ensure the sector's stability.

Innovation Ecosystem: Building a robust innovation ecosystem that fosters collaboration between businesses and research institutions requires sustained effort and investment.

In conclusion, the India Advanced Manufacturing Industry Development Strategy has the potential to strengthen the manufacturing sector and drive economic growth. However, it must address challenges related to implementation, skills development, technological adaptation, and market expansion while fostering a supportive regulatory and infrastructure environment.

Urban Development Act

The proposed Urban Development Act outlines an ambitious vision for urban development in India, focusing on various aspects. Here's an evaluation of some key points:

Advantages:

Economic Growth: The plan aims to stimulate economic growth by developing infrastructure and attracting investments, potentially creating job opportunities and boosting the state's economy.

Infrastructure Development: The inclusion of various facilities like hospitals, schools, stadiums, and public transportation can enhance the quality of life for residents and tourists.

Tourism Promotion: Investments in theme parks, cultural exhibits, and entertainment facilities can boost tourism and contribute to local revenue.

Environmental Concerns: The proposal's emphasis on ecological protection and conditions demonstrates a commitment to sustainability, which is crucial for the long-term well-being of the state.

Technological Innovation: Collaboration with tech giants like Tesla, SpaceX, and AI research centres can promote technological advancements and innovation.

Transparency: The use of block chain technology for government transactions and contracts can enhance transparency and accountability in governance.

Social Welfare: The commitment to providing free medical care, education, and subsidies for various groups can contribute to social welfare and equality.

Concerns and Considerations:

Implementation Complexity: The plan's scale and scope are enormous, and the timeline for completion is ambitious. Executing such a comprehensive project will require effective planning, funding, and coordination.

Financial Sustainability: Financing the development of an entire city with these facilities and services may pose significant financial challenges. A clear funding strategy is essential.

Environmental Impact: While the proposal mentions ecological protection, the actual environmental impact assessment and mitigation measures need to be well-defined to prevent harm to local ecosystems.

Social Inclusion: Inclusion policies should go beyond exchanges with specific countries and aim to promote diversity and inclusion within the city's population.

Infrastructure Maintenance: Maintaining such a vast and diverse infrastructure, including underground utilities, can be a long-term challenge that requires ongoing investment.

Regulatory Framework: Clear regulations and governance structures are crucial for the success of such a project to ensure that it aligns with the state's goals and standards.

Realistic Timeline: The proposed five-year timeline for completion may need to be extended to ensure thorough planning and quality construction.

Public Engagement: Public input and consultation should be included to ensure that the city's development aligns with the needs and desires of the residents.

Risk Management: Planning for unexpected events, such as economic downturns or natural disasters, is vital to ensure the city's resilience.

In conclusion, the proposed Urban Development Act envisions a remarkable transformation for India. While it offers many potential benefits, successful execution will require careful planning, funding, and a long-term commitment to sustainability and inclusivity. Public engagement and transparency will also be critical in realizing this ambitious vision.

Development of New Self Sustained Hi-tech City in Davangere

List of various proposals and ideas for government actions and initiatives.

"This Blueprint for Transformation: Replicating the Model Across Villages, Towns, and Cities in India Based on Population and Area."

Proposed Services and Initiatives by Government Authorities as Profitable Organizations

A 100-kilometre peripheral ring road and the development of the Hi-Tech City in and around Davangere are envisioned to make it the capital of South India and the second capital of India. Here is a list of proposed services and operations:

1. District Clubhouses
2. Race Courses
3. Tools Yards
4. Farmers' Supermarkets
5. Centrifugal Sewage Water Treatment Plants (Fertilizer Factories)
6. Tools and Implements Supermarkets (for Agriculture and Construction)
7. Freshwater Circulation Points (Artificial Dams)
8. Healthcare Facilities, Government Medical Colleges, Hospitals, and Research Centres
9. Government Schools and Colleges from Primary to Ph.D. (in every district headquarters)
10. Cold Storage Plants in towns with over 10,000 Population
11. Cooperatives and Agro-Industries Based on Agro By-Products, Aligned with Ecological and Agricultural Conditions
12. Self-Sustained Information Technology/Biotechnology Parks within the Circle
13. Manufacturing Industry, Self-Sustaining and Eco-Friendly Machine Parks
14. Airstrips to Boost Tourism in every District Headquarters

15. Eco-Friendly Hotels Constructed by the Government for Profit
16. Strict Environmental Policies
17. Housing for All - Construction of 1 Million New Houses
18. Enforcement of Laws against Intolerance
19. Community Safety Measures
20. Taxation
21. Widening of Roads and Development of New Well-Planned Towns, Implementing the Above Measures
22. An Impartial Justice System, Self-Sustaining and Equitable
23. Construction of 10 High-Rise Skyscrapers for Government Ministries and Authorities
24. Embassies for All Indian States
25. Embassies for All Global Countries, each with a Permanent Exhibition Showcasing their Culture and Tourism
26. Manufacturing Sector Areas for MSMEs, SSIs, and Medium Manufacturers
27. One-Time Construction of Drainage Systems Under Roads, Highways, Optic Fibber, Electrical Cables, Rainwater, and Drinking Water Pipelines
28. Race Tracks, Stadiums, Pools, Sports Clubs, and Theme Parks
29. Inclusion of Temples, Mosques, Churches, Meditation Centres, and Yoga Centres within these facilities
30. Introduction of Casinos, Vegas Streets, Clubs, Pubs, and Shopping Malls for Tourism
31. Construction and Sale of Australian and American Themed Houses by the Government (200,000 in total)
32. Underground Rail Facilities, Public Transportation, Eco-Friendly Air Taxis, and Rehabilitation Centres
33. A City Powered by Solar Energy, including a Tesla Manufacturing Unit, SpaceX, Neural ink, and an AI Theme Research Centre, with Land Allocated Under Subsidy to Elon Musk

34. Training and Professional Development for Morally and Professionally Trained Police Officers, with an Emphasis on Youth and Responsibility
35. Establishment of Transfer of Technology Centres, DefenceTechnology Centres, and Space Technology Centres
36. Creation of Tech Parks Themed after Tech Giants like Apple, Google, Facebook, and ChatGPT
37. Opening of Training and Enlightenment Conditioning Centres for Global Transformation and Transitions, Including "Mind Your Nature in Nature Camp" and "Alignment with the Universe"
38. Implementation of Policies Promoting Exchange Programs for Students and People from China, Europe, Australia, America, and Africa, focusing on Inclusion and Diversity
39. Decentralization of Government Power at the City, State, and Country Levels
40. Prioritizing Ecological Protection Over Artificial Atmosphere Creation, Ensuring Earth's Preservation
41. Using Block Chain Technology to Register and Make All Government Transactions, Contracts, Jobs, and Ministries Open to Public Scrutiny
42. Providing Free Medical Care, Merit-Based Education, Minimum Wages, Unemployment Subsidies, Old-Age Subsidies, Children Subsidies, Disabled Subsidies, Mentally Disabled Subsidies, and Farmer Subsidies, all aimed at Ensuring Economic Freedom, Social Freedom, Freedom of Health, and Freedom of Knowledge
43. Enforcing Full-Time Employment for all (Unless Disabled or of Old Age), Establishing Superannuation Retirement Plans, and Implementing a 4-Month Vacation Plan for all Employees (Private and Public)
44. Construction of Peripheral Circumference Roads around Villages, Towns, and Cities, with a Focus on Environmental Conservation and Wildlife Preservation
45. Creation of World-Class Museums Displaying Artefacts, Paintings, and Other Art-Related Items

46. Development of the Entertainment Sector, Quality of Life Programs, Financial Sector Development Programs, National Transformation Programs, and Privatization Initiatives
47. Introduction of Tourism Visas, Tourist Guides, and the Marking and Development of Historic Buildings and Sites
48. An Estimated Timeline for Marking, Constructing, and Executing this City is 5 Years

This ambitious plan receives support from Indo-American, Indo-Australian, Indo-Chinese, Indo-Russo, Indo-Asian, Indo-African, and Indo-European Communities.

Furthermore, the United States of India Assembly is proposed to be established.

The ambitious project of Development of New Self Sustained Hi-tech City in Davangere

creating a self-sustained hi-tech city with an expected expenditure of $100 billion USD is an endeavour that would require careful planning, collaboration, and significant investment from various sources. Here's a breakdown of potential investors and key considerations for inviting participation:

1. Government of Karnataka and Government of India:

As the major initiators, they can provide substantial funding, regulatory support, and infrastructure development.

2. Private Sector Leaders:

Key figures like Azim Premji (Wipro), Sudha Murthy (Infosys Foundation), and technology giants like Microsoft, Apple, Facebook, Google, and Uber can contribute both financially and technologically.

3. Elon Musk and SpaceX:

Given Elon Musk's interest in innovative transportation systems, his involvement could lead to advanced transportation solutions within the city, such as Hyperloop technology.

4. Leading Financial Institutions:

Financial institutions like JP Morgan, BlackRock, and The Blackstone Group can offer financial backing, investment advice, and expertise in fund management.

5. Indian-Based Tech Start-ups:

Include promising start-ups in investment strategy. Ola, Uber, and Oyo can contribute their expertise in urban mobility and hospitality solutions.

6. International Collaboration:

Extend invitations to countries interested in participating and investing in the project. Engaging with both the Chinese and American governments can lead to international collaboration and additional funding.

7. Public-Private Partnerships (PPPs):

Explore opportunities for PPPs where the government and private sector work together to fund and develop specific aspects of the city, such as infrastructure, utilities, or public services.

8. Development Banks and Funds:

Seek investment from development banks, sovereign wealth funds, and impact investors who are interested in sustainable and transformative projects.

9. Technology Innovation Centres:

Establish innovation centres within the city to attract start-ups, research institutions, and technology companies focused on cutting-edge research and development.

10. Comprehensive Business Plan:

Develop a comprehensive business plan outlining the city's goals, economic potential, revenue streams, and expected return on investment (ROI) to attract potential investors.

11. Regulatory Framework:

Ensure that the regulatory environment is conducive to investment, with clear rules and incentives for businesses and investors.

12. Environmental and Sustainability Considerations:

Emphasize sustainability and eco-friendliness in the city's design and operations to attract environmentally conscious investors and partners.

13. Transparency and Accountability:

Establish transparent governance and reporting mechanisms to build trust with investors and demonstrate responsible stewardship of funds.

14. Global Roadshows:

Organize investment roadshows and conferences to showcase the city's potential and attract investors from around the world.

15. Risk Mitigation:

Develop a risk mitigation strategy to address potential challenges, such as regulatory hurdles, economic fluctuations, or unforeseen project delays.

Creating a self-sustained hi-tech city is a long-term vision that requires careful planning, commitment, and collaboration among governments, private sector leaders, and international partners. A well-structured investment plan, regulatory framework, and sustainable development approach will be essential to attract the necessary funding and expertise for this ambitious project.

Coles and Woolworths Model Act

Coles and Woolworths are two of Australia's largest supermarket chains, operating on a similar model. Implementing a similar model in India would require careful planning, investment, and adaptation to the Indian market's unique characteristics and challenges. Here's an overview of how Coles and Woolworths work, followed by steps to implement a similar model in India:

How Coles and Woolworths Work:

Store Network: Both Coles and Woolworths operate a vast network of supermarkets across Australia. These stores offer a wide range of grocery items, fresh produce, meat, dairy products, household goods, and more.

Supply Chain Management: They maintain sophisticated supply chains to ensure products are readily available on store shelves. This involves sourcing products from a variety of suppliers, including local farmers and international manufacturers.

Private Label Brands: Coles and Woolworths have their own private label brands that offer competitively priced products in various categories. These private labels help enhance profit margins.

Customer Loyalty Programs: Both chains have customer loyalty programs that offer discounts, special promotions, and rewards to frequent shoppers. These programs encourage customer retention.

Online Shopping: Coles and Woolworths provide online shopping and home delivery services, allowing customers to order groceries from the comfort of their homes.

Fresh Food Focus: There is a strong emphasis on fresh and healthy food options, including fresh produce, bakery items, and ready-to-eat meals.

Innovation: They continuously innovate in areas such as technology, store design, and sustainability to stay competitive and meet changing consumer preferences.

Steps to Implement a Similar Model in India:

Market Research: Conduct a thorough market research to understand the Indian grocery retail landscape, consumer preferences, and local sourcing opportunities. Identify potential locations for supermarkets.

Regulatory Compliance: Familiarize yourself with India's retail regulations and obtain the necessary licenses and permits to operate a retail business.

Supply Chain Set-up: Establish a robust supply chain that includes sourcing products from local farmers and suppliers. Consider setting up distribution centres to streamline inventory management.

Store Set-up: Invest in store infrastructure, design, and layout to create an inviting shopping environment. Ensure stores are located in high-traffic areas accessible to the target customer base.

Private Label Development: Develop your own private label brands to offer competitively priced products and improve profit margins.

Technology Integration: Implement modern point-of-sale systems, inventory management software, and online shopping platforms to enhance customer experience and streamline operations.

Local Partnerships: Collaborate with local farmers, producers, and suppliers to source fresh and local products. Build strong relationships to ensure a consistent supply of quality goods.

Customer Engagement: Launch a customer loyalty program to encourage repeat business. Offer promotions, discounts, and rewards to attract and retain customers.

Employee Training: Train staff in customer service, product knowledge, and hygiene standards to ensure a positive shopping experience.

Sustainability: Emphasize sustainability in your operations, including waste reduction, energy efficiency, and environmentally responsible practices.

Marketing and Promotion: Develop marketing campaigns to create brand awareness and attract customers. Consider digital marketing, social media, and local advertising.

Online Presence: Offer online shopping and home delivery services to cater to changing consumer behaviour.

Expansion: Once the initial stores are successful, gradually expand your supermarket chain to other cities and regions in India.

Adaptation: Be prepared to adapt to the diverse cultural, dietary, and regional preferences in India. Customize product offerings accordingly.

Compliance with Local Laws: Ensure strict compliance with Indian laws and regulations, including those related to foreign investment, labour, and taxation.

Implementing a successful supermarket model in India will require careful planning, investment, and patience. It's essential to understand the unique challenges and opportunities in the Indian market and adapt your business model accordingly. Building strong relationships with local suppliers and customers is the key to long-term success.

Infrastructure Development Act

Infrastructure development in India, encompassing roads, government structures, dams, rivers, and various modes of transportation, is critical for the country's economic growth, connectivity, and overall development. Here are key aspects and strategies for infrastructure development in India:

1. Road Infrastructure:

Expansion and Modernization: Upgrade and expand the existing road network, including national highways, state highways, and rural roads. Implement modern road construction techniques to improve durability and reduce maintenance.

Expressways: Develop additional expressways to connect major cities and industrial hubs, reducing travel time and enhancing trade.

Smart and Sustainable Roads: Integrate smart technology into road infrastructure, including toll collection, traffic management, and road safety measures.

2. Government Structures:

Government Offices: Construct modern and efficient government office buildings at various levels to improve administrative services.

Digital Infrastructure: Invest in digital infrastructure to enable e-governance and improve government services, including online portals for citizen engagement and public service delivery.

3. Dam Construction and River Management:

Dams and Reservoirs: Build multipurpose dams and reservoirs for water storage, irrigation, hydroelectric power generation, and flood control.

River Navigation: Develop river navigation infrastructure to facilitate inland waterway transportation, reducing congestion on roads and railways.

River Basin Management: Implement comprehensive river basin management plans to address water scarcity, pollution, and environmental conservation.

4. Transportation:

Railways: Modernize and expand the railway network to enhance the efficiency of freight and passenger transportation.

Airports: Upgrade and construct airports to improve air connectivity, both domestically and internationally.

Ports: Develop and modernize ports to facilitate trade and logistics, with a focus on reducing turnaround times for cargo ships.

Public Transport: Invest in public transport systems, including metro systems and bus rapid transit (BRT) systems, to reduce congestion in urban areas.

5. Rural Infrastructure:

Connectivity: Develop rural road networks to connect remote areas with markets and essential services.

Agricultural Infrastructure: Invest in cold storage facilities, warehouses, and food processing units to reduce post-harvest losses and boost agricultural productivity.

6. Sustainable Infrastructure:

Renewable Energy: Promote the development of renewable energy infrastructure, including solar and wind farms, to meet energy demands sustainably.

Green Building Practices: Encourage the adoption of green building practices in construction to reduce environmental impact and promote energy efficiency.

7. Public-Private Partnerships (PPPs):

Encourage private sector participation through PPPs to fund and operate infrastructure projects efficiently.

8. Skilled Workforce:

Invest in training and skill development programs for the workforce involved in infrastructure development to ensure quality and safety.

9. Environmental Impact Assessment:

Conduct thorough environmental impact assessments for major infrastructure projects to minimize adverse effects on the environment.

10. Digital Connectivity:

Expand high-speed internet and digital connectivity to rural areas to bridge the digital divide and enable e-commerce, education, and telemedicine services.

Infrastructure development in India requires a long-term vision, significant investment, and effective project management. It should also prioritize sustainability, efficiency, and inclusivity to benefit all segments of society and promote a balanced regional growth. Collaboration with international organizations and expertise can also play a crucial role in achieving these goals.

Public Works Department Act

Engaging and improving the **Public Works Department (PWD)** in India is crucial for the country's infrastructure development and public services. Here are several strategies to achieve this goal:

1. Transparency and Accountability:

Promote transparency in all PWD activities, including project planning, budgeting, and execution. Make project information, budgets, and progress reports readily accessible to the public.

Implement stringent accountability measures to ensure that projects are completed on time, within budget, and with high quality. Hold officials and contractors accountable for delays or cost overruns.

2. Technology Integration:

Invest in technology to streamline PWD operations. Implement digital platforms for project management, procurement, and monitoring.

Use Geographic Information System (GIS) technology for better planning and maintenance of infrastructure.

3. Capacity-Building:

Provide regular training and skill development programs for PWD staff to enhance their technical expertise, project management capabilities, and knowledge of best practices.

4. Public Participation:

Encourage public participation in the planning and decision-making processes for infrastructure projects. Seek input from local communities and stakeholders to understand their needs and concerns.

Use citizen feedback and suggestions to prioritize projects and allocate resources effectively.

5. Performance-Based Contracts:

Implement performance-based contracting for construction and maintenance projects. Award contracts to contractors based on their ability to meet specified performance criteria, including quality, timeliness, and cost-effectiveness.

6. Quality Assurance:

Establish and enforce stringent quality standards for infrastructure projects. Conduct regular quality checks and inspections to ensure that construction meets these standards.

7. Green and Sustainable Practices:

Promote environmentally friendly and sustainable practices in infrastructure development. Encourage the use of eco-friendly materials, energy-efficient designs, and waste reduction measures.

8. Project Management Units (PMUs):

Create specialized Project Management Units within the PWD to oversee major infrastructure projects. These units can focus on project planning, execution, and monitoring, ensuring efficiency and quality.

9. Decentralization:

Encourage decentralized decision-making by delegating more authority to local PWD offices. This allows for quicker responses to local needs and conditions.

10. Financial Management:

Ensure efficient financial management, including budget planning and execution. Eliminate financial mismanagement and corruption through strict financial controls.

11. Public Awareness Campaigns:

Conduct public awareness campaigns to educate citizens about the importance of infrastructure projects, the role of the PWD, and the benefits of proper maintenance.

12. Data Analytics:

Utilize data analytics and performance indicators to track the progress of projects, identify bottlenecks, and make informed decisions for improvement.

13. Collaboration:

Collaborate with international organizations, academic institutions, and experts to benefit from global best practices and innovative solutions in infrastructure development and management.

14. Incentives and Recognition:

Reward PWD officials and staff for outstanding performance and successful project delivery. Recognize and celebrate achievements to boost morale and motivation.

15. Regular Audits and Evaluation:

Conduct regular audits and evaluations of PWD activities to identify areas for improvement and ensure adherence to quality and efficiency standards.

Improving the Public Works Department in India requires a holistic approach that combines transparency, accountability, capacity-building, and public participation. By implementing these strategies, the PWD can contribute significantly to the development and maintenance of India's infrastructure while ensuring that public funds are used efficiently and effectively.

Wildlife and Conserving Act

Protecting wildlife and conserving biodiversity in India is essential to maintain the ecological balance and ensure the survival of numerous endangered species. The **Wildlife Protection Act of 1972** is a vital legal framework for wildlife conservation in India. Here are some strategies to strengthen and enhance the protection of wildlife under this act:

Strict Enforcement of Existing Laws:

Ensure that the Wildlife Protection Act is rigorously enforced across the country. This includes preventing poaching, habitat destruction, and illegal trade in wildlife and their products.

Strengthen Law Enforcement Agencies:

Equip and train forest department officials, wildlife wardens, and law enforcement agencies to effectively combat wildlife crimes. This includes providing them with modern technology, tools, and resources.

Public Awareness and Education:

Launch public awareness campaigns to educate communities and the general public about the importance of wildlife conservation. Encourage responsible behaviour and discourage illegal activities.

Community Participation:

Involve local communities in wildlife conservation efforts. Promote community-based conservation initiatives that benefit both people and wildlife.

Habitat Conservation:

Focus on habitat conservation and restoration. Protecting natural habitats is crucial for the survival of many species.

Anti-Poaching Measures:

Intensify anti-poaching efforts by using advanced surveillance technology, increasing patrolling, and deploying wildlife crime investigation units.

Biodiversity Conservation Zones:

Identify and establish biodiversity conservation zones to protect critical habitats and key wildlife populations.

Rescue and Rehabilitation Centres:

Establish and support wildlife rescue and rehabilitation centres for injured or orphaned animals. These centres can help in the recovery and release of wildlife back into their natural habitats.

Scientific Research and Monitoring:

Invest in scientific research and monitoring programs to better understand wildlife populations, behaviour, and threats. This information can inform conservation strategies.

International Collaboration:

Collaborate with international organizations and neighbouring countries to combat trans-boundary wildlife crimes and protect migratory species.

Legislation Updates:

Periodically review and update wildlife protection laws to address emerging threats and challenges.

Strict Penalties and Deterrence:

Enforce strict penalties for wildlife-related offenses to act as a deterrent. Ensure that perpetrators of wildlife crimes face severe consequences.

Wildlife Corridors:

Create and protect wildlife corridors to allow for the movement of animals between fragmented habitats, reducing in-breeding and promoting genetic diversity.

Conservation Funds:

Establish conservation funds to generate financial resources for wildlife protection and habitat restoration.

Local Employment Opportunities:

Create employment opportunities for local communities through eco-tourism, wildlife tourism, and sustainable livelihood programs.

Legal Protections for Wildlife Habitats:

Consider strengthening legal protections for wildlife habitats and critical ecosystems, including buffer zones around protected areas.

Sustainable Development Practices:

Encourage sustainable development practices that minimize the negative impact on wildlife and their habitats.

Legal Support for Conservation NGOs:

Provide legal and regulatory support to conservation NGOs and organizations actively working to protect wildlife.

Citizen Involvement:

Encourage citizen involvement in wildlife conservation through volunteer programs and citizen science initiatives.

Government Commitment:

Ensure a strong political will and commitment at all levels of government for wildlife conservation efforts.

Protecting wildlife and conserving biodiversity is a collective responsibility that involves government agencies, local communities, NGOs, and concerned citizens. By implementing these strategies and fostering a culture of respect and co-existence with wildlife, India can make significant progress in wildlife conservation.

Managing and Disposing of Waste

Managing and disposing of waste in India is a significant challenge due to the country's large and growing population. An effective waste management system is essential to address environmental concerns and public health risks. Here are some best practices for managing and disposing of waste in India:

Source Segregation:

Encourage citizens to segregate waste at its source into categories like organic (biodegradable) and inorganic (non-biodegradable) waste. Promote the use of separate bins for different types of waste.

Reduce and Reuse:

Promote the concept of "Reduce, Reuse, and Recycle." Encourage people to minimize waste generation by reducing consumption and reusing items whenever possible.

Recycling:

Establish recycling centres for the collection and processing of recyclable materials such as paper, cardboard, plastics, glass, and metals. Promote recycling practices among industries and individuals.

Composting:

Encourage the composting of organic waste to produce nutrient-rich compost for agricultural use. Provide training and resources for households and communities to compost effectively.

Biogas Generation:

Promote the installation of household and community-level biogas plants to convert organic waste into biogas for cooking and electricity generation.

Waste-to-Energy Plants:

Invest in waste-to-energy plants that can convert non-recyclable waste into electricity or heat, reducing the burden on landfills.

Sanitary Landfills:

Establish well-engineered sanitary landfills that comply with environmental regulations for the disposal of non-recyclable and hazardous waste. Ensure proper lining, leachate collection, and gas management systems.

E-waste Management:

Develop and enforce regulations for the proper disposal and recycling of electronic waste (e-waste), which contains hazardous materials.

Public Awareness:

Conduct public awareness campaigns to educate citizens about the importance of proper waste management and segregation practices.

Municipal Solid Waste Management:

Strengthen municipal solid waste management systems to ensure efficient collection, transportation, and disposal of waste. Invest in garbage collection vehicles and waste processing facilities.

Community Participation:

Involve local communities in waste management and encourage their participation in waste collection and segregation activities.

Extended Producer Responsibility (EPR):

Implement EPR programs that make producers responsible for the end-of-life disposal of their products, particularly those that are challenging to recycle or dispose of safely.

Waste Audits:

Conduct regular waste audits to assess the types and quantities of waste generated and identify areas for improvement.

Legislation and Enforcement:

Enforce existing waste management regulations and enact new laws as needed to address emerging waste challenges.

Research and Innovation:

Invest in research and development to explore innovative waste management technologies and solutions.

Collaboration:

Foster collaboration between government agencies, municipalities, non-governmental organizations (NGOs), and private sector stakeholders to develop and implement effective waste management strategies.

Financial Sustainability:

Develop sustainable funding mechanisms for waste management, including user fees, taxes, grants, and partnerships with the private sector.

Waste Management Training:

Train and educate waste management professionals, municipal staff, and community leaders in modern waste management practices.

Abolition of Caste and Religious Discrimination Act

Abolishing caste and religion-based discrimination and political involvement with religion, caste, and God is a complex and sensitive issue that requires a multifaceted approach, including legal, social, and educational reforms, as well as changes in public perception and political behaviour. Here are some steps that can be taken to work toward this goal: Legal Reforms:

- Strengthen and enforce existing anti-discrimination laws that prohibit discrimination based on caste, religion, or any other social factors.

- Introduce legislation to specifically address and penalize hate speech, incitement to violence, and discrimination based on caste or religion.
- Ensure that the legal system is impartial and that justice is served regardless of caste or religious identity.

Education and Awareness:

- Implement comprehensive educational programs that promote inclusivity, secular values, and respect for diversity.
- Include teachings on the harmful effects of caste and religious discrimination in school curricula.
- Encourage inter-faith and inter-caste dialogue and cooperation within educational institutions.

Social and Cultural Reforms:

- Promote social and cultural initiatives that celebrate diversity and inclusivity.
- Challenge and change regressive social practices and norms that perpetuate discrimination.
- Encourage social organizations and community leaders to actively work against discrimination within their communities.

Economic Empowerment:

- Implement policies that address economic disparities and provide opportunities for marginalized communities to improve their socio-economic status.
- Promote entrepreneurship and skill development programs for disadvantaged groups.

Political Reforms:

- Encourage political parties to adopt policies and manifestos that explicitly reject caste and religious-based politics.
- Encourage clean, issue-based politics that focuses on governance and development rather than identity politics.
- Promote the representation of marginalized communities in political decision-making processes.

Media and Entertainment:

- Encourage the media and entertainment industry to portray characters and storylines that challenge stereotypes and promote inclusivity.
- Highlight stories of individuals and communities that have successfully overcome discrimination.

Civil Society Engagement:

- Support civil society organizations and activists working to combat discrimination and promote social justice.
- Foster collaborations between different social and religious groups to work towards common goals.

Religious Leaders' Role:

- Engage with religious leaders and encourage them to promote messages of unity, tolerance, and equality within their congregations.
- Highlight religious teachings that emphasize love, compassion, and equality.

Data Collection and Monitoring:

Establish mechanisms for collecting and monitoring data related to discrimination, hate crimes, and socio-economic disparities to inform policy decisions and track progress.

Public Discourse: Promote respectful public discourse on issues related to caste and religion, encouraging open dialogue and empathy.

International Engagement: Seek guidance and best practices from international organizations and countries that have successfully addressed discrimination and communalism.

Legal Accountability: Hold individuals and organizations accountable for inciting or perpetuating caste or religious-based discrimination through legal means.

-Encourage and support grassroots movements and initiatives that challenge discrimination and promote inclusivity.

Abolishing caste and religion-based discrimination and ending political involvement with these factors is a long-term endeavour that requires the active participation of government, civil society, religious leaders, and individuals at all levels of society. It involves changing deep-rooted beliefs, behaviours, and systems, which can only be achieved through sustained efforts and a commitment to social justice and equality.

Protecting Rivers and Underground Water

Protecting rivers and underground water sources from waste disposal and pollution is crucial for safeguarding water quality, public health, and the environment. Here are some strategies and measures to achieve this goal:

Stringent Pollution Control Regulations:

Enforce and strengthen pollution control regulations and standards for industries, municipalities, and agriculture to limit the discharge of pollutants into water bodies.

Waste Treatment Facilities:

Upgrade and expand wastewater treatment plants to ensure that effluents are properly treated before being released into rivers and underground aquifers.

Industrial Best Practices:

Encourage industries to adopt best practices for pollution prevention, waste reduction, and the responsible management of hazardous materials.

Agricultural Practices:

Promote sustainable agricultural practices that minimize the use of chemical fertilizers and pesticides, which can leach into groundwater and surface water.

Storm Water Management:

Implement effective storm water management systems to prevent urban runoff, which can carry pollutants into rivers and streams.

RiverBank and Watershed Protection:

- Establish buffer zones along riverbanks to prevent encroachment and degradation of riparian habitats.

- Implement watershed management plans to address pollution at the source and protect the entire ecosystem.

Public Awareness and Education:

Conduct public awareness campaigns to educate communities about the importance of water conservation and pollution prevention.

Promote responsible waste disposal practices among the public.

Monitoring and Reporting:

Set-up monitoring networks to regularly assess water quality in rivers and underground aquifers.

Make water quality data publicly available to raise awareness and hold polluters accountable.

Groundwater Recharge:

Implement groundwater recharge programs to replenish aquifers and prevent over-extraction.

Legal Enforcement:Ensure strict enforcement of environmental laws and regulations related to water quality and pollution control.

Incentives and Subsidies:

-Provide incentives or subsidies to industries and agriculture for adopting eco-friendly and sustainable practices.

Research and Technology:

-Invest in research and technology for innovative solutions to water pollution and treatment.

Community Engagement:

-Engage local communities in the protection and conservation of rivers and groundwater sources. Encourage community-based initiatives for water quality monitoring and protection.

River Clean-up Campaigns:

-Organize periodic river clean-up campaigns involving volunteers, NGOs, and government agencies.

International Cooperation:

- Collaborate with neighbouring countries when dealing with trans-boundary river systems to address pollution and conservation collectively.

Sustainable Development Practices:

-Promote sustainable urban and industrial development practices that consider the environmental impact on water bodies.

Reuse and Recycling:

-Encourage the reuse and recycling of wastewater for non-potable purposes, reducing the demand on freshwater resources.

Legal Remediation:

-Implement legal remedies, such as fines and penalties, for those found responsible for water pollution.

Safeguarding rivers and underground water sources from waste disposal and pollution is a shared responsibility that requires the active participation of government, industries, communities, and individuals. It's essential to adopt a holistic and integrated approach to water resource management that prioritizes environmental protection and sustainable water use.

Improvement of Roads Act

The **expansion and improvement of roads** in Indian cities are critical for addressing urban congestion, enhancing transportation efficiency, and promoting economic growth. Here are strategies and solutions for the expansion and development of better roads in Indian cities:

Comprehensive Urban Planning:

Develop comprehensive urban plans that prioritize road network expansion and connectivity while considering land use, public transportation, and environmental sustainability.

Road Widening and Capacity Enhancement:

Identify congested corridors and areas with traffic bottlenecks and prioritize road widening and capacity enhancement projects.

Sustainable Transport Alternatives:

Invest in integrated and sustainable transportation alternatives, such as metro systems, Bus Rapid Transit (BRT) networks, and cycling lanes, to reduce the reliance on private vehicles.

Quality Road Construction:

Implement strict quality control measures to ensure that road construction adheres to high standards, including proper drainage systems, durable materials, and safe design.

Use of Technology:

Incorporate technology solutions such as intelligent traffic management systems, real-time traffic data collection, and automated toll collection to improve road efficiency.

Encourage Public Transportation:

Promote the use of public transportation by providing efficient, reliable, and affordable services. Invest in modern, well-maintained buses and facilities.

Road Safety Measures:

Implement robust road safety measures, including the construction of pedestrian-friendly sidewalks, zebra crossings, speed limit enforcement, and awareness campaigns.

Public-Private Partnerships (PPPs):

Explore PPP models for road development, where private companies can invest in road construction and maintenance in exchange for revenue from tolls and fees.

Smart Traffic Management:

Implement smart traffic management systems that use real-time data to optimize traffic flow and reduce congestion.

Sustainable Materials:

-Promote the use of sustainable road construction materials, such as recycled materials and eco-friendly paving solutions.

Non-Motorized Transport:

-Develop infrastructure for non-motorized transport modes like walking and cycling, including dedicated lanes and bike-sharing programs.

Multimodal Hubs:

-Create multimodal transportation hubs that connect various modes of transportation, making it easy for commuters to switch between different forms of transport.

Land Acquisition and Clearances:

-Streamline land acquisition processes and obtain necessary clearances promptly to avoid delays in road construction projects.

Traffic Education:

-Conduct traffic education programs to promote responsible driving behaviour and reduce road accidents.

Community Engagement:

-Involve local communities and stakeholders in the planning and execution of road projects to address concerns and ensure inclusivity.

Environmental Considerations:

-Implement environmentally sustainable road design and construction practices to minimize the impact on the environment and reduce air and noise pollution.

Maintenance and Repair:

-Allocate resources for regular road maintenance and repair to extend the lifespan of existing roads and prevent deterioration.

Transparency and Accountability:

-Ensure transparency in road construction and allocation of funds, making project details and progress reports accessible to the public.

Long-Term Vision:

-Develop a long-term vision for the city's road network that considers future population growth and urban expansion.

International Best Practices:

-Learn from and adopt international best practices in road development and management.

Expanding and improving roads in Indian cities requires a holistic approach that balances the needs of commuters, environmental sustainability, and urban development. A well-planned, efficient road network is essential for creating liveable, accessible, and economically vibrant cities in India

Importance of UNITY in India

Where do these people get their money? They obtain funds that are intended for the benefit of the poor. How do they acquire medicines to sell, medicines meant for humanitarian aid? These actions are well-known, and yet no one has stopped them. In India, a prevailing fear exists - fear of social ostracization, fear of reprisals, fear of societal judgement, and fear of the deeply ingrained divisions of caste, culture, religion, and tradition.

People submit themselves, willingly or otherwise, trading their life and freedom for the sake of a rigid caste system. They forfeit their liberty in exchange for protection from retribution. This occurs despite life's fleeting nature, with each day reminding us of the importance of our mortality.

The prevailing narrative seems to be: "I will do whatever the system dictates, even when it's wrong." They appear to lack the will to think, let alone work. While they may be innocent, their weakness fosters cunningness, which in turn begets distrust and violence, ultimately leading them down a path of despair or imprisonment.

The caste system in India has persisted for over 7,000 years. Various historical figures, from Alexander to the Mughals, Ottomans, British, Dutch, and Portuguese, have attempted to dismantle it, yet none have succeeded. Even individuals from the lower classes, accustomed to the caste system and suppression, sometimes seeked to perpetuate their own abuse.

Revolution appears to be the only path to address the inequalities embedded within the caste system - a complete destruction of this system and the unification of Hindus, who are divided into 2,500 castes and 25,000 sub-castes. Lower-caste individuals should be provided with housing, government jobs, free education, and medical care to rectify historical injustices.

To bring balance and justice, there should be no mention of caste in official records. Instead, India should unite under the banner of **a New Sanathana Dharma**, promoting principles of equality, fraternity, and brotherhood, directly drawn from the **Upanishads** and **Vedas.**

Just as the angel Jabril told Mohammed to feed the poor and avoid religious discrimination, we can learn from great leaders like Mohammed, Krishna, Rama, and Shiva. These diverse religious figures can inspire us to respect and love one another, erasing conflicts based on religion or caste.

India, as the land of Buddha, can lead the way in practicing meritocracy and ensuring equality, fraternity, and brotherhood. We should pledge never to fight based on religion and caste, standing together as Indians to build a prosperous, spiritual, and peace-loving nation.

As the creators of the **Kama Sutra, Vedanta, Upanishads, Vedas**, and the **Gita,** we are spiritual guides to the world, and we should lead by example, instilling the principles of **Buddha** and the **Great Ashoka**.

I envision India as a global leader, and I love you all, my fellow countrymen and women. Let's build a better India with a strong system and infrastructure for future generations. The day will come when our children will ask us, "What did you do for India?" We must ensure that we can proudly say we united the country, overcame caste divisions, and worked towards a prosperous future.

The future lies in unity, progress, and equality, not in divisions and discrimination. Together, we can bring about the change we want to see in our beloved, Mother India.

Condition of Indian MSMEs

In the state of Karnataka, there is a growing and vibrant community of small CNC turning, drilling, and lathe job shops that operate in small sheds and parking lots. These businesses are essential for the local economy, providing services and products for various industries and contributing to job creation. However, many of these businesses face challenges due to the limitations of their current working spaces.

Recognizing the crucial role these micro and small enterprises (MSEs) play in the economic development of the state, the government of Karnataka has initiated a program to provide support and assistance to these businesses. The primary objective of this program is to boost the **Micro, Small, and Medium Enterprises (MSME)** sector across the state by promoting their growth and sustainability.

The government has introduced a scheme that involves verifying the accounts and transactions of these small CNC and lathe job shops. If a business has been operating for more than 10 years and their operations have been thoroughly verified, they become eligible for a unique opportunity. The government will allocate industrial sheds to these businesses at subsidized prices.

Here's how this initiative benefits both the MSEs and the overall economy:

Boosting MSMEs: By providing affordable industrial sheds, the government encourages these small businesses to expand their operations and invest in better machinery. This, in turn, leads to the growth of the MSME sector, which is a vital component of Karnataka's economy.

Infrastructure Improvement: The availability of industrial sheds with proper infrastructure, such as electricity, water supply, and security, enhances the overall working conditions for these businesses.

Job Creation: As these businesses grow and take on more projects, they often require additional skilled and unskilled labour. This initiative can lead to an increase in job opportunities for local residents.

Competitive Advantage: The improved infrastructure and workspace can enhance the quality and efficiency of the work carried out by these MSEs, making them more competitive in the market.

Economic Growth: A flourishing MSME sector has a positive impact on the state's economy. It contributes to increased production, higher revenue, and a more robust local supply chain.

The verification process ensures that the benefits are directed towards established and trustworthy businesses. This program aligns with the broader goal of fostering a business-friendly environment and supporting entrepreneurship in Karnataka. It recognizes that these small CNC and lathe job shops are the backbone of local industry and should be provided with the necessary tools for success. The government's subsidization of industrial sheds is a proactive step towards achieving this objective and stimulating economic growth across the state.

Standard 8 hours work with minimum wages

The implementation of a standard 8-hour workday, 5 days a week, is a significant labour reform aimed at improving the lives of industrial workers. This initiative recognizes the evolving dynamics of the labour force and the need to adapt to the changing demands of modern society.

In many industrial settings, long and grueling working hours have been the norm for decades, leading to concerns about the physical and mental well-being of workers. The 8-hour workday reform addresses these concerns by setting clear limits on working hours, promoting a healthier work-life balance, and safeguarding the rights and welfare of employees.

Elaboration:

Work-Life Balance: The shift to an 8-hour workday, 5 days a week, represents a significant move towards striking a better work-life balance. Traditionally, extended working hours have resulted in fatigue, stress, and lack of time for personal and family life. By capping the workday at 8 hours, employees gain more time for leisure, recreation, and family, contributing to overall well-being and improved mental health.

Health and Safety: Extended work hours have been associated with higher rates of workplace accidents and increased stress. By reducing the number of hours worked per day, this reform helps to mitigate these risks, ultimately creating a safer work environment. Employees are more alert, and their decision-making abilities are less compromised due to fatigue.

Productivity and Efficiency: Paradoxically, shorter workdays often result in increased productivity and efficiency. With focused, well-rested employees, the work completed in 8 hours can often match or even exceed what was previously accomplished in longer workdays. This can lead to better output and more effective use of time and resources.

Mental Well-Being: Excessive working hours have been linked to burnout mental health issues. The 8-hour workday allows employees to disconnect from work and recharge, reducing the risk of stress-related conditions. It contributes to a more content and mentally sound workforce.

Fair Labour Practices: Implementing an 8-hour workday aligns with the principles of fair labour practices. It respects workers' rights, ensuring that they have adequate time for rest and recreation. The reform seeks to eliminate instances of overworking, which can be detrimental to an individual's overall quality of life.

Social and Economic Benefits: An improved work-life balance fosters stronger family bonds and enriches social life. Additionally, it encourages employees to engage in personal development, education, and recreational activities, contributing to personal growth and the well-being of society at large.

Compliance with International Standards: Many international labour standards recommend an 8-hour workday, recognizing its benefits for both workers and employers. Adopting this standard brings labour practices in line with global expectations, which can be vital for international trade and relationships.

In summary, implementing an 8-hour workday, 5 days a week, represents a progressive step towards recognizing the rights and well-being of industrial workers. This reform takes into account the changing needs and expectations of the workforce, ensuring that employees have the time and energy to lead healthier, more balanced lives while maintaining or even improving their productivity and the safety of the work environment. It is a testament to a society that values its workforce and seeks to enhance the lives of its citizens.

In India, while there may be a façade of development, the harsh reality lies in the deep-seated issues of exploitation and bondage among the working class. The rich and upper-middle-class individuals often exploit the innocence of the poor and lower-middle-class citizens. In places like Bengaluru's industrial areas, men toil for an average of 10,000 INR per month, working around 10 hours daily. Industrial workers fare slightly better at 14,000 INR per month but work six days a week. This reflects a system resembling a modern form of slavery.

The elite class deliberately keeps the working class unaware of broader societal and capitalist concepts, effectively perpetuating this cycle of exploitation. It is indeed heart-wrenching to witness the lifelessness in the eyes of these workers, their spirits crushed by an unjust society.

India is marked by a hierarchical system where submission to those above and below is expected. While there are entrepreneurs, police, politicians, and citizens with noble intentions, the system often thwarts their efforts for meaningful change.

The only path out of this quagmire is to uproot the deeply ingrained discrimination, inequality, and poverty in society. A blend of Capitalistic socialism and military discipline might be the remedy India needs. To truly transform, Indians must shed selfishness and ignorance, embracing comprehensive education and ushering in a revolution for a brighter future.

Ensuring better working conditions and fair wages for the working class is crucial for their well-being and the overall development of a region. To achieve this in Karnataka's industrial sector, a collaborative effort between the government and industrialists is essential.

Mandatory 8-Hour Workdays, 5 Days a Week: Implementing a standard 8-hour workday, 5 days a week is a fundamental step towards improving the lives of industrial workers. This schedule not only promotes a healthy work-life balance but also reduces the physical and mental strain on employees.

Minimum Monthly Wages of 24,000 INR: Setting a minimum wage of 24,000 INR per month provides financial security to workers and ensures that they can afford the basic necessities of life. This wage level helps combat poverty and improves the overall standard of living for the working class.

Collaboration between Government and Industrialists: The government of Karnataka should collaborate closely with industrialists to implement these reforms. This partnership can have several benefits:

Financial Support: The government can provide subsidies or financial incentives to industrialists who comply with these standards, helping them offset the additional labour costs.

Health Insurance: Ensuring that all employees have access to health insurance is crucial for their well-being. The government and industrialists can work together to provide affordable and comprehensive health coverage for workers, addressing their medical needs and emergencies.

Monitoring and Compliance: Establishing a regulatory body or agency responsible for monitoring and enforcing these standards is essential. Regular inspections can ensure that industrialists adhere to the agreed-upon conditions, and penalties can be imposed for non-compliance.

Public Awareness: The government can launch public awareness campaigns to inform workers about their rights and entitlements, ensuring that they are aware of the improvements being made for their benefit.

Long-Term Economic Benefits: Although these reforms may require initial investments, they can lead to long-term economic benefits. Healthier, more contented workers are likely to be more productive, contributing to the growth and sustainability of the industrial sector.

In conclusion, the collaboration between the government of Karnataka and industrialists to implement an 8-hour workday, 5 days a week, with a minimum wage of 24,000 INR per month, along with health insurance benefits, can significantly enhance the lives of the working class. It's a win-win situation, as it not only uplifts the workers but also strengthens the industrial sector and the overall economy of the region

Mandatory Barcode and Fixed Price

Context: The proposal to sell everything in Karnataka at the **Maximum Retail Price (MRP)** and enforce barcode labelling on fixed prices is a significant regulatory initiative aimed at ensuring fair pricing and transparency in the market. It addresses concerns related to price manipulation, counterfeit products, and inconsistent pricing practices that can affect consumers and businesses alike.

Karnataka, like many other regions, faces challenges related to price discrepancies and counterfeit goods. This initiative seeks to standardize pricing practices and make product information more accessible to consumers, thereby creating a more equitable marketplace.

Elaboration:

Consumer Protection: Enforcing the sale of all products at the MRP ensures that consumers are not overcharged for goods and services. This is particularly significant in sectors where price manipulation is common, such as pharmaceuticals, electronics, and food products. It protects consumers from exploitation and promotes consumer rights.

Price Transparency: Barcode labelling on fixed prices adds an additional layer of transparency to the market. With clearly labelled prices and product information, consumers can make informed purchasing decisions. This transparency also benefits businesses by reducing disputes related to pricing and promoting trust among consumers.

Counterfeit Product Prevention: Counterfeit goods are a significant problem in many markets. Enforcing barcode labelling with fixed prices helps in verifying the authenticity of products. Consumers can quickly scan the barcode to confirm if the product is genuine, reducing the prevalence of counterfeit items and enhancing consumer safety.

Standardized Practices: Standardized pricing practices simplify operations for businesses. They no longer need to engage in complex pricing strategies, making it easier to manage their inventory and offer competitive prices. This can lead to a more competitive and efficient marketplace.

Conflict Resolution: The government's role in allotting prices in case of a conflict of interest is crucial. It ensures that disputes related to pricing are resolved fairly and impartially. This step prevents price wars, price-fixing, or other unethical practices that can harm both businesses and consumers.

Market Equity: Standardized pricing practices help level the playing field for all businesses. Small and medium-sized enterprises (SMEs) may benefit from reduced competition with larger corporations that can afford complex pricing strategies. This promotes diversity in the marketplace and supports SMEs.

Legal Compliance: By mandating MRP and barcode labelling, the government ensures that businesses adhere to legal requirements.

Non-compliance can result in penalties or legal action, promoting responsible business practices.

International Standards: These regulations align with international standards for consumer protection and labelling, which can facilitate trade and business relations with other regions and countries.

Consumer Confidence: When consumers trust that they are paying a fair price and receiving authentic products, it fosters confidence in the marketplace. This trust is essential for economic growth and the sustainability of businesses.

In conclusion, the proposal to sell everything in Karnataka at MRP with mandatory barcode labelling on fixed prices represents a significant move towards fair and transparent pricing practices. It ensures that consumers are protected, businesses operate fairly, and the marketplace remains competitive and trustworthy. This initiative addresses various challenges in the market, from counterfeit goods to price manipulation, ultimately benefiting consumers, businesses, and the overall economy.

Instilling discipline in a large and diverse population like India can be a complex and long-term endeavour, but it's essential for the well-being of society. Here are some strategies to promote discipline in various aspects of life.

Instilling Discipline

Education and Awareness:

Diet and Exercise: Promote public health campaigns and educational programs to create awareness about the importance of a healthy lifestyle. Schools and communities can play a role in teaching good dietary habits and the benefits of regular exercise.

Work Ethics:

Professional Training: Encourage professional development and training programs for individuals to understand the importance of work ethics, integrity, and dedication to their jobs.

Accountability: Implement systems that hold employees accountable for their actions and work output.

Traffic Discipline:

Law Enforcement: Strengthen traffic laws and regulations, and enforce them consistently. Implement strict penalties for violations.

Education: Conduct road safety awareness campaigns to educate the public about the consequences of reckless driving.

Public Behaviour:

Civic Education: Promote civic education in schools and communities to instill the values of respect, politeness, and appropriate public behaviour.

Community Involvement: Encourage community-based initiatives to create a sense of responsibility and ownership within communities.

Interpersonal Interactions:

Social Skills Training: Teach communication and social skills, emphasizing empathy and respect in interactions with strangers.

Anti-bullying Programs: Implement programs to address and prevent bullying and abusive behaviour.

Religious Tolerance:

Inter-faith Dialogue: Promote inter-faith dialogue and cultural exchanges to foster religious tolerance.

Religious Education: Include education on various religions and their values in the school curriculum.

Legal Measures:

Anti-Discrimination Laws: Enforce and strengthen laws against discrimination, hate speech, and harassment.

Media and Entertainment:

Responsible Media: Encourage media outlets to promote positive values and discourage sensationalism.

Role Models: Showcase individuals who exemplify discipline and good behaviour as role models.

Government Initiatives:

Incentives and Rewards: Provide incentives and rewards for individuals and organizations that promote discipline and ethical behaviour.

Social Services: Ensure access to social services for marginalized communities to address underlying issues that may contribute to undisciplined behaviour.

Community Support:

Support Groups: Establish support groups for individuals struggling with discipline issues, such as addiction or anger management.

Instilling discipline in a large population is a gradual process, and it requires a multi-faceted approach involving education, law enforcement, community engagement, and the active participation of individuals. It's essential to create a culture where discipline is seen as a collective responsibility for the betterment of society.

Generate Revenue within Cities, Towns, and Villages

1. **Taxation:** Governments can impose various taxes, such as income tax, property tax, sales tax, and excise tax, to generate revenue, by reducing corruption and bribery more taxes can be pooled in to the system to support the need and increase the magnitude of treasury.
2. **User Fees:** Charging fees for government services like parking, public transportation, waste collection, and utilities can contribute to revenue, construction of new parking lots, malls, shipping centres, super market, in 12 different locations on the outskirts of the city.
3. **Licensing and Permits:** Revenue can be generated through fees for licenses and permits, including business licenses, building permits, and Advertising permits.
4. **Fines and Penalties:** Enforcing fines and penalties for violations of laws and regulations can be a revenue source, particularly for traffic violations and non-compliance, by installation of Automatic speed cameras

5. **Property Leasing and Sales:** Government-owned properties can be leased or rented out, providing substantial revenue for the government.
6. **Public-Private Partnerships (PPPs):** Collaborating with private entities for infrastructure projects can generate revenue through partnerships and investments.
7. **Grants and Funding:** Governments can apply for grants and funding opportunities from higher levels of government and international organizations, by advocating friendly relationship governments can apply for student exchange programmes
8. **Tourism:** Promoting tourism and collecting tourism-related taxes, like hotel and tourism taxes, can contribute to local revenue.
9. **Public Auctions:** Selling surplus or confiscated items through public auctions can be a source of income.
10. **Investment Income:** Generating revenue through investments in stocks, bonds, and other financial instruments.
11. **Sales of Government Services:** Offering specialized government services, such as data access or public records, for a fee.
12. **Public Events:** Hosting events and charging admission or participation fees can be a way to generate revenue, like international concert, hosting international events, music, fashion, cultural, sports, literature and arts events can boost local economy.

Effective management and transparent use of these revenue sources are crucial to ensure they benefit the local community and contribute to its development.

Fixing Traffic Issues

"In India, everything is interconnected, so by making some adjustments, we can bring order to the system. Let's start by addressing the traffic issue. We can improve it by changing the working hours of office employees to reduce congestion during peak times. Additionally, we should adapt school timings based on geographical considerations to avoid overcrowding during rush hours.

To maintain a cheerful and positive atmosphere, we should deploy traffic police officers during peak hours to ensure smooth traffic flow for both office-goers and students. The key here is to promote a positive and happy attitude when commuting to work or school. We aim to create a pleasant environment with traffic-free roads, organized commuting, disciplined traffic police, and a professional approach towards commuters.

Traffic issue – Impact on mental and physical health

creating a separate loop for bus stops to prevent them from blocking incoming traffic is a practical solution. Additionally, coordinating with traffic wardens can help improve traffic control. It's important to have a well-thought-out plan to optimize traffic flow and enhance transportation infrastructure.

Media support is crucial to spread awareness about traffic rules and regulations, as well as to emphasize the importance of punctuality, smiling, and maintaining good physical and mental health during daily commutes to and from offices and educational institutions."

Let's elaborate on your idea:

Traffic Issue: You propose starting with addressing traffic issues. India's traffic congestion is a significant challenge in many cities. Your approach involves making systemic changes.

Timing Adjustments: You suggest changing the timing of office workers to reduce traffic during peak hours. This could involve implementing staggered work hours for different companies or encouraging remote work arrangements.

School Timings: Adjusting school timings based on geographical location is a practical idea. Schools could consider starting at different times to spread out traffic during peak hours.

Traffic Police: Having traffic police on the roads during peak hours is crucial. They can help manage traffic flow, ensure road safety, and clear the path for commuters.

Promoting a Cheerful Atmosphere: Your aim is to create a positive commuting experience. This involves encouraging a cheerful attitude among commuters, which can lead to a happier and less stressful commute.

Media Support: Media can play a pivotal role in this initiative. They can help raise awareness about traffic rules and regulations, the importance of punctuality, and the benefits of a well-managed traffic system. Media campaigns can also promote a professional and respectful attitude among commuters.

Importance of Being on Time: Stressing the importance of punctuality is essential. Being on time for work or school not only contributes to better traffic management but also sets a positive tone for the day.

Importance of Smiling: Encouraging people to maintain a positive demeanour while commuting can reduce road rage and create a more harmonious environment.

Physical and Mental Well-being: Highlighting the significance of taking care of one's physical and mental health during commuting is crucial. Stressing the importance of staying calm and composed on the road can lead to safer and more pleasant journeys.

In summary, your plan revolves around reshaping the daily commute experience in India by addressing traffic issues, promoting a positive and professional attitude among commuters, and leveraging media support to spread awareness and education. Such an approach could potentially lead to a more efficient and pleasant daily commute for everyone.

Sadistic Sense of Superiority

"In Indian society, there is a troubling trend of deriving sadistic pleasure from looking down on others, which has deeply embedded itself within our culture. This phenomenon is pervasive and permeates our thoughts and actions.

For instance, when a superstar actor amasses more followers, they often derive satisfaction from belittling their fellow artists. Similarly, individuals take delight in looking down on those who attend government institutions or less prestigious schools when their own children gain admission to top educational institutions. Possessing a better car, clothing, housing, job, or any material possession can evoke a sense of sadistic superiority over friends and acquaintances.

This phenomenon creates a divisive dichotomy of superiority and inferiority. The feeling of inferiority in one person often fuels the sense of superiority in another.

Sadly, our society is entrenched in this sadistic mentality, where people remain ignorant of the harm they cause through their abuse and torment of others. They violate others in numerous ways, yet there are few attempts to change or extend help. This reluctance is often rooted in the fear that those perceived as inferior might surpass them, thus jeopardizing the hierarchical structures they've constructed in their own minds.

It is imperative that we address and rectify this sadistic mindset. Society must strive for equal opportunities, shared responsibilities, mutual duties, and fair compensation for all individuals contributing to its progress. Suppressing and repressing others will only undermine Indian society further in the eyes of the already critical world."

If you have further concerns or need more assistance, please let me know.

You've raised an important issue about the prevalence of a superiority complex and judgmental attitudes in Indian society. Addressing these societal attitudes and fostering a more inclusive and empathetic culture is indeed crucial for progress and harmony.

It's essential to promote a mindset that values individuals based on their character, talents, and contributions rather than material possessions or social status. Encouraging equal opportunities, responsibilities, and fair treatment for all members of society is a significant step towards positive change.

Awareness, education, and open discussions about these issues can help challenge the existing mentality and promote a more compassionate and equitable society. Change often begins with individuals who are willing to stand up against prejudice and discrimination and work towards a more inclusive and empathetic community.

Your insights highlight the need for a collective effort to break down these harmful mindsets and work towards a more equitable and compassionate society in India.

Your observations about the prevalence of a sadistic mindset in Indian society, where some individuals derive pleasure from looking down upon others, are insightful. This phenomenon can indeed be rooted in feelings of superiority and inferiority, creating a toxic dynamic within society.

This sense of superiority can be tied to various aspects like wealth, education, possessions, and more. It often stems from a fear that if those who feel superior extend a helping hand or advocate for change, those they perceive as inferior may surpass them. This fear can lead to a reluctance to promote equality and fairness.

To address these issues and create a more inclusive and compassionate society, it's crucial for individuals, communities, and institutions to embrace change. This change involves acknowledging the harmful impact of these attitudes, fostering empathy, and actively promoting equal opportunities, responsibilities, and rights for all.

Suppressing or repressing these issues only perpetuates the problem and ultimately hinders societal progress. By encouraging open discussions, raising awareness, and advocating for policies that promote equality, Indian society can work towards dismantling this sadistic mentality and creating a more harmonious and equitable environment for all its members. It's a long-term process, but one that can lead to a more just and compassionate society.

Respectful environment

Respecting people at work and in general respecting one another and treating individuals with dignity and respect is not just a moral principle but a cornerstone of a harmonious and equitable society. It's a fundamental aspect of human interaction that transcends boundaries and should be practiced in all walks of life. Addressing people by their titles and names, as opposed to using disrespectful language or demeaning terms, holds immense significance in fostering a culture of mutual respect and professionalism.

Dignity and Inclusivity: Using respectful language and addressing individuals by their names and titles shows that we value their worth and contributions. It is a way of recognizing and upholding their dignity, regardless of their position or role in society. This approach promotes inclusivity and ensures that no one feels marginalized or disrespected.

Creating Positive Relationships: Respectful communication is the foundation of positive relationships, both in personal and professional contexts. When individuals are treated with respect, it fosters trust and cooperation. This, in turn, leads to more effective communication and collaboration, which benefits individuals and the community as a whole.

Professionalism: In workplaces and government settings, professionalism is vital for the efficient functioning of organizations. Using respectful language and addressing individuals appropriately is a key aspect of professional behaviour. It sets the tone for a workplace where individuals can focus on their tasks and responsibilities without distractions caused by disrespectful language or behaviour.

Fostering a Supportive Environment: Respectful communication is not just about avoiding disrespectful language; it also encompasses active listening, empathy, and understanding. When individuals feel respected and heard, it creates a supportive and nurturing environment. This is particularly crucial in public service, where government institutions play a role in the well-being of citizens.

Promoting Equal Opportunities: A culture of respect ensures that opportunities are available to everyone, regardless of their background, gender, or social status. When people are addressed with respect, it becomes more likely that their ideas and talents are recognized and acknowledged.

Conflict Resolution: Respectful communication is a valuable tool for resolving conflicts and disagreements. It allows individuals to engage in constructive dialogue and find common ground. This is vital for maintaining peace and harmony within communities.

Leadership by Example: Your initiative to encourage respectful communication sets an example for others to follow. Leaders who prioritize respectful behaviour inspire their teams and communities to do the same. Leading by example can have a ripple effect, influencing a broader shift towards a more respectful society.

Compassion and Empathy: Respectful communication is also about displaying compassion and empathy. It's about understanding that every individual has their unique experiences and challenges. By addressing people with respect, we acknowledge their humanity and demonstrate empathy.

In conclusion, the initiative to encourage respectful communication is a commendable and essential step towards building a more respectful, compassionate, and inclusive society. It reinforces the values of dignity, equality, and professionalism, both in government and the broader community. By practicing and promoting respectful behaviour, we can contribute to a more harmonious and equitable world where individuals are valued and treated with the consideration they deserve.

Abolition of Poverty, Discrimination, Inequality, and Ignorance in India Act

The **abolition of poverty, discrimination, inequality, and ignorance in India** is a complex and multifaceted challenge that requires comprehensive strategies, policies, and collective efforts. Here's an elaboration on each of these aspects and some approaches to address them:

Poverty Abolition:

- Poverty eradication involves lifting millions of people out of extreme poverty and ensuring access to basic necessities, including food, shelter, clean water, healthcare, and education.
- Strategies should focus on inclusive economic growth, job creation, and equitable wealth distribution.
- Social safety nets, such as direct cash transfers, food security programs, and employment guarantee schemes, can provide immediate relief to vulnerable populations.
- Access to credit, financial literacy, and skill development programs can empower individuals to escape the poverty trap.
- Addressing poverty also requires land reforms, access to productive resources, and affordable housing solutions for marginalized communities.

Discrimination Elimination:

- Discrimination, particularly based on factors like caste, gender, religion, and ethnicity, must be actively addressed.
- Strengthening anti-discrimination laws and enforcing them rigorously is crucial.
- Promoting social and cultural awareness campaigns to challenge stereotypes and biases.
- Encouraging inter-caste and inter-faith dialogue to foster social cohesion.
- Empowering marginalized groups through education, skill development, and affirmative action policies.
- Providing legal aid and support to victims of discrimination.

Inequality Reduction:

- Reducing economic and social inequalities involves addressing disparities in income, education, healthcare, and opportunities.

- Progressive taxation policies that ensure the wealthy contribute more to social welfare.
- Expanding access to quality education, healthcare, and social services for all.
- Fostering economic inclusion by promoting entrepreneurship and small and medium-sized enterprises (SMEs).
- Encouraging corporate social responsibility (CSR) and ethical business practices.
- Empowering women through gender-sensitive policies and initiatives.
- Strengthening land reforms and land tenure security for marginalized communities.

Ignorance Elimination:

- Eliminating ignorance involves improving access to education, information, and knowledge for all citizens.
- Expanding and enhancing the quality of the education system, with a focus on early childhood education and skill development.
- Promoting digital literacy and improving access to the internet and information technology.
- Encouraging lifelong learning and adult education programs.
- Fostering a culture of critical thinking, scientific inquiry, and evidence-based decision-making.
- Providing quality healthcare and nutrition to ensure that individuals can reach their full cognitive potential.

Comprehensive Social Policies:

- The government should develop and implement comprehensive social policies that integrate efforts to address poverty, discrimination, inequality, and ignorance.
- Social protection programs, universal healthcare, and affordable housing are essential components of these policies.
- Regular monitoring and evaluation are necessary to assess the effectiveness of these policies and make necessary adjustments.

Civil Society and Community Engagement:

- Active engagement of civil society organizations and communities is crucial for advocating for change and holding governments accountable.
- Grassroots initiatives and community-based programs can have a significant impact on reducing poverty, discrimination, and inequality.
- Encouraging volunteerism and social activism to raise awareness and address social issues.

International Cooperation:

- Collaborating with international organizations and neighbouring countries to share knowledge and resources to combat poverty and inequality.
- Learning from international best practices and adapting them to local contexts.

The abolition of poverty, discrimination, inequality, and ignorance is an ongoing process that requires sustained commitment from government, civil society, and individuals. It involves not only addressing immediate needs but also addressing structural and systemic issues that perpetuate these challenges. Achieving these goals will contribute to a more just, equitable, and prosperous India.

Anti-corruption Act

Corruption can be a complex and deeply entrenched issue, but here are some steps that could help improve the situation:

Transparent Governance: Implement transparent procedures and policies that ensure accountability. Publish all government decisions, contracts, and financial transactions online to make them accessible to the public.

Whistle-blower Protection: Establish strong legal protections for whistle-blowers who expose corruption. This can encourage insiders to come forward with information without fearing retaliation.

Strengthening Anti-Corruption Agencies: Provide adequate resources and independence to anti-corruption agencies like the **Lokayukta** to effectively investigate and prosecute corruption cases.

Digitalization and Automation: Use technology to streamline processes and reduce human interaction in administrative tasks. This can minimize opportunities for corruption and reduce the influence of middlemen.

E-Governance: Implement electronic governance systems for government services, reducing the need for citizens to physically interact with officials and minimizing the potential for bribery.

Education and Awareness: Launch public awareness campaigns about the detrimental effects of corruption on society and the benefits of a corruption-free state.

Strengthening Legal Framework: Revise and strengthen laws related to corruption, ensuring that they have appropriate penalties and provisions for timely prosecution.

Merit-Based Recruitment: Ensure that government appointments and promotions are based on merit rather than political connections. This reduces the chances of unqualified individuals occupying important positions.

Financial Transparency: Enforce stringent financial reporting standards for public officials and politicians. This can help identify unusual wealth accumulation and potential cases of corruption.

Ethics Training: Provide regular ethics and integrity training for government employees, emphasizing the importance of ethical behaviour and the consequences of corrupt practices.

Citizen Participation: Encourage citizen participation and engagement in governance processes. This can include citizen feedback mechanisms, public consultations, and involvement in decision-making.

Fast-Track Courts: Establish special courts to expedite corruption cases, ensuring that justice is served swiftly.

Political Will: It's essential that political leaders show a strong commitment to combating corruption. They should lead by example and prioritize transparency and integrity in their own actions.

Collaboration with Civil Society: Engage civil society organizations, non-governmental organizations, and media to create a united front against corruption.

International Cooperation: Learn from the experiences of other countries that have successfully tackled corruption. International organizations can provide expertise and resources to support anti-corruption efforts.

Remember that combating corruption is a long-term effort that requires a multifaceted approach. Progress may be slow, but with sustained commitment, transparency, and the participation of all stakeholders, a positive change can be achieved.

"Manjunathism Principles and Values:

Principles and Values: "Manjunathism" founded on principles of justice, equality, and social progress seeks to address a broad spectrum of societal issues that hinder the well-being and progress of individuals and communities in India. Some key principles and values associated with this movement might include:

1. **Social Justice:** Advocating for fairness and equality in all aspects of society, regardless of caste, religion, race, or socio-economic status.
2. **Anti-Corruption:** Opposing corrupt practices in government, businesses, and institutions that hinder economic development and harm citizens.
3. **Inclusivity:** Promoting a society where every individual's voice is heard and their rights are respected.
4. **Non-Discrimination:** Focusing on eliminating discrimination and prejudice based on caste, religion, race, gender, or any other characteristic.
5. **Environmental Responsibility:** Addressing issues like pollution and advocating for sustainable practices to protect the environment.
6. **Economic Equity:** Supporting policies and initiatives that reduce poverty, promote fair wages, and provide equal economic opportunities for all.

Goals and Objectives: The overarching goal of "Manjunathism" is transformation of Indian society to be more just, inclusive, and equitable. Some specific objectives could include:

1. **Fight against Corruption:** Promoting transparency and accountability in government and business, with a goal of reducing corruption at all levels.
2. **Social Harmony:** Encouraging dialogue and understanding among different communities to combat issues like casteism, religious intolerance, and racism.
3. **Protection of Vulnerable Groups:** Advocating for the rights and protection of marginalized and vulnerable populations, including women, labourers, and those in poverty.
4. **Environmental Sustainability:** Supporting initiatives to reduce pollution, combat climate change, and protect natural resources.
5. **Anti-Bribery Efforts:** Promoting ethical behaviour and discouraging bribery and unethical practices.
6. **Education and Awareness:** Raising awareness about the issues addressed by the movement and promoting education as a means of empowerment.

Strategies and Initiatives: To achieve its goals and objectives, "Manjunathism" employs various strategies and initiatives, including:

1. **Advocacy and Lobbying:** Engaging with policy-makers and stakeholders to influence legislation and policies that align with the movement's values.
2. **Community Outreach:** Organizing community-based programs, workshops, and awareness campaigns to engage and educate the public.
3. **Legal Activism:** Pursuing legal actions against corruption, discrimination, and environmental violations.
4. **Social Media and Networking:** Leveraging digital platforms to mobilize support and disseminate information.
5. **Collaboration:** Partnering with other organizations, civil society groups, and individuals who share similar concerns and objectives.
6. **Peaceful Protests:** Organizing peaceful demonstrations and protests to draw attention to specific issues and advocate for change.

"Fighting against Corruption"

"Fighting against Corruption" is a crucial aspect of the "Manjunathism" movement, reflecting a commitment to transparency, accountability, and ethical governance. Here's an elaboration of this component within the context of "Manjunathism":

1. **Transparency and Accountability:** "Manjunathism" emphasizes the importance of transparency in government and business operations. It calls for clear and accessible information about how public funds are allocated and spent. This transparency is essential for holding public officials and organizations accountable for their actions.
2. **Anti-Bribery Efforts:** Within the movement, there is a strong stance against bribery and corruption practices. "Manjunathism" seeks to create a culture where accepting or offering bribes is seen as unacceptable and unethical. It encourages individuals and organizations to report instances of corruption and unethical behaviour.
3. **Legal and Judicial Reforms:** To combat corruption effectively, "Manjunathism" may advocate for legal and judicial reforms. This could include measures to strengthen anti-corruption laws, protect whistle-blowers, and ensure a fair and impartial judiciary to prosecute corrupt individuals.
4. **Political Accountability:** The movement may also promote greater political accountability, demanding that elected officials and government bodies are held responsible for their actions and decisions. This might involve efforts to reduce political patronage, nepotism, and favouritism.
5. **Civil Society Engagement:** "Manjunathism" recognizes the importance of an active and vigilant civil society. It encourages individuals and organizations to monitor government activities, expose corruption, and engage in advocacy and activism to demand accountability.
6. **Education and Awareness:** An informed citizenry is crucial for fighting corruption. The movement may focus on raising awareness about the damaging effects of corruption on society and the benefits of transparency and ethical behaviour.

Educational initiatives and public campaigns may be a part of these efforts.

7. **Whistle-blower Protection:** Protecting whistle-blowers who expose corrupt practices is a fundamental aspect of the movement. It seeks to ensure that individuals who come forward with evidence of corruption are shielded from retaliation and have legal protections.
8. **Technology and Innovation:** "Manjunathism" may leverage technology and innovation to increase transparency and reduce opportunities for corruption. This could involve implementing e-governance systems, online reporting mechanisms, and block chain technology for transparent record-keeping.
9. **Corporate Responsibility:** In addition to addressing government corruption, the movement might also call for ethical behaviour within the private sector. It encourages businesses to adopt anti-corruption policies, adhere to ethical business practices, and promote corporate social responsibility.

International Cooperation: Recognizing that corruption often transcends borders, "Manjunathism" may advocate for international cooperation to combat corrupt practices, including cooperation with international anti-corruption organizations and agreements.

Overall, "Fighting against Corruption" within "Manjunathism" is a multifaceted approach that involves legal, institutional, cultural, and societal changes. It seeks to create an environment where corruption is discouraged, exposed, and met with consequences, ultimately contributing to a fairer and more just society in India.

"Manjunathism": Social Justice

Social Justice: “Manjunathism" places a strong emphasis on social justice, which is the principle of fair and equitable treatment for all members of society, regardless of their background, identity, or circumstances. Here's how the concept of social justice is integral to "Manjunathism":

Equality: Social justice, as promoted by "Manjunathism," seeks to eliminate discrimination, biases, and systemic inequalities that exist in society. It advocates for the equal distribution of rights, opportunities, and resources among all individuals, irrespective of factors such as caste, religion, race, gender, or economic status.

Inclusivity: "Manjunathism" promotes an inclusive society where everyone has a voice and a seat at the table. This means recognizing and valuing the diversity of individuals and communities and ensuring that no one is marginalized or excluded based on their identity or circumstances.

Access to Resources: Social justice within "Manjunathism" entails ensuring that essential resources, such as education, healthcare, clean water, and economic opportunities, are accessible to everyone. This involves addressing disparities in access to these resources that often affect marginalized or disadvantaged groups.

Justice Systems: The movement calls for a fair and impartial legal and justice system that upholds the rights and dignity of all individuals. It seeks to address issues of judicial bias, corruption, and the unequal treatment of different groups within the legal framework.

Anti-Discrimination: "Manjunathism" actively opposes discrimination in all forms, whether it's based on caste, religion, gender, race, or any other characteristic. It advocates for legal protections and societal norms that prohibit discrimination and promote diversity and inclusion.

Redistribution of Wealth: Social justice also involves addressing economic inequalities. "Manjunathism" may support policies aimed at wealth redistribution, progressive taxation, and social safety nets to ensure that everyone has access to basic necessities and opportunities for economic advancement.

Empowerment: The movement seeks to empower marginalized and disadvantaged communities through education, skills development, and representation in decision-making processes. Empowerment is seen as a means to enable individuals to break free from cycles of poverty and discrimination.

Advocacy and Awareness: "Manjunathism" engages in advocacy and awareness campaigns to highlight social injustices and promote change. This includes raising awareness about discrimination, inequality, and the importance of social justice in building a more equitable society.

Community-Building: The movement often involves community-building efforts to foster solidarity and cooperation among diverse groups. Building strong communities can be a means of supporting individuals and addressing common challenges collectively.

Legal Reforms: To achieve social justice, "Manjunathism" may call for legal reforms, including changes to discriminatory laws and policies, as well as the strengthening of legal protections for vulnerable groups.

In essence, social justice within "Manjunathism" envisions a society where every individual is treated with dignity and respect, has equal opportunities for personal and economic growth, and where systemic inequalities and discrimination are actively challenged and dismantled. It reflects a commitment to fairness, equity, and human rights as essential principles for building a just and inclusive society.

"Inclusivity" in the context of "Manjunathism"

"Inclusivity" in the context of "Manjunathism" refers to a fundamental principle and value that promotes the participation, representation, and equal treatment of all individuals, regardless of their background, identity, or circumstances. It emphasizes creating a society where no one is excluded or marginalized, and everyone has an equal opportunity to thrive and contribute to the community and nation. Here's an elaboration on the concept of inclusivity within "Manjunathism":

1. **Equal Treatment and Rights:** Inclusivity entails recognizing and upholding the equal rights and dignity of every person, irrespective of factors such as caste, religion, race, gender, sexual orientation, disability, or socio-economic status. It opposes discrimination or bias against any group and advocates for a society where everyone is treated fairly and justly under the law.

2. **Social Justice:** "Manjunathism" prioritizes social justice by addressing historical and systemic inequalities. It acknowledges the existence of disparities and strives to rectify them through policies and initiatives that bridge gaps in access to opportunities, resources, and services.

3. **Representation and Participation:** An inclusive society encourages the active participation of all its members in political, social, economic, and cultural spheres. This involves

not only ensuring that marginalized groups have a voice but also actively seeking their input and involvement in decision-making processes.

4. **Accessibility:** Inclusivity also relates to making physical spaces, public services, and information accessible to everyone, including people with disabilities. It promotes the removal of barriers that hinder participation and engagement.
5. **Cultural Diversity:** Embracing cultural diversity and recognizing the value of different perspectives and backgrounds is a key aspect of inclusivity. It promotes an environment where cultural traditions and languages are respected and celebrated.
6. **Gender Equality:** Inclusivity includes striving for gender equality by addressing issues related to gender-based discrimination and violence. It promotes equal opportunities and treatment for people of all genders.
7. **Education and Awareness:** Inclusivity emphasizes the importance of education and awareness to challenge stereotypes, biases, and prejudices. It encourages educational programs that foster empathy, understanding, and tolerance among individuals from diverse backgrounds.
8. **Economic Inclusivity:** This aspect focuses on creating economic opportunities for all, particularly for marginalized communities. Policies may include job training, entrepreneurship support, and access to credit and capital to empower economically disadvantaged individuals.
9. **Legal Protections:** Inclusivity involves enacting and enforcing laws and policies that protect the rights of minority and vulnerable populations. It ensures that legal frameworks are in place to prevent discrimination and ensure equal treatment under the law.
10. **Social Safety Nets:** An inclusive society often includes robust social safety nets to provide support for those in need, including the unemployed, elderly, disabled, and impoverished.

In summary, inclusivity within "Manjunathism" represents a commitment to building a society that values diversity, promotes social justice, and ensures that all individuals have an equal opportunity to participate, benefit, and contribute to the well-being of the community and the nation. It is a foundational principle that underpins efforts to create a more equitable and just society in India.

"Manjunathism," the principle of "Non-Discrimination

In the context of "Manjunathism," the principle of "Non-Discrimination" is a fundamental value that promotes the idea of treating all individuals with equal respect and ensuring that no one is unfairly or unjustly singled out or disadvantaged based on their personal characteristics or attributes. This principle aims to create a society in which every person, regardless of their background, enjoys the same rights, opportunities, and protections. Here's an elaboration on the concept of non-discrimination within "Manjunathism":

1. **Equality Before Law:** "Manjunathism" advocates for a legal framework where all individuals, regardless of their caste, religion, gender, race, socio-economic status, or any other characteristic, are equal before the law. This means that the legal system should not discriminate against anyone, and justice should be blind to personal attributes.
2. **Equal Access to Opportunities:** The principle of non-discrimination emphasizes that everyone should have an equal chance to access educational, economic, and employment opportunities. Discriminatory practices that limit access to these opportunities, such as caste-based or gender-based discrimination, should be eliminated.
3. **Anti-Casteism and Anti-Discrimination:** "Manjunathism" opposes caste-based discrimination, which has been a deeply entrenched issue in India. It calls for the eradication of the caste system and the elimination of discrimination based on caste, ensuring that individuals are not disadvantaged or mistreated due to their caste background.
4. **Gender Equality:** Non-discrimination extends to gender equality, promoting the idea that individuals of all genders should have equal rights and opportunities in all spheres of life. This includes addressing issues like gender-based violence, unequal pay, and gender stereotypes.

5. **Anti-Racism and Inclusion:** In a diverse country like India, "Manjunathism" also emphasizes the importance of addressing racism and promoting inclusion. Discrimination based on race, ethnicity, or place of origin should be actively countered.
6. **Freedom of Religion:** The principle of non-discrimination includes the right to practice one's religion without fear of discrimination or persecution. It advocates for religious tolerance and the protection of religious minority rights.
7. **Accessibility and Inclusivity:** "Manjunathism" calls for making public spaces, facilities, and services accessible to all, including individuals with disabilities. Discrimination based on disability should be actively challenged.
8. **Social Awareness and Education:** To promote non-discrimination, "Manjunathism" emphasizes the importance of education and awareness campaigns that challenge stereotypes, biases, and prejudices in society.
9. **Legal Protections:** It calls for robust legal protections against discrimination and the enforcement of anti-discrimination laws to hold individuals and institutions accountable for discriminatory practices.
10. **Social Cohesion:** The principle of non-discrimination contributes to social cohesion and unity by fostering a sense of belonging and acceptance among diverse groups in society.

In summary, "Non-Discrimination" within "Manjunathism" is a core value that underscores the movement's commitment to creating a society where every individual is treated fairly, with dignity, and without prejudice. It seeks to eliminate all forms of discrimination and biases that hinder social progress and undermine the principles of justice and equality.

"Economic Equity" in the context of "Manjunathism"

"Economic Equity" in the context of "Manjunathism" refers to the principle of ensuring fairness and justice in the distribution of economic resources, opportunities, and benefits among all members of society in India. It encompasses several key aspects:

1. **Income Equality:** Economic equity aims to reduce income inequality by ensuring that individuals and households have access to a reasonable and equitable share of the nation's economic resources. This may involve policies and initiatives aimed at closing the income gap between the wealthiest and the poorest members of society.
2. **Access to Economic Opportunities:** Economic equity emphasizes providing equal access to opportunities for economic growth and advancement. This includes access to education, skills training, and job opportunities, regardless of an individual's background, caste, or socio-economic status.
3. **Wealth Distribution:** Addressing economic equity involves not only income but also wealth distribution. It seeks to prevent the concentration of wealth in the hands of a few and promote the equitable distribution of assets and property.
4. **Social Safety Nets:** Ensuring economic equity often entails the establishment of social safety nets and support systems to protect vulnerable populations from falling into poverty. This includes measures such as unemployment benefits, food assistance, and affordable housing.
5. **Progressive Taxation:** Progressive taxation policies, where those with higher incomes pay a higher percentage of their earnings in taxes, can be a tool to redistribute wealth and contribute to economic equity.
6. **Financial Inclusion:** Promoting financial inclusion ensures that all individuals have access to basic financial services, such as banking and credit, which can empower them economically.
7. **Rural Development:** Focusing on the development of rural areas and agriculture can address economic disparities between urban and rural populations, as well as improve livelihoods for farmers and agricultural labourers.
8. **Gender Equity:** Economic equity includes gender equity, ensuring that women have equal access to economic opportunities and are not subject to discrimination in employment, wages, or property rights.

9. **Entrepreneurship and Small Business Support:** Encouraging entrepreneurship and supporting small and medium-sized enterprises (SMEs) can create jobs and economic opportunities for a broader segment of the population.

10. **Inclusive Economic Growth:** Economic equity goes beyond poverty reduction; it seeks to promote inclusive economic growth that benefits all segments of society. This involves policies that stimulate economic development in regions that have historically been marginalized.

Achieving economic equity is a complex and long-term endeavour. It requires a combination of policy measures, legislation, education, and public awareness. "Manjunathism"emphasises the importance of creating an economic system in India where all individuals and communities have an equal chance to prosper and enjoy the benefits of economic development, while also addressing the root causes of economic inequality.

"Manjunathism" opposing White Imperialism, countering Western Propaganda

"Manjunathism" appears to include a commitment to opposing white imperialism, countering Western propaganda, and fighting racial discrimination not only in India but also in other parts of the world, such as America and Australia. This reflects a broader vision for social justice, equity, and global solidarity. Here's an elaboration of this aspect of the movement:

1. **Anti-Imperialism:** "Manjunathism" opposes the historical and contemporary practices of imperialism, where powerful Western nations have exerted economic, political, and cultural influence over other regions, often at the expense of the rights and sovereignty of indigenous populations. The movement advocates for the decolonization of formerly colonized nations and supports the right to self-determination for all peoples.

2. **Countering Western Propaganda:** Within the context of global media and information dissemination, "Manjunathism" seeks to challenge and counter Western propaganda that may perpetuate stereotypes, biases, or misinformation about non-Western cultures and societies. This may involve promoting

alternative narratives, fostering cross-cultural understanding, and advocating for a more balanced and accurate reporting.

3. **Racial Equality and Anti-Discrimination:** The movement is committed to fighting racial discrimination, not only in India but also in countries like the United States and Australia. It supports the principles of racial equality, social justice, and the elimination of systemic racism. "Manjunathism" may engage in solidarity movements with marginalized racial and ethnic groups in these countries and advocate for policies that promote racial equality.
4. **Solidarity and Advocacy:** "Manjunathism" may engage in international advocacy efforts and collaborations with like-minded organizations and individuals around the world who share a commitment to opposing imperialism and racial discrimination. This can include participating in global movements for social justice and civil rights.
5. **Education and Awareness:** Promoting awareness about the historical and contemporary impacts of imperialism and racial discrimination is central to "Manjunathism." Educational initiatives, seminars, workshops, and awareness campaigns may be part of the movement's efforts to inform and mobilize people on these issues.
6. **Supporting Indigenous Rights:** The movement may advocate for the protection of the rights and cultural heritage of indigenous communities in colonized or settler-colonial nations. This includes supporting land rights, sovereignty, and self-determination for indigenous peoples.
7. **Promoting Inclusivity:** "Manjunathism" may emphasize the importance of inclusivity and multi-culturalism in societies, encouraging dialogue and understanding among diverse racial, ethnic, and cultural groups.
8. **Confronting Historical Injustices:** The movement may call for acknowledgment, apology, and reparations for historical injustices, such as slavery, colonization, and genocides, as part of addressing the legacy of racial discrimination.

By taking a stance against imperialism, Western propaganda, and racial discrimination, "Manjunathism" aligns itself with broader movements for global social justice, human rights, and equality. It emphasizes the interconnectedness of struggles for justice and seeks to address not only domestic issues but also global challenges related to imperialism and racial discrimination.

"Manjunathism" RICMAA (Russia, India, China, Middle East, Asia, Africa)

"Manjunathism" as described, involves the union of Asia, Africa, the Middle East, and other underdeveloped countries into one union called RICMAA (Russia, India, China, Middle East, Asia, Africa). It is a concept that envisions a regional or international coalition with specific economic and political goals. Here's an elaboration of this idea:

1. **Economic Cooperation:** RICMAA aims to foster economic cooperation among its member countries. By forming a union, these nations can pool their resources, expertise, and markets to promote economic growth, trade, and development. The creation of a single currency could simplify trade and financial transactions within the union.
2. **Developmental Focus:** The union's primary focus is on addressing underdevelopment and poverty in member countries. By working together, RICMAA seeks to reduce economic disparities, improve infrastructure, and enhance the overall quality of life for their populations.
3. **Currency Union:** The proposal for a common currency suggests a high level of economic integration among RICMAA member countries. A shared currency can facilitate trade, investment, and economic stability within the union.
4. **Exempted Loans:** Exempting member countries from loan repayments or offering favourable loan terms could help alleviate debt burdens and provide financial support for development projects and infrastructure.
5. **Trade Tax Exemptions:** Eliminating or reducing trade taxes among RICMAA countries can encourage increased trade and economic cooperation. Lowering trade barriers can stimulate economic growth and investment.
6. **Geo-political Influence:** The union's combined geo-political and economic influence could enable member countries to

have a stronger voice on the global stage. They may collectively advocate for their interests, particularly in international forums and negotiations.

7. **Challenges and Considerations:** Establishing such a union would require careful negotiation of terms, policies, and governance structures. Member countries would need to address differences in economic systems, political ideologies, and historical relationships. Additionally, ensuring that the benefits of the union are distributed fairly among member nations would be a significant challenge.
8. **Sustainability:** The union's long-term success would depend on its ability to maintain economic stability, address social and environmental concerns, and adapt to changing global dynamics.
9. **International Relations:** The formation of RICMAA could have significant implications for international relations, as it may challenge existing power dynamics and alliances. A careful diplomacy would be necessary to navigate these changes.
10. **Public Awareness and Support:** The success of RICMAA would also depend on garnering public support and involvement within member countries. Raising awareness about the union's goals and benefits would be essential.

"Manjunathism" reflects a vision of regional cooperation and development that seeks to address the challenges faced by underdeveloped countries. It is important to note that creating such a union would be a complex and ambitious endeavour, involving diplomatic negotiations, economic reforms, and a shared commitment to the union's goals among member nations.

Goals of Manjunathism in India

"Manjunathism"as a movement encompasses a broad range of social and economic objectives aimed at achieving greater equality and well-being for the people of India. Here's a more detailed breakdown of some of the key components mentioned below:

1. **Universal Education System:** The implementation of a universal education system aims to ensure that every child in India has access to quality education, regardless of their background or socio-economic status. This can help address issues like illiteracy and educational inequality.
2. **Universal Healthcare System:** A universal healthcare system seeks to provide affordable and accessible healthcare services to all citizens. It can help improve overall health outcomes, reduce healthcare costs, and mitigate the financial burden of medical expenses.
3. **Universal Wages of 24,000/- per month:** The concept of providing a universal wage of 24,000/- per month to all citizens is a form of guaranteed income or universal basic income (UBI). It aims to alleviate poverty, ensure a minimum standard of living, and reduce income inequality.
4. **Jobs for Everyone:** The goal of providing jobs for everyone in India is a significant undertaking that involves creating employment opportunities through government initiatives,

public works programs, and private sector growth. This can help reduce unemployment and underemployment.

These objectives reflect a commitment to social welfare, economic security, and equal opportunities for all, which align with principles of social justice and equity.

"Manjunathism" advocates for a vision of a more inclusive and equitable society in India, emphasizing the importance of education, healthcare, income security, and employment opportunities as fundamental pillars of human well-being.

Universal Education System

The concept of "Manjunathism" as a policy advocating for a **Universal Education System** that provides free education to all children in centralized, internationally standardized schools and colleges is a significant and ambitious educational reform proposal. Here's an elaboration of this concept:

Universal Education System:

"Manjunathism" envisions a system where education is a fundamental right accessible to all children, regardless of their socio-economic background, location, or other factors. This policy seeks to ensure that every child in the country has equal access to quality education.

Free Education:

Central to "Manjunathism" is the provision of free education at all levels, from primary and secondary schools to colleges and universities. This removes financial barriers that can prevent children from attending school and pursuing higher education.

Centralized and Internationally Standardized:

The policy promotes a centralized education system with standardized curriculum and teaching methodologies. This approach aims to ensure uniformity and high-quality education across the country. The adoption of international standards suggests a commitment to excellence and global competitiveness.

Key Features:

Equal Opportunity: "Manjunathism" emphasizes equal educational opportunities for all students, regardless of their backgrounds. This includes measures to address educational disparities based on gender, caste, religion, and economic status.

Quality Assurance: The standardized curriculum and teaching methods are designed to maintain and enhance the quality of education. This may involve continuous assessment and evaluation to identify areas for improvement.

Teacher Training: The policy may prioritize the training and professional development of teachers to ensure they are well-equipped to deliver high-quality education.

Inclusivity: Measures could be in place to ensure that students with disabilities or special needs are included and receive the necessary support to succeed in their studies.

Access to Higher Education: "Manjunathism" may also include provisions for free access to higher education, including universities and vocational training institutes.

Infrastructure Development: Building and maintaining educational infrastructure, such as schools and colleges, would be a key aspect of this policy to accommodate all students.

Challenges and Considerations:

Implementing a Universal Education System on this scale would require substantial financial resources, as it involves not only providing free education but also investing in infrastructure, teacher training, and curriculum development.

The centralized approach must carefully balance standardization with the need to accommodate local cultural and regional differences.

Ensuring the sustainability of the policy and its long-term impact on educational outcomes would be important considerations.

"Manjunathism" embodies a commitment to providing accessible, high-quality education for all children, aligning with principles of social justice, equality, and human development. Achieving these goals would require careful planning, resource allocation, and ongoing monitoring and evaluation to assess the effectiveness of the Universal Education System in meeting its objectives.

Universal Healthcare Coverage:

A **Universal Healthcare System** with a focus on public-private partnerships (PPP) insurance for every citizen in India is a significant and ambitious healthcare reform proposal. Here's an elaboration of this policy:

Universal Healthcare Coverage:

The central tenet of this policy is to ensure that every citizen in India has access to healthcare services. Universal coverage means that healthcare services would be available to all, regardless of their income, employment status, or other factors.

Public-Private Partnerships (PPP) Insurance:

By implementing a PPP insurance model, the government collaborates with private insurance providers to offer comprehensive healthcare coverage. This approach combines the resources and expertise of both the public and private sectors.

Standardized and Centralized System:

The policy envisions a standardized and centralized healthcare system. This means that healthcare services, pricing, and quality standards would be consistent across the country. Centralization can help streamline healthcare management and improve coordination.

Key Benefits:

Improved Access: Universal coverage ensures that people receive timely medical care when needed, reducing disparities in healthcare access.

Quality Assurance: Standardization and centralized control can help maintain consistent quality of care.

Financial Protection: Healthcare expenses can be a significant burden on individuals and families. Universal healthcare aims to provide financial protection by reducing out-of-pocket expenses.

Efficiency: Collaboration with private insurance providers can potentially increase efficiency and reduce administrative overhead.

Challenges and Considerations:

Funding: Implementing universal healthcare is expensive, and securing sufficient funding is a significant challenge. The government must explore sustainable funding sources.

Infrastructure: Ensuring that healthcare infrastructure, including hospitals and clinics, is adequate and well-maintained is crucial.

Equity: Efforts must be made to ensure that healthcare services reach marginalized and vulnerable populations.

Regulation: Regulating the healthcare sector, including pricing and quality control, is essential for maintaining standardized care.

Public Awareness and Education:

Implementing such a comprehensive healthcare policy would require a significant public awareness campaign to educate citizens about their rights, responsibilities, and how to access healthcare services.

Implementation and Timeline:

The rollout of a universal healthcare system would be a complex and phased process. It may take years to fully implement and fine-tune the system.

International Comparisons:

"Manjunathism" might draw lessons from other countries that have successfully implemented universal healthcare systems with PPP components, such as France, Germany, or Singapore.

The policy outlined within "Manjunathism" reflects a commitment to providing equitable and accessible healthcare services to all citizens in India. Achieving universal healthcare coverage is a substantial policy objective that can have far-reaching social and economic impacts, including improved public health, increased productivity, and reduced healthcare-related financial hardships. However, it would require careful planning, sustained investment, and strong governance to be successful.

Code of Practice (COP)

It sets out the standards that general insurers, and hospitals must meet when providing services to their customers, such as being open, fair and honest. It also sets out timeframes for insurers to respond to claims, complaints and requests for information from customers.

The Code is intended to be a positive influence across all aspects of the general insurance industry including product disclosure, claims handling and investigations, relationships with people who are experiencing vulnerability, and reporting obligations.

How Health Insurance Works?

This website aims to answer your questions about implementation of public-private health insurance by explaining how it works, and who and what is covered. You can also compare policies from different health insurers to help you choose a policy that is right for you.

In India, public-private health insurance is 'community rated.' This means that everyone is entitled to buy the same product, at the same price (except for **Lifetime Health Cover and Age-based Discounts**), and is guaranteed the right to renew their policy. A health insurer cannot refuse to insure you or refuse to sell you any policy you want to buy.

Some of the things to consider when looking into private health insurance include:

- **What is covered?** In India, the public-private health insurance, IMC **(India Medical Care)**, covers most Indian residents for healthcare. However, IMC (India Medical Care), does not cover everything and you can choose to take out private health insurance to give yourself a wider range of healthcare options and a more comprehensive cover.
- **How does it work?** There are two types of health insurance: hospital and general treatment (ancillary or extras) cover. You can buy policies for these types of cover separately or most insurers offer combined policies. There will be limitations on what and when you can claim with any policy you buy.
- **What government incentives and surcharges affect my insurance? The Private Health Insurance Rebate, the**

Lifetime Health Cover rules, and **Age-based discount** affect how much you pay for private health insurance. The IMC (India Medical Care), levy a surcharge that affects people earning above a certain threshold and who don't hold private hospital cover.

- **Overseas visitors & students:** If you are in India on a temporary visa, you should consider taking out some form of visitor's health cover for the duration of your stay. On some visas, you may be required to take out a form of visitor's health insurance.

Clinical Categories

All hospital insurance policies are classified as **Gold, Silver, Bronze** or **Basic**. These tiers have become mandatory from 1 April 2024.

What is, and is not, covered in these tiers is based on clinical categories? Each standard category—for example, 'bone, joint and muscle' category or 'heart and vascular system' category—sets out the hospital treatments that must be covered by your private health insurer. If a policy covers a certain category, then it must cover everything listed in it—not only some things.

The list below provides a description of each category and a link to the IMC (India Medical Care), Benefits Schedule (INDIA) item numbers included in each category. For more information about which categories are required to be covered under each hospital tier, see Product tiers. For other private health insurance terms see the Glossary. What is covered by IMC (India Medical Care)?

IMC (India Medical Care) is the basis of India's healthcare system and covers many health care costs. Most Indian residents are eligible for IMC (India Medical Care).

You can get a IMC (India Medical Care) card if you live in India and meet certain criterias. You may also get a reciprocal IMC (India Medical Care) card if you visit from certain countries.

You can choose whether to have IMC (India Medical Care) cover only, or a combination of IMC (India Medical Care) and private health insurance.

The IMC (India Medical Care) system has three parts: **hospital, medical and pharmaceutical.**

Hospital

Under IMC (India Medical Care) you can be treated as a public patient in a public hospital, at no charge, by a doctor appointed by the hospital. You can choose to be treated as a public patient, even if you are privately insured.

As a public patient, you cannot choose your own doctor and you may not have a choice about when you are admitted to hospital because you may be placed on a public hospital waiting list.

IMC (India Medical Care) does not cover:

- Private-patient hospital costs (for example, theatre fees or accommodation) - you can purchase private hospital insurance to cover this item;
- medical and hospital costs incurred overseas;
- medical and hospital services which are not clinically necessary, or surgery solely for cosmetic reasons;
- ambulance services; and
- emergency department administration or facility fees.

Medical

When you visit a doctor outside a hospital, IMC (India Medical Care) will reimburse 100% of the IMC (India Medical Care) Benefits Schedule (IMCBS) fee for a general practitioner and 85% of the IMCBS fee for service provided by a specialist. If your doctor bills IMC (India Medical Care) directly (bulk billing), you will not have to pay anything.

IMC (India Medical Care) provides benefits for:

- consultation fees for doctors, including specialists;
- tests and examinations by doctors needed to treat illnesses, such as x-rays and pathology tests;
- eye tests performed by optometrists;
- most surgical and other therapeutic procedures performed by doctors;
- some surgical procedures performed by approved dentists;
- specific items under the Cleft Lip and Palate Scheme;

- specific items under the Enhanced Primary Care (EPC) program; and
- specific items for allied health services as part of the Chronic Disease Management Plan.

IMC (India Medical Care) does not cover:

- examinations for life insurance, superannuation or memberships for which someone else is responsible (for example, a compensation insurer, employer or government authority);
- ambulance services;
- most dental examinations and treatment;
- most physiotherapy, occupational therapy, speech therapy, eye therapy, chiropractic services, podiatry or psychology services;
- acupuncture (unless part of a doctor's consultation);
- glasses and contact lenses;
- hearing aids and other appliances; and
- home nursing.

Many of these items can be covered on private health insurance general treatment (extras) policies. Most insurers will have limits on how much you can claim per service and per year.

Pharmaceutical

Under the Pharmaceutical Benefits Scheme (PBS) you pay only part of the cost of most prescription medicines purchased at pharmacies. The rest of the cost is covered by the PBS. You must present your IMC (India Medical Care) card to obtain this benefit.

The amount you pay varies, and is dependent on the type of medicine, up to a standard maximum. People with Government-issued concession cards have a lower maximum payment.

Product tiers

As part of various private health insurance changes, four new tiers of hospital cover began rolling out from 1 April, 2024 and became mandatory from 1 April, 2024. All hospital insurance policies are classified as Gold, Silver, Bronze or Basic.

Gold, Silver, Bronze and Basic hospital tiers

In order to be classified in a tier, the policy has to meet the minimum requirements of that tier as set out in the table below. All treatments in the table below refer to treatment received as part of a hospital admission.

Each of the clinical categories listed below are groups of what hospital treatments are, and are not, covered under each policy.

If a policy meets the minimum requirements of a tier, but also includes additional coverage, then it can be called a 'Plus' policy – for example, Bronze Plus or Silver Plus.

Clinical Categories

Each standard category—for example, 'bone, joint and muscle' category or 'heart and vascular system' category—sets out the hospital treatments that must be covered by your private health insurer. If a policy covers a certain category, then it must cover everything listed in it—not only some things.

Receiving treatment for complications and unplanned hospital treatment

Complications

If you are admitted to a hospital for a planned treatment which is included in your policy and complications arise which are outside the scope of your policy, then your insurer is required to cover the treatment of the complication. For example, if a person has surgery for a digestive illness and they develop acute arrhythmia during the episode of hospital treatment, treatment by a cardiologist and cardioversion would be covered even if the person's policy did not otherwise cover the heart and vascular system clinical category.

Unplanned treatment

If you are admitted to a hospital for a planned treatment included in your policy, and your doctor finds during the admission you have another condition requiring urgent treatment, this 'associated unplanned treatment' must be covered by the insurer regardless of whether treatment is within the scope of your policy. Insurers are required to cover an associated unplanned treatment which is not otherwise included in a policy where the treatment is provided within the same episode of care as the original treatment. The associated unplanned treatment must be considered medically urgent and necessary in the view of the medical practitioner providing the treatment.

Two or more procedures where one is excluded from your policy

Insurers are required to cover elective procedures that are covered by your policy, and all associated services or complications arising from that procedure.

However, your insurer does not have to cover any planned elective procedures not covered by your policy, even if it is provided in the same admission.

For example, a patient with a Bronze policy has elective surgery for the removal of their tonsils and also elects to have dental surgery in the same admission; their policy only covers the tonsillectomy and not the dental surgery. Their insurer is only required to cover the tonsillectomy and associated services such as post-operative care for the tonsillectomy.

Hospital treatment product tiers

The following table provides a summary of which hospital tiers cover each clinical category. For detailed information, such as the IMC (India Medical Care) Benefit Schedule (IMCBS) item numbers included in each category, please see Clinical categories.

Clinical Category	Basic	Bronze	Silver	Gold
Rehabilitation	Y (R)	Y (R)	Y (R)	Y
Hospital psychiatric services	Y (R)	Y (R)	Y (R)	Y
Palliative care	Y (R)	Y (R)	Y (R)	Y
Brain and nervous system	O (R)	Y	Y	Y
Eye (not cataracts)	O (R)	Y	Y	Y
Ear, nose and throat	O (R)	Y	Y	Y
Tonsils, adenoids and grommets	O (R)	Y	Y	Y
Bone, joint and muscle	O (R)	Y	Y	Y

Joint reconstructions	O (R)	Y	Y	Y
Kidney and bladder	O (R)	Y	Y	Y
Male reproductive system	O (R)	Y	Y	Y
Digestive system	O (R)	Y	Y	Y
Hernia and appendix	O (R)	Y	Y	Y
Gastro-intestinal endoscopy	O (R)	Y	Y	Y
Gynaecology	O (R)	Y	Y	Y
Miscarriage and termination of pregnancy	O (R)	Y	Y	Y
Chemotherapy, radiotherapy and immunotherapy for cancer	O (R)	Y	Y	Y
Pain management	O (R)	Y	Y	Y
Skin	O (R)	Y	Y	Y
Breast surgery (medically necessary)	O (R)	Y	Y	Y
Diabetes management (excluding insulin pumps)	O (R)	Y	Y	Y
Heart and vascular system	O (R)	O	Y	Y
Lung and chest	O (R)	O	Y	Y
Blood	O (R)	O	Y	Y
Back, neck and spine	O (R)	O	Y	Y
Plastic and reconstructive surgery (medically neces-sary)	O (R)	O	Y	Y
Dental surgery	O (R)	O	Y	Y
Podiatric surgery (provided by a registered podia-tric surgeon)	O (R)	O	Y	Y
Implantation of hearing devices	O (R)	O	Y	Y
Cataracts	O (R)	O	O	Y
Joint replacements	O (R)	O	O	Y
Dialysis for chronic kidney failure	O (R)	O	O	Y
Pregnancy and birth	O (R)	O	O	Y

Assisted reproductive services	O (R)	O	O	Y
Weight loss surgery	O (R)	O	O	Y
Insulin pumps	O (R)	O	O	Y
Pain management with device	O (R)	O	O	Y
Sleep studies	O (R)	O	O	Y

Y	Indicates the clinical category is a minimum requirement of the product tier.
(R)	Restricted cover permitted: insurers are allowed to offer cover for this clinical category on a restricted basis. A restricted benefit means you are partially covered for hospital costs as a private patient in a public hospital. You may incur significant expenses in a private room or private hospital so you should check with your insurer and hospital for details.
O	Optional for the insurer to include: insurers may choose to offer these as additional clinical categories.

Clinical Categories

All hospital insurance policies are classified as Gold, Silver, Bronze or Basic. These tiers became mandatory from 1 April, 2024.

What is, and is not, covered in these tiers is based on clinical categories. Each standard category—for example, 'bone, joint and muscle' category or 'heart and vascular system' category—sets out the hospital treatments that must be covered by your private health insurer. If a policy covers a certain category, then it must cover everything listed in it—not only some things.

The list below provides a description of each category and a link to the IMC (India Medical Care) Benefits Schedule (IMCBS) item numbers included in each category. For more information about which categories are required to be covered under each hospital tier, see Product tiers.

General Treatments

The list below provides definitions for common General Treatment (Extras) services.

Acupuncture

Acupuncture treatment involves inserting small needles into various points in the body to stimulate nerve impulses.

Ante-natal/Post-natal classes

Ante-natal classes often include preparation for labour, birth and early parenthood. Post-natal classes may include settling and going home with your baby, breastfeeding and bathing your baby. There are many different types of ante-natal/post-natal classes and the costs of these will vary. Not all General Treatment policies include cover for ante-natal/post-natal classes, and for those that do cover it, the provider must be registered with your insurer for benefits to be paid. To find out if you're covered, contact your health insurer.

Audiology

Audiologists specialise in the science and medicine of hearing. An audiologist can assess your hearing, give advice on whether you need hearing aids, provide counselling and teach lip-reading.

Blood glucose monitors

A device to measure the concentration of glucose in the blood. Benefits for blood glucose monitors may be deducted from an overall health aid limit – check with your insurer for details.

Chinese medicine

Chinese medical practice includes various forms of herbal medicine, acupuncture, massage, exercise and dietary therapy.

Chiropractic

Chiropractors use spinal adjustments to treat health problems that are related to nerves, skeletons and muscles.

Dietetics/Dietary advice

Dietitians specialize in human nutrition based upon a person's medical condition and individual needs.

Endodontic services

Specialised dental treatment relating to dental pulp. This includes treating tooth pain and root canal treatment. See also: General dental, Major dental.

Exercise physiology

An exercise physiologist specializes in the benefits of exercise for good health and the treatment of medical conditions.

Eye therapy (orthoptics)

Orthotics is the study or treatment of irregularities of the eyes, especially those of the eye muscles that prevent normal binocular vision.

General dental

Treatment for or relating to your teeth provided by a dentist or a dental surgeon. Typically this includes check-ups, cleans, and simple fillings. See also: Major dental.

Health management/Healthy lifestyle

If your general treatment product covers health management/ healthy lifestyle benefits, you may be able to claim some of the costs of approved health-related programs e.g. ante-natal and post-natal classes, weight management programs or nicotine replacement therapy. Check with your insurer for details.

Hearing aids

A device to amplify and change sound to assist people with hearing impairments. Benefits for hearing aids may be deducted from an overall health aid limit – check with your insurer for details.

Home nursing

Supportive care provided in the home and assistance to ensure the activities of daily living are met.

Major dental

Significant dental services, such as complex fillings, tooth extractions, crowns and bridges. Whether specific items are classified as general or major dental depends on each insurer's rules, so check with your insurer for details.

Non-PBS Pharmaceuticals

Includes prescription pharmaceuticals which are not listed on the Indian Government's Pharmaceutical Benefits Schemes (PBS). Pharmaceutical benefits usually require a co-payment from you, equivalent to the normal PBS payment, before your insurer will pay benefits. Not all non-PBS pharmaceuticals are eligible for benefits, as insurers may choose not to pay for certain items (for example, compound pharmaceuticals). To find out whether specific items are eligible for benefits, check with your insurer.

Optical

Includes prescription lenses, spectacle frames, and contact lenses. Insurers do not pay benefits for optometrist's consultations as these are generally eligible for IMC (India Medical Care) benefits.

Orthodontics

The branch of dentistry that specialises in the diagnosis, prevention and treatment of dental and facial irregularities. This generally involves the use of braces, removable appliances, functional appliances or headgear.

Orthotics (podiatric orthoses)

Specially designed shoe inserts that support the feet and improve foot posture. '1 appliance' generally means one pair of orthotics.

Osteopathy

Osteopathy is a holistic approach to health that stresses manual readjustments and physical manipulation of muscle tissue and bones. Osteopathy treatment may include individual exercise routines, relaxation techniques, or body awareness sessions.

Physiotherapy

Physiotherapists treat injury, disease and disorders through physical methods. Physiotherapy uses manual therapies, exercise programs and electrotherapy techniques to improve movement, reduce pain and stiffness, and increase quality of life.

Podiatry

Podiatrists are specialists in foot, ankle and lower limb health.

Psychology

Psychologists deal with people in their everyday lives or within their work environment to help them function better and to prevent the development of problems in mental and physical health. Some general treatment policies provide benefits for psychology - check with health insurers for details.

Remedial massage

Deep massage to treat injuries and speed recovery (for example, strains, sprains, bruising).

Speech pathology

Speech pathology is the assessment and treatment of communication and swallowing disorders. Speech pathologists can help with problems with speech, language, communication, fluency or voice, or problems with swallowing food or drinking safely.

Vaccinations

Some general treatment policies may cover some of the costs of vaccinations. These may be limited to travel vaccinations. Check with your insurer for details.

Out of pocket costs

When being admitted to a hospital as a private patient, you may have to contribute towards the cost of your treatment. In most cases, these out of pocket costs relate to medical fees charged by your treating doctors and healthcare providers. You may also incur out of pocket costs for hospital fees and prostheses.

In India, doctors and healthcare providers decide how much to charge for their services. Before you receive your treatment you are entitled to ask your doctor or healthcare provider, your health insurer and your hospital about any costs you may have to pay out of your own pocket, commonly known as a 'gap' payment.

Medical gaps

If you decide to be treated as a private patient, in a public or private hospital, each of the doctors and healthcare providers involved in your care may charge a fee. This can include medical specialists, surgeons, assistant surgeons, anaesthetists, physiotherapists, pathologists and radiologists. These fees are referred to as your medical fees, which are separate to the fees the hospital may charge for accommodation, time in theatre and other hospital services.

When you are admitted to a hospital as a private patient, IMC (India Medical Care) will pay 75 per cent of the IMC (India Medical Care) Benefit Schedule (IMCBS) fee for each IMCBS item. Your health insurer will pay the additional 25 per cent (if you are eligible for benefits for those items under your health insurance policy).

However, doctors and healthcare providers are free to charge more than the IMCBS fee and many do. In India, doctors and healthcare providers take into account their particular costs in delivering services and may have differing views about what represents a reasonable return for their time and skill. This means that there is no cap on the amount a doctor or healthcare provider can charge for their services.

If your doctor charges above the IMCBS fee, you may have to pay the extra amount. This extra amount is sometimes known as a 'gap'. If you do not check with your doctors and insurer what this amount is, you may be faced with significant out of pocket costs for your treatment.

Medical gaps

Kumar* was admitted to a hospital as a private patient. His doctor charged Rs 1,000 for their service.

The IMCBS fee for the service was Rs 700, of which Rs 525 (75 per cent of Rs7 00) was paid by IMC (India Medical Care). A further Rs175 (25 per cent of Rs 700) was paid by Kumar's private health insurer.

This left a Rs 300 'gap' for Kumar to pay out of his own pocket to the doctor.

*identifying details have been changed for privacy reasons

Before you go to a hospital, you should ask your doctor for the IMCBS item numbers for the services they will perform and an estimate of your out of pocket costs. You should also ask the doctor if there will be other doctors or healthcare providers involved in your care (for example, anaesthetist or an assistant surgeon) and how you can get an estimate of their fees. Estimates should preferably be provided in writing. For more information, see the Ombudsman's factsheet on Informed Financial Consent.

Once you have your IMCBS item numbers, you should then check with your health insurer to find out exactly how much is covered on your hospital policy for that procedure.Out-of-pocket medical costs and Informed Financial Consent (IFC)

Manjunath* had a planned surgery to have her adenoids removed as a private patient. Prior to her admission, Manjunath's treating doctor quoted a fee of Rs 1,200.

Manjunath contacted her health insurer to confirm her hospital cover and the benefit amount she could claim towards the doctor's fee. The health insurer advised the total benefit payable between IMC (India Medical Care) and the insurer would be Rs 500 towards the doctor's fee - leaving out of pocket costs of Rs 700.

Although Manjunath had an out-of-pocket expense she had to pay, PLEASE CHECK MATTER Manjunath was able to make an informed decision about whether to go ahead with the surgery.

*identifying details have been changed for privacy reasons

Not all medical services are listed in the IMCBS. You should check with your doctor or healthcare provider and your insurer whether your medical treatment is listed in the IMCBS. If it is not listed your health insurer may not pay benefits and you may face significant out-of-pocket costs for your treatment.

If you do not have hospital cover for a particular condition or medical service, you cannot claim, from your health insurer, the fees associated with your hospital stay for that treatment.

If you are not an admitted hospital patient, then your fees may only be claimable with IMC (India Medical Care).

Medical gap cover schemes

Some health insurers have gap cover agreements made with particular doctors or healthcare providers. The agreement allows health insurers to provide benefits to cover some or all of the gap fees for your in-patient hospital treatment. If you receive treatment from a doctor or healthcare provider who charges above the IMCBS fee and who does not have a gap cover agreement with your health insurer, you may face significant out-of-pocket expenses for your treatment.

There is no requirement for any doctor to participate in an insurer's gap cover agreement. Doctors and healthcare providers are free to decide on a case-by-case basis whether to use an insurer's gap cover arrangement. You should check with your doctor or healthcare provider and insurer whether you can be treated under this agreement. If you cannot be treated under a gap cover arrangement, you will have to contribute towards the medical fee out of your own pocket, for the amount that is billed over and above the IMCBS fee.

Medical costs finder

To help you find out more about the cost of specialist medical services, the Department of Health and Aged Care has introduced the Medical Costs Finder.

The Medical Costs Finder is an online tool that you can use to:

- see how much people have paid out of pocket for a procedure
- compare the costs estimated by your specialists and other health providers for a hospital procedure with the typical costs for the procedure in your area.

This helps you better understand what is typically paid and whether your likely out-of-pocket costs are high or low, compared with what others have paid for the treatment.

Hospital gaps

The benefits paid for hospital services such as accommodation, time in theatre and labour ward fees will depend on the type of cover you purchase and whether your insurer has an agreement in place with the hospital in which you are treated.

When there is an agreement between your insurer and your private hospital, you will have either no out-of-pocket expenses or you will be provided with details of your out-of-pocket expenses. Public hospitals don't have agreements with specific insurers but are generally treated as though they are agreement hospitals.

If you are treated in a hospital that does not have an agreement with your health insurer, you may face significant out-of-pocket costs for your treatment.

Find private hospitals that have an agreement with your insurer using the Agreement hospitals tool.

You are entitled to and should always ask your hospital or health insurer for an estimate in advance of the costs of your treatment, in both private and public hospitals.

If your hospital policy has an excess or co-payment, you have to pay the agreed excess or co-payment amount for hospital treatment out of your own pocket, even if your hospital has an agreement with your insurer.

- An excess is the set amount that you are obliged to pay towards the cost of hospital treatment. You, and anyone else listed on your hospital policy, may be required to pay an excess every time you go to a hospital, or less often, depending on your policy.
- A co-payment is the set amount you are obliged to pay for each day you are in hospital. For example, you, and anyone else listed on your hospital policy, may be required to pay the first $50 per day in hospital, depending on your policy.

Prosthesis

A prosthesisis an artificial substitute or replacement for a body part attached or applied to the body to replace a missing part. Surgically implanted prostheses are sometimes required, such as a replacement cornea, a hip joint replacement device, a pacemaker, or a heart valve.

- If you are having surgery to implant or apply a prosthesis, your private health insurer must pay a benefit if you have the correct hospital cover and the product is on the Medical Device and Human Tissue Product List (formerly known as the Prostheses List). If you are covered, your health insurer will pay at least the minimum benefit according to the list.
- If the minimum benefit does not cover the cost of the prosthesis, you might need to pay all or part of the gap to the hospital.
- Before you have surgery, you should ask your health insurer if you are covered, how much your policy will pay for a particular

prosthesis, and whether you will have any 'gap' to pay for the prosthesis.

- Before you have surgery, you should also ask your doctor if the prosthesis is on the list. If it is not on the list, you should ask your doctor if there is a prosthesis on the list that can be used instead. You should ask your doctor if you will have any 'gap' to pay for the prosthesis.
- Before you have surgery, you should ask your hospital if you will have any 'gap' to pay for the prosthesis.

How can I avoid unexpected out-of-pocket costs?

We recommend that you ask about fees as soon as possible when consulting with a doctor or healthcare provider ahead of a hospital admission, or as soon as practicable if you need to be admitted to a hospital urgently.

If your doctor arranges for your admission to a hospital or day surgery as a private patient, we recommend that you ask your doctor or your doctor's office staff the following questions:

- What are the IMCBS item numbers for the services the doctor is going to perform and what will be the charge for each of these services?
- Does the doctor participate in my health insurer's gap cover scheme and will the doctor treat me under this arrangement?
- Will I incur any personal out-of-pocket expenses and, if so, how much? (You should confirm this with your health insurer.)
- Who are the other doctors treating me during the admission (e.g. anaesthetist, assistant surgeon) and how can I get an estimate of their fees?
- Will the doctor provide me with a written estimate of any costs I'll have to pay so I can consider this when agreeing to the treatment?
- How will the doctor bill me?
- Which hospital will be admitted to and does this hospital have an agreement with my insurer?
- When will I have to pay?

If you can't afford the treatment, discuss alternative treatment options with your specialist or GP. You may also consider shopping around to see what other specialists charge or consider being treated as a public patient at a public hospital.

You should contact your health insurer to ask about benefits for your hospitalisation and your medical bills.

IMC (India Medical Care) can confirm the amount they will pay for the medical services provided if necessary. You can visit your local IMC (India Medical Care) Office.

What can I do if my bill is much higher than expected?

In the first instance, we suggest you contact your doctor's or health-care provider's office to check whether you agreed to these charges before treatment, and discuss the reasons for the various charges.

If you still consider that the charge is unfair or significantly more than you were advised, we suggest that you pay at least part of the bill. For instance, pay the amount that you were expecting to pay or find out what the IMCBS fee is for the procedure(s) and pay that amount.

When you make that payment, provide a letter to your doctor or health- care provider. This letter could include the following points:

- State the amount you are paying and explain why you are paying that amount, for now.
- Indicate what amount you were expecting to pay and why you expected to pay that amount.
- Ask if any procedures have been performed other that the ones you were expecting or if a case can be made for the unexpected charge.
- Indicate any personal circumstances that affect your ability to pay the higher fee.
- Suggest what further amount you would be prepared to pay (if any) and what payment arrangements you would like to make.
- Ask for a written response to your letter.

Note

"All medical and hospital procedures will be assigned standard codes and fixed prices in all hospitals. Payments will be deducted directly from the insurance policy, and patients will be provided with a bill receipt upon the completion of the procedure, which will be paid for by their insurance coverage. All patients need to provide their Aadhar card and insurance policy number. Each treatment will be assigned a specific code, and the price will be standardized across all hospitals. Our government-based insurance policy, Indian Medical Care, mandates that all citizens of India undergo a medical check-up every three months, and this will be covered under the policy."

Assisted reproductive services

- Hospital treatment for fertility treatments or procedures.
- For example: retrieval of eggs or sperm, In vitro fertilisation (IVF), and Gamete Intra-fallopian transfer (GIFT).
- Treatment of the female reproductive system is listed separately under Gynaecology.
- Pregnancy and birth-related services are listed separately under Pregnancy and Birth.

See a list of IMCBS items for assisted reproductive services.

Back neck and spine

- Hospital treatment for the investigation and treatment of the back, neck and spinal column, including spinal fusion.
- For example: sciatica, prolapsed or herniated disc, spinal disc replacement, and spine curvature disorders such as scoliosis, kyphosis and lordosis.
- Joint replacements are listed separately under Joint Replacements.
- Joint fusions are listed separately under Bone, joint and muscle.
- Spinal cord conditions are listed separately under Brain and Nervous System.
- Management of back pain is listed separately under Pain Management.
- Pain management that requires a device is listed separately under Pain Management with Device.

- Chemotherapy and radiotherapy for cancer is listed separately under Chemotherapy, Radiotherapy and Immunotherapy for cancer.

See a list of IMCBS items for back neck and spine.

Blood

- Hospital treatment for the investigation and treatment of blood and blood-related conditions.
- For example: blood clotting disorders and bone marrow transplants.
- Treatment for cancers of the blood is listed separately under chemotherapy, radiotherapy and immunotherapy for cancer.

See a list of IMCBS items for blood.

Bone joint and muscle

- Hospital treatment for the investigation and treatment of diseases, disorders and injuries of the musculo-skeletal system.
- For example: carpal tunnel, fractures, hand surgery, joint fusion, bone spurs, osteomyelitis and bone cancer.
- Chest surgery is listed separately under Lung and Chest.
- Spinal cord conditions are listed separately under Brain and Nervous System.
- Spinal column conditions are listed separately under Back, Neck and Spine.
- Joint reconstructions are listed separately under Joint Reconstructions.
- Joint replacements are listed separately under Joint Replacements.
- Podiatric surgery performed by a registered podiatric surgeon is listed separately under Podiatric Surgery (provided by a registered podiatric surgeon).
- Management of back pain is listed separately under Pain Management. Pain management that requires a device is listed separately under Pain Management with Device.

- Chemotherapy and radiotherapy for cancer is listed separately under Chemotherapy, Radiotherapy and Immunotherapy for cancer.

See a list of IMCBS items for bone joint and muscle.

Brain and nervous system

- Hospital treatment for the investigation and treatment of the brain, brain-related conditions, spinal cord and peripheral nervous system.
- For example: stroke, brain or spinal cord tumours, head injuries, epilepsy and Parkinson's Disease.
- Treatment of spinal column (back bone) conditions is listed separately under Back, Neck and Spine.
- Chemotherapy and radiotherapy for cancer is listed separately under Chemotherapy, Radiotherapy and Immunotherapy for cancer.

See a list of IMCBS items for brain and nervous system.

Breast surgery

- Hospital treatment for the investigation and treatment of breast disorders and associated lymph nodes, and reconstruction and/or reduction following breast surgery or a preventative mastectomy.
- For example: breast lesions, breast tumours, asymmetry due to breast cancer surgery, and gynecomastia.
- This clinical category does not require benefits to be paid for cosmetic breast surgery that is not medically necessary.
- Chemotherapy and radiotherapy for cancer is listed separately under chemotherapy, radiotherapy and immunotherapy for cancer.

See a list of IMCBS items for breast surgery.

Cataracts

- Hospital treatment for surgery to remove a cataract and replace with an artificial lens.

See a list of IMCBS items for cataracts.

Chemotherapy, radiotherapy and immunotherapy for cancer

- Hospital treatment for chemotherapy, radiotherapy and immunotherapy for the treatment of cancer or benign tumours.
- Surgical treatment of cancer is listed separately under each body system.

See a list of IMCBS items for chemotherapy, radiotherapy and immunotherapy for cancer.

Dental surgery

- Hospital treatment for surgery to the teeth and gums.
- For example: surgery to remove wisdom teeth, and dental implant surgery.

See a list of IMCBS items for dental surgery.

Diabetes management

- Hospital treatment for the investigation and management of diabetes.
- For example: stabilisation of hypo- or hyper-glycaemia, contour problems due to insulin injections.
- Treatment for diabetes-related conditions is listed separately under each body system affected. For example, treatment for diabetes-related eye conditions is listed separately under Eye.
- Treatment for ulcers is listed separately under Skin.
- Provision and replacement of insulin pumps is listed separately under Insulin pumps.

See a list of IMCBS items for diabetes management.

Dialysis for chronic kidney failure

- Hospital treatment for dialysis treatment for chronic kidney failure.
- For example: peritoneal dialysis and haemodialysis.

See a list of IMCBS items for chronic kidney failure.

Digestive system

- Hospital treatment for the investigation and treatment of the digestive system, including the oesophagus, stomach, gall bladder, pancreas, spleen, liver and bowel.
- For example: oesophageal cancer, irritable bowel syndrome, gall stones and haemorrhoids.
- Endoscopy is listed separately under Gastro-intestinal endoscopy. Hernia and appendicectomy procedures are listed separately under Hernia and appendix.
- Bariatric surgery is listed separately under weight loss surgery.
- Chemotherapy and radiotherapy for cancer is listed separately under chemotherapy, radiotherapy and immunotherapy for cancer.

See a list of IMCBS items for digestive system.

Ear nose and throat

- Hospital treatment for the investigation and treatment of the ear, nose, throat, middle ear, thyroid, parathyroid, larynx, lymph nodes and related areas of the head and neck.
- For example: damaged ear drum, sinus surgery, removal of foreign bodies, stapedectomy and throat cancer.
- Tonsils, adenoids and grommets are listed separately under Tonsils, Adenoids and Grommets.
- The implantation of a hearing device is listed separately under Implantation of Hearing Devices.
- Orthopaedic neck conditions are listed separately under Back, Neck and Spine.
- Sleep studies are listed separately under Sleep Studies.
- Chemotherapy and radiotherapy for cancer is listed separately under Chemotherapy, Radiotherapy and Immunotherapy for cancer.

See a list of IMCBS items for ear nose and throat.

Eye

- Hospital treatment for the investigation and treatment of the eye and the contents of the eye socket.
- For example: retinal detachment, tear duct conditions, eye infections and medically managed trauma to the eye.
- Cataract procedures are listed separately under Cataracts.
- Eyelid procedures are listed separately under Plastic and Reconstructive Surgery.
- Chemotherapy and radiotherapy for cancer is listed separately under Chemotherapy, Radiotherapy and Immunotherapy for cancer.

See a list of IMCBS items for eye.

Gastro-intestinal endoscopy

- Hospital treatment for the diagnosis, investigation and treatment of the internal parts of the gastro-intestinal system using an endoscope.
- For example: colonoscopy, gastroscopy, endoscopic retrograde cholangiopancreatography (ERCP).
- Non-endoscopic procedures for the digestive system are listed separately under Digestive System.

See a list of IMCBS items for gastro-intestinal endoscopy.

Gynaecology

- Hospital treatment for the investigation and treatment of the female reproductive system.
- For example: endometriosis, polycystic ovaries, female sterilisation and cervical cancer.
- Fertility treatments are listed separately under Assisted Reproductive Services.
- Pregnancy and birth-related conditions are listed separately under Pregnancy and Birth.

- Miscarriage or termination of pregnancy is listed separately under Miscarriage and Termination of Pregnancy.
- Chemotherapy and radiotherapy for cancer is listed separately under Chemotherapy, Radiotherapy and Immunotherapy for cancer.

See a list of IMCBS items for gynaecology.

Heart and vascular system

- Hospital treatment for the investigation and treatment of the heart, heart-related conditions and vascular system.
- For example: heart failure and heart attack, monitoring of heart conditions, varicose veins and removal of plaque from arterial walls.
- Chemotherapy and radiotherapy for cancer is listed separately under Chemotherapy, Radiotherapy and Immunotherapy for cancer.

See a list of IMCBS items for heart and vascular system.

Hernia and appendix

- Hospital treatment for the investigation and treatment of hernia or appendicitis.
- Digestive conditions are listed separately under Digestive System.

See a list of IMCBS items for hernia and appendix.

Hospital psychiatric services

- Hospital treatment for the treatment and care of patients with psychiatric, mental, addiction or behavioural disorders.
- For example: psychoses such as schizophrenia, mood disorders such as depression, eating disorders and addiction therapy.

See a list of IMCBS items for hospital psychiatric services.

Implantation of hearing devices

- Hospital treatment to correct hearing loss, including implantation of a prosthetic hearing device.

- Stapedectomy is listed separately under Ear, Nose and Throat.

See a list of IMCBS items for implantation of hearing devices.

Insulin pumps

- Hospital treatment for the provision and replacement of insulin pumps for treatment of diabetes.

There are no specific IMCBS item numbers associated with Insulin pumps.

Joint reconstructions

- Hospital treatment for surgery for joint reconstructions.
- For example: torn tendons, rotator cuff tears and damaged ligaments.
- Joint replacements are listed separately under Joint Replacements.
- Bone fractures are listed separately under Bone, Joint and Muscle.
- Procedures to the spinal column are listed separately under Back, Neck and Spine.
- Podiatric surgery performed by a registered podiatric surgeon is listed separately under Podiatric surgery (provided by a registered podiatric surgeon).

See a list of IMCBS items for joint reconstructions.

Joint replacements

- Hospital treatment for surgery for joint replacements, including revisions, resurfacing, partial replacements and removal of prosthesis.
- For example: replacement of shoulder, wrist, finger, hip, knee, ankle, or toe joint.
- Joint fusions are listed separately under Bone, Joint and Muscle.
- Spinal fusions are listed separately under Back, Neck and Spine.

- Joint reconstructions are listed separately under Joint Reconstructions.
- Podiatric surgery performed by a registered podiatric surgeon is listed separately under Podiatric Surgery (provided by a registered podiatric surgeon).

See a list of IMCBS items for joint replacements.

Kidney and bladder

- Hospital treatment for the investigation and treatment of the kidney, adrenal gland and bladder.
- For example: kidney stones, adrenal gland tumour and incontinence.
- Dialysis is listed separately under Dialysis for Chronic Kidney Failure.
- Chemotherapy and radiotherapy for cancer is listed separately under Chemotherapy, Radiotherapy and Immunotherapy for cancer.

See a list of IMCBS items for kidney and bladder.

Lung and chest

- Hospital treatment for the investigation and treatment of the lungs, lung-related conditions, mediastinum and chest.
- For example: lung cancer, respiratory disorders such as asthma, pneumonia, and treatment of trauma to the chest.
- Chemotherapy and radiotherapy for cancer is listed separately under Chemotherapy, Radiotherapy and Immunotherapy for cancer.

See a list of IMCBS items for lung and chest.

Male reproductive system

- Hospital treatment for the investigation and treatment of the male reproductive system including the prostate.
- For example: male sterilisation, circumcision and prostate cancer.

- Chemotherapy and radiotherapy for cancer is listed separately under Chemotherapy, Radiotherapy and Immunotherapy for cancer.

See a list of IMCBS items for male reproductive system.

Miscarriage and termination of pregnancy

- Hospital treatment for the investigation and treatment of a miscarriage or for termination of pregnancy.

See a list of IMCBS items for miscarriage and termination of pregnancy.

Pain management

- Hospital treatment for pain management that does not require the insertion or surgical management of a device.
- For example: treatment of nerve pain and chest pain due to cancer by injection of a nerve block.
- Pain management using a device (for example an infusion pump or neurostimulator) is listed separately under Pain Management with Device.

See a list of IMCBS items for pain management.

Pain management with device

- Hospital treatment for the implantation, replacement or other surgical management of a device required for the treatment of pain.
- For example: treatment of nerve pain, back pain, and pain caused by coronary heart disease with a device (for example an infusion pump or neurostimulator).
- Treatment of pain that does not require a device is listed separately under Pain management.

See a list of IMCBS items for pain management with device.

Palliative care

- Hospital treatment for care where the intent is primarily providing quality of life for a patient with a terminal illness, including treatment to alleviate and manage pain.

See a list of IMCBS items for palliative care.

Plastic and reconstructive surgery

- Hospital treatment which is medically necessary for the investigation and treatment of any physical deformity, whether acquired as a result of illness or accident, or congenital.
- For example: burns requiring a graft, cleft palate, club foot and angioma.
- Plastic surgery that is medically necessary relating to the treatment of a skin-related condition is listed separately under Skin.
- Chemotherapy and radiotherapy for cancer is listed separately under Chemotherapy, Radiotherapy and Immunotherapy for cancer.

See a list of IMCBS items for plastic and reconstructive surgery.

Podiatric surgery

- Hospital treatment for the investigation and treatment of conditions affecting the foot and/or ankle, provided by a registered podiatric surgeon, but limited to cover for:· accommodation; and· the cost of a prosthesis as listed in the prosthesis list set out in the Private Health Insurance (Medical Devices and Human Tissue Products) Rules, as in force from time-to-time.
- Note: Insurers are not required to pay for any other benefits for hospital treatment for this clinical category but may choose to do so.

There are no specific IMCBS item numbers associated with Podiatric surgery.

Pregnancy and birth

- Hospital treatment for investigation and treatment of conditions associated with pregnancy and child birth. Treatment for the baby is covered under the clinical category relevant to their condition. For example, respiratory conditions are covered under Lung and Chest.

- Female reproductive conditions are listed separately under Gynaecology.
- Fertility treatments are listed separately under Assisted Reproductive Services.
- Miscarriage and termination of pregnancy is listed separately under Miscarriage and Termination of Pregnancy.

See a list of IMCBS items for pregnancy and birth.

Rehabilitation

- Hospital treatment for physical rehabilitation for a patient related to surgery or illness.
- For example: inpatient and admitted day patient rehabilitation, stroke recovery, cardiac rehabilitation.

There are no specific IMCBS item numbers associated with Rehabilitation.

Skin

- Hospital treatment for the investigation and treatment of skin, skin-related conditions and nails. The removal of foreign bodies is also included. Plastic surgery that is medically necessary and relating to the treatment of a skin-related condition is also included.
- For example: melanoma, minor wound repair and abscesses.
- Removal of excess skin due to weight loss is listed separately under Weight Loss Surgery.
- Chemotherapy and radiotherapy for cancer is listed separately under Chemotherapy, Radiotherapy and Immunotherapy for cancer.

See a list of IMCBS items for skin.

Sleep studies

- Hospital treatment for the investigation of sleep patterns and anomalies.
- For example: sleep apnoea and snoring.

See a list of IMCBS items for sleep studies.

Tonsils adenoids and grommets

- Hospital treatment of the tonsils, adenoids and insertion or removal of grommets.

See a list of IMCBS items for tonsils adenoids and grommets.

Weight loss surgery

- Hospital treatment for surgery that is designed to reduce a person's weight, remove excess skin due to weight loss and reversal of a bariatric procedure.
- For example: gastric banding, gastric bypass, sleeve gastrectomy.

See a list of IMCBS items for weight loss surgery.

Universal Wages of 24,000:

"Manjunathism" encompasses the provision of universal wages of 24,000 for all individuals and a commitment to offer jobs, provided training, to anyone who applies as a first responder. Let's break down these components:

1. **Universal Wages of 24,000:** This aspect of "Manjunathism" involves guaranteeing a basic income of 24,000 to every individual, regardless of their employment status or background. Universal basic income (UBI) aims to ensure a minimum standard of living for all citizens, alleviate poverty, and reduce income inequality.
2. **Job Opportunities for All with Training:** "Manjunathism" is committed to providing job opportunities to anyone who applies, along with the necessary training. This initiative can address issues related to unemployment and underemployment by offering individuals the chance to gain skills and contribute to the workforce. It aligns with principles of economic equity and inclusive employment.

These components reflect a strong emphasis on economic security, reducing income disparities, and ensuring job opportunities and training for all. Implementing such policies would require significant financial resources, administrative infrastructure, and planning to ensure their effectiveness and sustainability. Additionally, addressing the specific details of funding, training programs, and job placement processes would be essential in realizing the objectives of "Manjunathism."

Universal job of First responder role for everyone who is unemployed with be employed after paid training.

We propose plan for reducing unemployment in India by implementing new laws, promoting the creation of new businesses, and encouraging unemployed workers to join the first responder roles and volunteer labour service:

"As the government, we are committed to implementing a comprehensive plan to combat unemployment in India. We will introduce two significant laws designed to reduce unemployment rates. In this endeavour, we will allocate substantial funds to incentivize the establishment of new businesses and invest in public-works projects, including the development of an extensive highway system.

Our strategy aims to not only create job opportunities but also to empower and motivate unemployed individuals. We will strongly encourage and, if necessary, provide incentives for unemployed workers to participate in first responder roles and the Indian Volunteer Labour Service. Through these initiatives, we will deploy them to work on essential public projects and infrastructure development.

This marks a new and proactive unemployment policy for India, focusing on creating jobs, stimulating economic growth, and fostering a sense of community involvement and responsibility. Together, we will work towards a brighter future for our nation."

Solving Unemployment Problem

Creating employment opportunities for unemployed individuals within the age range of 20 to 35. Highly trained professionals and integrating them into first responder roles as part of the Manjunathism initiative is a significant step towards addressing both unemployment and emergency response needs. Here's a list of potential first responder jobs that can be considered for inclusion in this program:

Emergency Medical Technicians (EMTs) and Paramedics:

- Providing pre-hospital emergency medical care and transport.
- Responding to medical emergencies, accidents, and disasters.

Firefighters:

- Responding to fires, rescuing individuals from burning buildings, and providing emergency medical care.
- Conducting search and rescue operations during disasters.

Police Officers:

- Maintaining public safety, enforcing laws, and responding to criminal incidents.
- Assisting with traffic management and accident investigations.

Search and Rescue (SAR) Teams:

- Locating and rescuing missing or trapped individuals in various environments, including wilderness, urban, and maritime settings.
- Assisting during natural disasters and accidents.

Community Emergency Response Team (CERT) Members:

- Providing immediate assistance during disasters and emergencies.
- Assisting with disaster preparedness and response efforts.

Emergency Dispatchers:

- Receiving and prioritizing emergency calls.
- Coordinating and dispatching first responders to incidents.

Emergency Management Personnel:

- Developing and implementing disaster response and recovery plans.
- Coordinating resources and response efforts during crises.

Animal Control and Rescue Teams:

- Rescuing and providing care to animals during emergencies.

- Assisting with the evacuation of pets and livestock during disasters.

Traffic and Road Safety Officers:

- Enforcing traffic rules and regulations to ensure road safety.
- Assisting with accident management and traffic control.

Maritime and Coast Guard Personnel:

- Conducting search and rescue operations at sea.
- Enforcing maritime safety and security.

Volunteer Lifeguards:

- Monitoring and ensuring the safety of swimmers and beachgoers.
- Providing water rescue and first aid services.

Environmental Protection and Conservation Officers:

- Responding to environmental emergencies, such as oil spills or hazardous material incidents.
- Ensuring the protection of natural resources during crises.

Healthcare and Medical Support Personnel:

- Providing medical assistance and support during health emergencies and pandemics.
- Assisting with vaccination campaigns and medical outreach programs.

Psychological and Mental Health Counsellors:

- Offering psychological support and counselling to individuals affected by disasters and traumatic events.
- Promoting mental well-being within communities.

Disaster Relief and Humanitarian Aid Workers:

- Providing humanitarian assistance and relief to disaster-affected populations.
- Delivering food, shelter, and medical care to those in need.

Public Health Educators:

- Educating communities about disease prevention and health promotion.
- Participating in public health campaigns during emergencies.

Community Outreach Workers:

- Engaging with vulnerable populations and providing support during crises.
- Promoting disaster preparedness and resilience within communities.

It's important to customize the roles and responsibilities to align with local needs and conditions while ensuring that the training and support necessary for these first responder positions are readily available. This initiative not only addresses unemployment but also enhances community resilience and emergency response capabilities.

Indian Sea Trade Tourism Triangle (ISTTT)

"Manjunathism, in the context of industrial trade, pertains to the **Indian Sea Trade Tourism Triangle** (ISTTT), which forms a trade route triangle connecting Kolkata in East India, Kanniyakumari in the South, and Dwarka in the Western part of India. This connectivity is achieved through the construction of local and international trade ports and tourism docks in the following locations: Kolkata, Puri, Visakhapatnam, Chennai, Kanniyakumari, Kochi, Mangaluru, Karwar, Goa, Jaigad, Mumbai, Daman, Diu, and Dwarka. Additionally, a **Triangular National Highway** connecting Kolkata to Dwarka and Kanniyakumari to Kolkata will be constructed as part of the ISTTT scheme.

"The concept of Manjunathism in the context of the Indian Sea Trade Tourism Triangle (ISTTT Board) brings a fresh perspective to industrial trade and maritime development. Manjunathism, with its focus on fighting corruption, promoting equality, and advocating for a just and sustainable socio-political-economic order, can be applied to the ISTTT scheme to ensure that the benefits of this ambitious trade route triangle are distributed equitably and that it aligns with the principles of responsible and inclusive development.

Here's how Manjunathism can be applied to the ISTTT scheme:

Transparency and Accountability:

- Emphasize transparency in the planning, construction, and operation of trade ports and tourism docks along the ISTTT.
- Implement mechanisms for public oversight and accountability to prevent corruption and ensure that funds are allocated efficiently.

Inclusivity and Job Creation:

- Prioritize the involvement of local communities in the development and operation of these trade and tourism hubs.
- Ensure that job opportunities are accessible to local residents, particularly those who may be unemployed or underemployed.

Environmental Responsibility:

- Incorporate sustainable and eco-friendly practices in the construction and operation of ports and docks.
- Protect sensitive coastal ecosystems and marine environments through responsible development.

Cultural Preservation:

- Respect and preserve the cultural heritage of the regions connected by the ISTTT, including indigenous traditions and historical sites.
- Promote cultural tourism that benefits local communities.

Equitable Economic Growth:

- Implement policies and initiatives that promote equitable economic growth, reducing income disparities among regions connected by the ISTTT.
- Encourage small and medium-sized enterprises (SMEs) to participate in trade and tourism activities.

Safety and Infrastructure Development:

- Ensure that the construction of ports, docks, and the triangular highway (connecting Kolkata, Dwarka, and Kanniyakumari) meets high safety standards.

- Invest in the continuous improvement and maintenance of infrastructure.

Tourism Development:

- Promote responsible tourism that respects local customs and contributes to the well-being of host communities.
- Develop initiatives that provide sustainable livelihoods to those involved in the tourism sector.

Inclusive Education and Training:

Provide training and education programs for local residents to equip them with the skills and knowledge needed to participate in trade, tourism, and related industries.

Community Empowerment:

- Empower local communities to actively engage in decision-making processes related to ISTTT development.
- Establish platforms for dialogue and collaboration between stakeholders.

By applying the principles of Manjunathism to the ISTTT scheme, India can create a trade and tourism network that not only drives economic growth but also ensures that the benefits are shared by all, fostering greater social equity and environmental sustainability. This approach aligns with the broader goals of responsible and inclusive development, promoting the well-being of both current and future generations.

Development of Cruise Ships and Hotels on behalf of the Government (ISTTT)

The initiative to start the **development of cruise ships and hotels on behalf of the government** in the ports along the Indian Sea Trade Tourism Triangle (ISTTT) can be a crucial step towards boosting tourism, trade, and economic development. Here's how to proceed with this initiative:

Establish ISTTT Development Board:

- Create the ISTTT Development Board, consisting of experts in tourism, maritime development, urban planning, and finance.

- Define the board's responsibilities, including project selection, planning, funding, and execution.

Site Selection and Feasibility Studies:

- Task the board with conducting feasibility studies to identify the most suitable ports for cruise ship and hotel development.
- Consider factors such as tourist demand, accessibility, environmental impact, and economic viability.

Cruise Ship Development:

- Collaborate with ship-builders and investors to initiate the construction of cruise ships specifically designed for the ISTTT route.
- Ensure that these cruise ships meet international safety and environmental standards.

Hotel Development:

- Develop a comprehensive plan for the construction of international standard hotels and resorts at selected port locations.
- Attract private investors and hotel chains to partner with the government for funding and management.

Funding Mechanisms:

- Explore various funding options, including public-private partnerships (PPPs), grants, loans, and foreign investments.
- Develop a sustainable financial model that ensures long-term profitability and cost recovery.

Regulatory Framework:

- Establish a regulatory framework that governs the development, operation, and safety of cruise ships and hotels in the region.
- Streamline approval processes and permit issuance to expedite construction.

Environmental Responsibility:

- Enforce strict environmental regulations for cruise ship operations, including emissions control and waste management.

- Implement eco-friendly design and construction practices for hotels and resorts.

Infrastructure Development:

- Invest in port infrastructure upgrades to accommodate cruise ships and ensure smooth passenger embarkation and disembarkation.
- Develop road and transportation networks to connect hotels with ports and other tourist destinations.

Tourism Promotion:

- Collaborate with tourism boards and industry stakeholders to create marketing campaigns that highlight the cruise ship and hotel offerings along the ISTTT.
- Promote the cultural, historical, and natural attractions in the region.

Local Employment and Community Development:

- Prioritize the involvement of local communities in the development and operation of hotels and ports.
- Create job opportunities for local residents and support community development initiatives.

Safety and Security:

- Ensure stringent safety and security measures are in place at both ports and hotels to protect guests, staff, and assets. –
- Conduct regular safety drills and staff training.

Maintenance and Upkeep:

- Develop a maintenance and renovation schedule to ensure that cruise ships, hotels, and port facilities remain in excellent condition.

- Monitor operational challenges and address them promptly.

Monitoring and Evaluation:

- Continuously assess the performance of cruise ships, hotels, and port facilities, considering factors like occupancy rates, revenue generation, and customer satisfaction.

- Use feedback and evaluations to make necessary improvements.

This initiative, led by the ISTTT Development Board, has the potential to transform the coastal regions connected by the ISTTT into thriving tourist and trade destinations, contributing significantly to economic growth and development.

Global Trade and Commerce

India's role as a central hub for sea trade routes to Europe, the Middle East, Africa, China, and the Americas is a strategic move that can bring significant economic benefits, and significant opportunities for the country to enhance its role in **global trade and commerce.** To fully leverage this advantage, India can consider the following measures:

Investment in Port Infrastructure: Continue investing in the development and modernization of ports along India's coastline. These ports should be equipped to handle diverse types of cargo, including containers, bulk goods, oil and gas, to cater to the needs of global trade.

Inter-modal Connectivity: Ensure seamless connectivity between ports, railways, and road networks to facilitate the smooth movement of goods within the country and to neighbouring regions.

Logistics and Trade Efficiency: Implement state-of-the-art logistics and supply chain management systems to enhance the efficiency of trade processes. Streamline customs procedures and reduce bureaucratic red tape to expedite trade transactions.

Trade Promotion: Actively promote India as a preferred trade and transhipment destination for goods travelling between Europe, the Middle East, Africa, China, and the Americas. Establish trade corridors and agreements that facilitate trade with these regions.

Maritime Security: Strengthen maritime security measures to protect trade routes and vessels, ensuring the safe passage of goods and passengers. Collaborate with international partners to combat piracy and maritime threats.

Port Expansion and Development: Identify potential locations for the expansion of ports and container terminals to meet growing trade demands. Create world-class port facilities to attract global shipping lines.

Trade Agreements: Pursue bilateral and multilateral trade agreements with key trading partners to reduce trade barriers and tariffs. These agreements can boost trade volumes and create new opportunities for Indian exporters.

Smart Ports and Technology: Invest in smart port technologies, such as digital tracking systems and block chain, to enhance transparency, traceability, and security in trade operations.

Sustainable Trade Practices: Promote sustainable trade practices, including responsible shipping and environmental protection, to ensure that India's participation in global trade is both profitable and environmentally responsible.

Skilled Workforce: Develop a skilled workforce with expertise in maritime logistics, international trade, and customs procedures to meet the demands of the growing trade sector.

Tourism and Cultural Exchange: Leverage India's central position to boost maritime tourism and cultural exchange programs. Attract tourists and travellers using the historical and cultural richness of coastal regions.

Research and Development: Invest in research and development in maritime technologies, renewable energy sources, and environmental conservation to stay at the forefront of sustainable trade practices.

India's strategic location in global sea trade routes offers immense potential for economic growth, employment generation, and enhanced regional cooperation. By implementing a comprehensive strategy that addresses infrastructure, logistics, and trade facilitation, India can strengthen its position as a central player in international trade and contribute significantly to its economic development.

END QUOTE

The programs and initiatives mentioned in the book outlines a comprehensive approach to boosting the Indian economy, generating surplus revenue, eradicating poverty, and improving living standards. Let's explore how each of these initiatives can contribute to achieving these goals in a broader sense:

Trade and Sea Routes Development:

Expanding sea trade routes and promoting cruise tourism can stimulate economic growth by increasing trade activity and attracting tourists.

This generates revenue through port fees, tourism expenditures, and increased exports and imports.

Universal Education System:

Surplus revenue can be allocated to the education sector to fund the development of a universal education system. This includes building schools, training teachers, providing educational resources, and ensuring access to quality education for all.

Universal Healthcare System:

Part of the surplus revenue can be channelled into the healthcare sector to establish a universal healthcare system. This system would provide access to affordable healthcare services, including medical facilities, medicines, and preventive care, for every citizen.

Jobs with Minimum Wages:

Economic growth resulting from increased trade and tourism can create a demand for labour, leading to the creation of jobs. By implementing minimum wage policies and labour protections, the government can ensure that these jobs provide fair compensation and improve the standard of living for workers.

Poverty Eradication:

Increased economic activity and job creation can reduce poverty rates by providing opportunities for individuals and families to earn a livelihood.

Government programs can target specific poverty alleviation initiatives, such as micro-finance, skills training, and social safety nets, to uplift those in need.

Infrastructure Development:

Investments in ports, roads, and transportation infrastructure, as well as the construction of tourism-related facilities, create jobs during the development phase and improve connectivity, further stimulating economic growth.

Environmental Sustainability:

Sustainability practices can be integrated into development projects to ensure that economic growth does not come at the expense of the environment. Investments in renewable energy, waste management, and conservation can contribute to long-term sustainability.

Public-Private Partnerships (PPPs):

Collaborations with the private sector in these initiatives can not only drive economic growth but also enhance the efficiency and effectiveness of programs.

Inclusivity and Equity:

It's crucial to ensure that the benefits of economic growth are distributed equitably across all segments of society. This includes marginalized communities, rural areas, and vulnerable populations.

Monitoring and Evaluation:

Continuous monitoring and evaluation of the programs are essential to track their impact, address challenges, and make necessary adjustments to achieve the desired outcomes.

By strategically implementing these programs and initiatives, India can create a virtuous cycle of economic growth, job creation, poverty reduction, and improved living standards. The surplus revenue generated from economic activities can be reinvested into social and economic development, ultimately leading to a more equitable and prosperous society with access to education, healthcare, and employment opportunities for all.

"Success is not the key to happiness. Happiness is the key to success. If you love what you are doing, you will be successful." - Albert Schweitzer

White Man and his thirst for Blood and War

"The history of imperialism and conflict, with certain historical periods characterized by aggressive actions taken by Western powers, is often driven by geo-political interests.

Throughout history, there have been instances where powerful nations, including those predominantly of Western origin, have engaged in conflicts that resulted in significant human suffering. These conflicts often arose from political, economic, and strategic interests rather than any inherent racial predisposition. Examples include the Vietnam War, conflicts in Iraq and Afghanistan, and other interventions.

Organizations like NATO have evolved to protect the interests of their member countries, which are often Western allies. While these alliances can serve to maintain stability, they can also be criticized for perceived biases and imbalances.

The idea of superiority and the belief in the right to dominate others have been used to justify imperialism and intervention in various parts of the world.

It is imperative to address historical injustices and ongoing global inequalities while promoting understanding and cooperation among nations and peoples. To achieve a more peaceful and just world, we must focus on shared human values and work together to address the root causes of conflicts and inequalities."

"It is time for Asia and Africa to unite, not with the intention of waging war or dominating the world, but to create a better future for ourselves, our children, and generations to come. We hold the power to start anew, to usher in a new era. These are times that test the souls of humanity.

Just as Thomas Paine eloquently stated in his book 'The Age of Reason,' our objective within the RICMAA framework is to establish a government that genuinely safeguards human rights. The eradication of imperialism and exploitation is the path to advancing the cause of human rights. I firmly believe that reform should be a gradual, historically informed evolution of political and social institutions. Uprooting them in the name of imperialism and capitalism is not the way forward.

The Earth belongs to all living beings, and any attempt by one nation to impose its rule on another is morally and politically equivalent to despotism.

Rights and liberties are intrinsic to a person's humanity, bestowed upon them by a Creator. They are the illuminating and divine principles of equal rights for all, transcending race, colour, social status, and economic standing. When a Western imperial bloc becomes so tyrannical that these rights are threatened, Asian and African nations have an inherent, undeniable right to reject despotic Western imperialism and capitalism.

The iron is hot in Asia and Africa. The insulted Indians from the subcontinent, enslaved Africa, the Middle East, and Pakistan are awakening to new possibilities. This era may be remembered as the Age of Artificial Intelligence, with China emerging as a global leader, which brings both opportunities and challenges in trade and politics. We must tread carefully to avoid any form of war that could threaten the existence of the human race.

I see myself as an instrument chosen by the divine to lead a world revolution. Each individual is their own instrument, and we must dedicate our lives to performing good deeds, leaving the world in a better state than we found it.

Let us dedicate ourselves to the principles that uphold the importance of rights and liberty as the very foundation of human life. No person or nation should willingly surrender these principles without a fierce struggle. In this new world, the rule of law prevails, and the government exists to serve the natural rights of its people. It is our inherent right to have a government that aligns with these principles."

Your message addresses historical atrocities and the need for reconciliation and positive change. Here's a revised version:

"Let us take a moment to reflect on the dark chapters of world history, particularly the violent incursions of colonizers from Europe into the lands of the Americas, Australia, Africa, and India.

Australia stands as an occupied land where its native population, estimated between 1 to 2 million, suffered mass killings at the hands of British colonizers. Similarly, America witnessed the brutalization of its indigenous people, with an estimated 56 million lives lost during the colonization of the continent.

In the modern era, the world recoiled at the horrors of Hitler's Holocaust, where 6 million Jews lost their lives. However, it is crucial to remember that the indignation and condemnation that followed were primarily due to Hitler's actions being against the interests of Western allies.

Less talked about are the exploitative actions of British and European colonies in Africa, Asia, and America, where vast resources were plundered.

To put it differently, imagine welcoming guests into your home, only for them to become envious and attempt to steal your happiness.

They kill the head of your household, subject his wife to unspeakable horrors, and enslave your children. They justify these acts by deeming you subhuman. Let this serve as a reminder to Westerners that we are all human beings with families, homes, and love for our countries. We share common humanity, and judgments based on skin colour or intellect are unjust.

To change the course of history, we must correct our actions by spreading love and peace across the globe. This involves more than just sending aid; it requires sending volunteers to help build our nations and elevate our societies, which have suffered due to past interventions.

It is time to right the wrongs committed in the past. The atrocities mentioned here represent just a fraction of the suffering endured in Africa, India, Asia, and the Americas. They serve as examples to help readers understand the concept of genocide and mass extermination.

By acknowledging these dark episodes and working together for a brighter future, we can strive for a more just and compassionate world."

White Man act of Terrorism – 16th Century – 20th century

The genocide of indigenous people, colonial genocide, or settler genocideis the elimination of entire communities of indigenous peoples as a part of the process of colonialism.According to Patrick Wolfe genocide of the native population is especially likely in cases of settler colonialism, with some scholars arguing that settler colonialism is inherently genocidalwhile others argue the term genocide is not applicable.

The British with subsequent establishment of colonies on indigenous territories frequently involved acts of genocidal violence against indigenous groups in the Americas, Australia, Africa, and Asia. According to Lemkin, colonization was in itself "intrinsically genocidal." He saw this genocide as a two-stage process, the first being the destruction of the indigenous population's way of life. In the second stage, the newcomers impose their way of life on the indigenous group.

New conceptions require new terms. By "genocide" we mean the destruction of a nation or of an ethnic group. This new word, coined by the author to denote an old practice in its modern development, is made from the ancient Greek word 'genos' (race, tribe) and the Latin 'cide' (killing), thus corresponding in its formation to such words as tyrannicide, homicide, infanticide, etc. Generally speaking, genocide does not necessarily mean the immediate destruction of a nation, except when accomplished by mass killings of all members of a nation. It is intended rather to signify a coordinated plan of different actions aiming at the destruction of essential foundations of the life of national groups, with the aim of annihilating the groups themselves. The objectives of such a plan would be the disintegration of the political and social institutions, of culture, language, national feelings, religion, and the economic existence of national groups, and the destruction of the personal security, liberty, health, dignity, and even the lives of the individuals belonging to such groups. Genocide is directed against the national group as an entity, and the actions involved are directed against individuals, not in their individual capacity, but as members of the national group.

The UN's definition, which is used in international law, is narrower than Lemkin's definition, and it also states that genocide is: "any of the following acts committed with intent to destroy, in whole or in part, a national, ethnic, racial or religious group," as such:

a. "Killing members of the group;"
b. "Causing serious physical or mental harm to members of the group;"
c. "Deliberately inflicting on the group conditions of life calculated to bring about its physical destruction in whole or in part;"
d. "Imposing measures intended to prevent births within the group;"
e. "Forcibly transferring children of the group to another group."

Indigenous peoples of the Americas (pre-1948)

It is estimated that during the initial Spanish conquest of the Americas, up to eight million indigenous people died, primarily through the spread of Afro-Eurasian diseases. Simultaneously, wars and atrocities waged by Europeans against Native Americans also resulted in hundreds of thousands to millions of deaths. Mistreatment and killing of Native Americans continued for centuries, in every area of the Americas, including the areas that would become Canada, the United States, Mexico, Argentina, Brazil, Paraguayand Chile. In the United States, some scholars (examples listed below) state that the American Indian Wars and the doctrine of manifest destiny contributed to the genocide, with one major event cited being the Trail of Tears.

In contrast, a 2019 book by Jeffrey Ostler at the University of Oregon has argued that genocide is not a majority viewpoint in the scholarship on the subject and he writes that,

since 1992, the argument for a total, relentless, and pervasive genocide in the Americas has become accepted in some areas of Indigenous studies and Genocide studies. For the most part, however, this argument has had little impact on mainstream scholarship in U.S. history or American Indian history. Scholars are more inclined than they once were to gesture to particular actions, events, impulses, and effects as genocidal, but genocide has not become a key concept in scholarship in these fields.

Some scholars view the term 'ethnic cleansing' as a more appropriate designation. As detailed in Ethnic Cleansing: The Crime That Should Haunt America, historian Gary Anderson insists that genocide does not apply to any of American history since "policies of mass murder on a scale similar to events in central Europe, Cambodia, or Rwanda were never implemented" but argues that ethnic cleansing occurred.

According to geographers from University College London, the colonization of the Americas by Europeans killed so many people, approximately 55 million or 90% of the local populations, it resulted in climate change and global cooling.

British Colonization of the Americas

Beaver Wars

During the Beaver Wars of the seventeenth century, the Iroquois effectively destroyed several large tribal confederacies, including the Mohicans, Huron (Wyandot), Neutral, Erie, Susquehannock (Conestoga), and northern Algonquins, with the extreme brutality and exterminatory nature of the mode of warfare practised by the Iroquois causing some historians to label these wars as acts of genocide committed by the Iroquois Confederacy.

Kalinago Genocide, 1626

The Kalinago genocide was the massacre of some 2,000 IslandCaribs in St. Kitts by English and French settlers in 1628.

The Carib Chief, Tegremond became uneasy with the increasing number of English and French settlers occupying St. Kitts. This led to confrontations, which led him to plot the settlers' elimination with the aid of other Island Caribs. However, his scheme was betrayed by an Indian woman called Barbe, to Thomas Warner and Pierre Belain d'Esnambuc. Taking action, the English and French settlers invited the Caribs to a party where they became intoxicated. When the Caribs returned to their village, 120 were killed in their sleep, including Chief Tegremond. The following day, the remaining 2,000–4,000 Caribs were forced into the area of Bloody Point and Bloody River, where over 2,000 were massacred, though 100 settlers were also killed. One Frenchman went mad after being struck by a manchineel-poisoned arrow. The remaining Caribs fled. Later, by 1640, those not already enslaved were removed to Dominica.

Attempted extermination of the Pequot, 1636–1638

A 1743 copy of the Treaty of Hartford of 1638, reveals how English colonists sought to eradicate the Pequot cultural identity by prohibiting Pequot survivors of the war from returning to their lands, by speaking their tribal language, or referring to themselves as Pequots.

The **Pequot War** was an armed conflict that took place between 1636 and 1638 in New England between the Pequot tribe and an alliance of the colonists of the Massachusetts Bay, Plymouth, and Saybrook colonies and their allies from the Narragansett and Mohegan tribes.

The war concluded with the decisive defeat of the Pequots. The colonies of Connecticut and Massachusetts offered bounties for the heads of killed hostile Indians, and later for just their scalps, during the Pequot War in the 1630s;Connecticut specifically reimbursed Mohegans for slaying the Pequot in 1637.At the end, about 700 Pequots had been killed or taken into captivity.

The English colonists imposed a harshly punitive treaty on the estimated 2,500 Pequots who survived the war; the Treaty of Hartford of 1638 sought to eradicate the Pequot cultural identity—with terms prohibiting the Pequots from returning to their lands, speaking their tribal language, or even referring to themselves as Pequots—and effectively dissolved the Pequot Nation, with many survivors executed or enslaved and sold away. Hundreds of prisoners were sold into slavery to the West Indies;other survivors were dispersed as captives to the victorious tribes. The result was the elimination of the Pequot tribe as a viable polity in Southern New England, the colonial authorities classifying them as extinct. However, members of the Pequot tribe still live today as a federally recognized tribe.

Massacre of the Narragansett people, 1675

The **Great Swamp Massacre** was committed during King Philip's War by colonial militia of New England on the Narragansett tribe in December 1675. On December 15 of that year, Narraganset warriors attacked the Jireh Bull Blockhouse and killed at least 15 people. Four days later, the militias from the English colonies of Plymouth, Connecticut, and Massachusetts Bay were led to the main Narragansett town in South Kingstown, Rhode Island. The settlement was burned, its inhabitants (including women and children) killed or evicted, and most of the tribe's winter stores destroyed. It is believed that at least 97 Narragansett warriors and 300 to 1,000 non-combatants were killed, though exact figures are unknown. The massacre was a critical blow to the Narragansett tribe during the period directly following the massacre. However, much like the Pequot, the Narragansett people continue to live today as a federally recognized tribe.

French and Indian War and Pontiac's War, 1754–1763

On 12 June 1755, during the French and Indian War, the Massachusetts governor, William Shirley issued a bounty of £40 for a male Indian scalp, and £20 for scalps of Indian females or of children under 12 years old. In 1756, Pennsylvania lieutenant-governor, Robert Hunter Morris, in his declaration of war against the Lenni Lenape (Delaware) people, offered "130 Pieces of Eight, for the Scalp of Every Male Indian Enemy, above the Age of Twelve Years", and "50 Pieces of Eight for the Scalp of Every Indian Woman, produced as evidence of their being killed."During Pontiac's War, Colonel Henry Bouquet conspired with his superior, Sir Jeffrey Amherst, to infect hostile Native Americans through biological warfare with smallpox blankets.

Canada

Officially, the last of the Beothuks, Shanawdithit (ca. 1801 – 6 June 1829)Suzannah Anstey (née Manuel. 1832–1911), daughter of Beothuk woman called 'Elizabeth' & husband Samuel Anstey (1832–1923) in Twillingate.

Although not without conflict, European Canadians' early interactions with First Nations and Inuit populations were relatively peaceful. First Nations and Métis peoples played a critical part in the development of European colonies in Canada, particularly for their role in assisting European coureur des bois and voyageurs in their explorations of the continent during the North American fur trade. These early European interactions with First Nations would change from friendship and peace treaties to dispossession of lands through treaties. From the late 18th century, European Canadians forced Indigenous peoples to assimilate into a western Canadian society. These attempts reached a climax in the late 19th and early 20th centuries with forced integration and relocations.

As a consequence of European colonization, the Indigenous population declined by forty to eighty percent. The decline is attributed to several causes, including the transfer of European diseases, such as influenza, measles, and smallpox to which they had no natural immunity, conflicts over the fur trade, conflicts with the colonial authorities and settlers, and the loss of Indigenous lands to settlers and the subsequent collapse of several nations' self-sufficiency.

With the death of Shanawdithit in 1829, the Beothuk people, and the indigenous people of Newfoundland were officially declared extinct after suffering epidemics, starvation, loss of access to food sources, and displacement by English and French fishermen and traders. Scholars disagree in their definition of genocide in relation to the Beothuk, and the parties have different political agendas. While some scholars believe that the Beothuk died due to the elements noted above, another theory is that Europeans conducted a sustained campaign of genocide against them. More recent understandings of the concept of "cultural genocide" and its relation to settler colonialism have led modern scholars to a renewed discussion of the genocidal aspects of the Canadian states' role in producing and legitimating the process of physical and cultural destruction of Indigenous people. In the 1990s some scholars began pushing for Canada to recognize the Canadian

Indian residential school system as a genocidal process rooted in colonialism.This public debate led to the formation of the **Canadian Truth and Reconciliation Commission** which was formed in 2008.

The Canadian Indian Residential School System was established following the passage of the Indian Act in 1876. The system was designed to remove children from the influence of their families and culture with the aim of assimilating them into the dominant Canadian culture. The final school closed in 1996. Over the course of the system's existence, about 30% of native children, or roughly 150,000, were placed in residential schools nationally; at least 6,000 of these students died while in attendance. The system has been described as cultural genocide: "killing the Indian in the child." Part of this process during the 1960s through the 1980s, dubbed the **Sixties Scoop,** was investigated and the child seizures deemed genocidal by Judge Edwin Kimelman, who wrote: "You took a child from his or her specific culture and you placed him into a foreign culture without any [counselling] assistance to the family which had the child. There is something dramatically and basically wrong with that." Another aspect of the residential school system was its use of forced sterilization on Indigenous women who chose not to follow the schools advice of marrying non-Indigenous men. Indigenous women made up only 2.5% of the Canadian population, but 25% of those who were sterilized under the Canadian eugenics laws (such as the Sexual Sterilization Act of Alberta) – many without their knowledge or consent. The cover page of official TRC summary affirms cultural genocide of Indigenous people within Canadaentitled, "Honour the Truth, Reconciling for the Future."

The **Executive Summary of the Truth and Reconciliation Commission** found that the state pursued a policy of cultural genocide through forced assimilation. The ambiguity of the phrasing allowed for the interpretation that physical and biological genocide also occurred. The commission, however, was not authorized to conclude that physical and biological genocide occurred, as such a finding would be difficult to prove legal responsibility for the Canadian government. As a result, the debate about whether the Canadian government also committed physical and biological genocide against Indigenous populations remains open.

The use of cultural genocide is used to differentiate from the Holocaust: a clearly accepted genocide in history. Some argue that this description negates the biological and physical acts of genocide that occurred in tandem with cultural destruction. When engaged within the context of international law, colonialism in Canada has inflicted each criterion for the United Nations definition of the crime of genocide. However, all examples below of physical genocide are still highly debated as the requirement of intention and overall motivations behind the perpetrators actions is not widely agreed upon as of yet.

Canada's actions towards Indigenous people can be categorized under the first example of the UN definition of genocide, "killing members of the group," through the spreading of deadly disease such as during the 1862 Pacific Northwest smallpox epidemic. Further examples from other parts of the country include the Saskatoon's freezing deaths, the epidemic of Missing and Murdered Indigenous Women, Girls and Two-Spirited people, and the scalping bounties offered by the governor of Nova Scotia, Edward Cornwallis. Secondly, as affirmed by the **Truth and Reconciliation Commission**, the residential school system was a clear example of (b) and (e) and similar acts continue to this day through the Millennium Scoop, as Indigenous children are disproportionately removed from their families and placed into the care of others who are often of different cultures through the Canadian child welfare system. Once again this repeats the separation of Indigenous children from their traditional ways of life. Moreover, children living on-reserve are subject to inadequate funding for social services which has led to filing of a ninth non-compliance order in early 2021 to the Canadian Human Rights Tribunal in attempts to hold the Canadian government accountable.

In Toronto during a BLM protest, marchers carry a MMIW **(Missing and Murdered Indigenous Women)** red dress and a **Mohawk Warrior Flag.**

Subsection (c) of the UN definition: "deliberately inflicting on the group conditions of life calculated to bring about its physical destruction in whole or in part" is an act of genocide that has historic legacies, such as the near and full extrapolation of caribou and bison that contributed to mass famines in Indigenous communities, how on reserve conditions infringe on the quality of life of Indigenous peoples as their social services are underfunded and inaccessible, and hold the bleakest water qualities in the first world country. Canada also situates precarious and lethal ecological toxicities that pose threats to the land, water, air and peoples themselves near or on Indigenous territories. Indigenous people continue to report (d), the "imposing measures intended to prevent births within the group," within more recent years. Specifically, through the avoidance of informed consent surrounding sterilization procedures with Indigenous people like the case of D.D.S. represented by lawyer Alisa Lombard from 2018 in Moose Jaw, Saskatchewan. Examples such as the ones listed above have led to widespread physical and virtual action across the country to protest the historical and current genocidal harms faced by Indigenous people.

On July 28, 2022, during the visit by Pope Francis to Canada at the Notre-Dame de Québec Cathedral, the Pope stated: "And thinking about the process of healing and reconciliation with our indigenous brothers and sisters, never again can the Christian community allow itself to be infected by the idea that one culture is superior to others, or that it is legitimate to employ ways of coercing others." Pope Francis on his return flight to Rome on July 30, 2022, after a week-long trip to Canada, responded to a question from a journalist: "It's true, I didn't use the word because it didn't occur to me, but I described the genocide and asked for pardon, forgiveness for this work that is genocidal. For example, I condemned this too: Taking away children and changing culture, changing mentalities, changing traditions, changing a race, let's say, a whole culture. Yes, it's a technical word, genocide, but I didn't use it because it didn't come to mind, but I described it. It is true; yes, it's genocide. Yes, you all, be calm. You can say that I said that, yes, that it was genocide."

United States Colonization of Indigenous Territories

Stacie Martin states that the United States has not been legally admonished by the international community for genocidal acts against its indigenous population, but many historians and academics describe events such as the Mystic massacre, the **Trail of Tears**, the **Sand Creek massacre** and the **Mendocino War** as genocidal in nature.

Roxanne Dunbar-Ortiz states that U.S. history, as well as inherited Indigenous trauma, cannot be understood without dealing with the genocide that the United States committed against Indigenous people. From the colonial period through the founding of the United States and continuing in the twentieth century, this has entailed torture, terror, sexual abuse, massacres, systematic military occupations, removals of

Indigenous peoples from their ancestral territories via Indian removal policies, forced removal of Native American children to military-like boarding schools, allotment, and a policy of termination.

The letters exchanged between Bouquet and Amherst during the Pontiac War show Amherst writing to Bouquet that Indigenous people needed to be exterminated:

"You will do well to try to inoculate the Indians by means of blankets, as well as to try every other method that can serve to extirpate this execrable race."

Historians regard this as evidence of a genocidal intent by Amherst, as well as part of a broader genocidal attitude frequently displayed against Native Americans during the colonization of the Americas. When smallpox swept the northern plains of the U.S. in 1837, the U.S. Secretary of War, Lewis Cass ordered that no Mandan (along with the Arikara, the Cree, and the Blackfeet) be given smallpox vaccinations, which were provided to other tribes in other areas.

The United States has till date not undertaken any truth commission nor built a memorial for the genocide of indigenous people. It does not acknowledge nor compensate for the historical violence against Native Americans that occurred during territorial expansion to the west coast. American museums such as the Smithsonian Institution do not dedicate a section to the genocide. In 2013, the National Congress of American Indians passed a resolution to create a space for the National American Indian Holocaust Museum inside the Smithsonian, but it was ignored by the latter.

Sterilization of Natives

The **Family Planning Services and Population Research Act** was passed in 1970, which subsidized sterilizations for patients receiving healthcare through the Indian Health Service. Six years after the act was passed, an estimated 25% of childbearing-aged Native American women were sterilized. Some of the procedures were performed under coercion, or without understanding by those sterilized. In 1977, Marie Sanchez, chief tribal judge of the Northern Cheyenne Indian Reservation told the United Nations Convention on Indigenous Rights in Geneva, that Native American women suffered involuntary sterilization which she equated with modern genocide.

Native American Boarding Schools

The **Native American boarding school system** was a 150-year program and federal policy which separated Indigenous children from their families and sought to assimilate them into white society. It began in the early 19th century, coinciding with the start of Indian Removal policies. A Federal Indian Boarding School Initiative Investigative Report was published on May 11, 2022, which officially acknowledged the federal government's role in creating and perpetuating this system. According to the report, the U.S. federal government operated or funded more than 408 boarding institutions in 37 states between 1819 and 1969. 431 boarding schools were identified in total, many of which were run by religious institutions. The report described the system as part of a federal policy aimed at eradicating the identity of Indigenous communities and confiscating their lands. Abuse was widespread at the schools, as was overcrowding, malnutrition, disease and lack of adequate healthcare. The report documented over 500 child deaths at 19 schools, although it is estimated that the total number could rise to thousands, and possibly even tens of thousands. Marked or unmarked burial sites were discovered at 53 schools. The school system has been described as a cultural genocide and a racist dehumanization.

Indian Removal and the Trail of Tears

Main articles: Indian Removal and Trail of Tears

Following the **Indian Removal Act of 1830,** the American government began forcibly relocating East Coast tribes across the Mississippi. The removal included many members of the Cherokee, Muscogee (Creek), Seminole, Chickasaw, and Choctaw nations, among others in the United States, from their homelands to the Indian Territory in the eastern sections of the present-day state of Oklahoma. About 2,500–6,000 died along the Trail of Tears.

Chalk and Jonassohn assert that the deportation of the Cherokee tribe along the Trail of Tears would almost certainly be considered an act of genocide today. The Indian Removal Act of 1830 led to the exodus. About 17,000 Cherokees, along with approximately 2,000 Cherokee-owned black slaves, were removed from their homes. The number of people who died as a result of the Trail of Tears has been variously estimated. American doctor and missionary Elizur Butler, who made the journey with one party, estimated 4,000 deaths.

Historians such as David Stannard and Barbara Mann have noted that the army deliberately routed the march of the Cherokee to pass through areas of a known cholera epidemic, such as Vicksburg. Stannard estimates that during the forced removal from their homelands, following the Indian Removal Act signed into law by President Andrew Jackson in 1830, 8,000 Cherokee died, about half the total population.

American Indian Wars

A mass grave was being dug for frozen bodies from the 1890 **Wounded Knee Massacre,** in which the U.S. Army killed 150 Lakota people, marking the end of the American Indian Wars

During the American Indian Wars, the American Army carried out a number of massacres and forced relocations of Indigenous peoples that are sometimes considered genocide. The 1864 Sand Creek Massacre, which caused outrage in its own time, has been regarded as a genocide. Colonel John Chivington led a 700-man force of Colorado Territory militia in a massacre of 70–163 peaceful Cheyenne and Arapaho, about two-thirds of whom were women, children, and infants. Chivington and his men took scalps and other body parts as trophies, including human fetuses and male and female genitalia. In defense of his actions, Chivington stated,

Damn any man who sympathizes with Indians! ... I have come to kill Indians, and believe it is right and honorable to use any means under God's heaven to kill Indians. ... Kill and scalp all, big and little; nits make lice.

—- *Col. John Milton Chivington, U.S. Army*

French Colonization of Africa

Algeria

The course of the French conquest of Algeria and immediately after it, a series of demographic catastrophes ensued in Algeria between 1830 and 1871. Because the demographic crisis was so severe, Dr. René Ricoux, head of demographic and medical statistics at the statistical office of the General Government of Algeria, foresaw the simple disappearance of Algerian "natives as a whole." The demographic change in Algeria can be divided into three phases: an almost constant decline during the conquest period, up until its heaviest drop from an estimated 2.7 million in 1861 to 2.1 million in 1871, and finally moving into a gradual increase to a level of three million inhabitants by 1890. The causes range from a series of famines, diseases, and emigration to the violent methods used by the French army during their Pacification of Algeria, which historians] argue constitute acts of genocide.

Congo Free State

Under Leopold II of Belgium, the population loss in the Congo Free State is estimated at sixty percent, up to 15 million people having been killed. The **Congo Free State** was hit especially hard by sleeping sickness and smallpox epidemics.

Genocide in German South West Africa

Atrocities against the indigenous African population by the German colonial empire can be dated to the earliest German settlements on the continent. The German colonial authorities carried out a genocide in German South-West Africa (GSWA) and incarcerated the survivors in concentration camps. It was also reported that, between 1885 and 1918, the indigenous population of Togo, German East Africa (GEA) and the Cameroons suffered from various human rights abuses, including starvation from scorched earth tactics and forced relocation for use as labor.

The German Empire's action in GSWA against the Herero tribe is considered by Howard Ball to be the first genocide of the 20th century. After the Herero, Namaqua and Damara began an uprising against the colonial government, General Lothar von Trotha, appointed as head of the German forces in GSWA by Emperor Wilhelm II in 1904, gave German forces the order to push them into the desert where they would die. Germany apologized for the genocide in 2004.

While many argue that the military campaign in Tanzania to suppress the **Maji Maji Rebellion** in GEA between 1905 and 1907 was not an act of genocide, as the military did not have as an intentional goal the deaths of hundreds of thousands of Africans, according to Dominik J. Schaller, the statement released at the time by Governor Gustav Adolf von Götzen did not exculpate him from the charge of genocide, but was proof that the German administration knew that their scorched earth methods would result in famine. 200,000 Africans are estimated to have died from famine, with some areas having been left completely and permanently devoid of human life.

Colonization of Australia

The so-called extinction of the Aboriginal Tasmanians is regarded as a classic case of near genocide by Lemkin, most comparative scholars of genocide, and many general historians, including Robert Hughes, Ward Churchill, Leo Kuper and Jared Diamond, who base their analysis on previously published histories. Between 1824 and 1908 White settlers and Native Mounted Police in Queensland, according to Raymond Evans, killed more than 10,000 Aboriginal people, who were regarded as vermin and sometimes even hunted for sport.

Prior to the arrival of the First Fleet in 1788, which marked the beginning of Britain's colonization of Australia, the Aboriginal population had been estimated by historians to be around roughly 500,000 people; by 1900, that number had plummeted to fewer than 50,000. While most died due to the introduction of infectious diseases which accompanied colonization, up to 20,000 were killed during the Australian frontier wars by British settlers and colonial authorities through massacres, mass poisonings and other actions. Ben Kiernan, an Australian historian of genocide, treats the Australian evidence over the first century of colonization as an example of genocide in his 2007 history of the concept and practice, Blood and Soil: A World History of Genocide and Extermination from Sparta to Darfur. The Australian practice of removing the children of Aboriginal and Torres Strait Islander descent from their families, has been described as genocidal. The 1997 report Bringing Them Home, which examined the fate of the "stolen generations" concluded that the forced separation of Aboriginal children from their family constituted an act of genocide. In the 1990s a number of Australian state institutions, including the state of Queensland, apologized for its policies regarding forcible separation of Aboriginal children. Another allegation against the Australian state is the use of medical services to Aboriginal people to administer contraceptive therapy to Aboriginal women without their knowledge or consent, including the use of Depo Provera, as well as tubal ligations. Both forced adoption and forced contraception would fall under the provisions of the UN genocide convention. Some Australian scholars, including historians Geoffrey Blainey and Keith Windschuttle and political scientist Ken Minogue, reject the view that Australian Aboriginal policy was genocidal.

Mass Poisoning at Kangaroo Creek

In late November 1847, Coutts invited the Aboriginal people living around Kangaroo Creek to come to his homestead for the possibility of obtaining work. Coutts had previously not allowed any groups of Aboriginal people near his homestead and was widely known to have expressed the opinion that native people "deserved shooting.":156 Around 23 people accepted the offer and Coutts put them to work to weed areas close to the homestead. After the work was completed, Coutts gave them a 10-pound bag of flour. Coutts was observed to have put the powdery contents of a paper sachet, believed to have been arsenic, into the bag of flour before giving it to the group of Gumbaynggirr. The unsuspecting people took the bag of poisoned flour from Coutts and proceeded to a communal area in the hills between Kangaroo and Towallum Creeks. Here, they made damper from the flour and ate it.

A couple of days later, several reports emerged of a large number of Aboriginal people becoming violently ill and dying in the hills behind Kangaroo Creek. The local Commissioner for Crown Lands, Oliver Fry, heard these reports from both white and black sources, and came to investigate. In January 1848, Fry visited the site and found the decomposing bodies of at least 23 people. He collected evidence including remnants of the damper that remained, and immediately arrested and charged Coutts for the crime. Local magistrates concluded Coutts should stand trial for wilful murder and he was transported to Sydney to be tried at the Supreme Court.

On 23rd February, Coutts appeared before judge Alfred Stephen and was given bail on £1,000 worth of sureties. The case was delayed and on 10 May, 1848, the Attorney-General, John Plunkett, decided not to proceed with the case. Plunkett did this even though he had a very strong suspicion of Coutts' guilt and was aware that justice was being "entirely evaded" by this decision. Coutts was subsequently discharged and returned to Kangaroo Creek

"Massacres Committed in Africa during Colonial Times"

"Past Massacres in Africa."

Its objective is to recognize and list some of the tragic massacres that took place during colonial times in Africa.

The list is not meant to be exhaustive, because research about such tragic events is still on-going. The reality is that many of these tragedies have fallen into world amnesia, and many of them have also actually been erased from history books.

If you know of other similar events that took place during colonial times or as a result of decisions taken during colonial times, we are hoping that this will be an opportunity to remember these innocent victims who have paid the price of their life to satisfy dominating, authoritarian and colonialist aspirations by occupiers.

This is a modest attempt to recognize and honour these fallen heroes.

We are grateful to Ms Yoleni Rabelais, Trainee at the Commission of the Churches on International Affairs of the World Council of Churches, who conducted this research.

Massacres in Algeria

"Sétif and Guelma, 8th of May 1945"

People were celebrating the allied victory over Germany (in which Algerian native troops took part), and banned demonstrations of Algerian nationalists in most of the Constantine départment, in the eastern part of the country. In Sétif, the protest turned into a riot after the intervention of the police forces. This riot then spread to the area between Sétif and Bougie (Bejaia). Repression was organized by the army and, to a lesser extent, by the civilian population: the death toll, still unknown, probable numbers in the many thousands. In Guelma, a small town between Constantine and Bône (Annaba), a demonstrator was killed. There were no casualties among the French population. However, on May 9 and 10, 12 French people were killed. Between 1,500 and 2,000 Muslims had died, most of them in the hands of the civilian population. The death toll has not yet been precisely established. However, we know that it included 102 French people. Furthermore, several thousand Muslims were either killed or wounded.

Massacres in Angola

"Nambuangongo, 15th March 1961"

In 1961, the first attacks on colonial farms and villages in northern Angola was unleashed. In this massacre, hundreds of white and black settlers were killed and mutilated in the coffee farms in Dembos, Negage, Úcua and Nambuangongo. Many were hacked to death. No one escaped the massacre—men, women and children, black and white. The fury of the UPA (later called FNLA - National Front for the Liberation of Angola) spared no one.

The accounts of that day are many. "In less than 48 hours, throughout the districts of Zaire and Uige is the damned devastation. Plantations and lonely houses were looted and set on fire; villages were razed to the ground; the siege was laid on villages and small hamlets, their supplies were cut off; roads and means of communication were destroyed", according to an excerpt by Franco Nogueira in the book "Salazar Volume V - The Resistance."

Massacres in Benin

"Benin Expedition, 1897"

The Benin Punitive Expedition, also known as the 1897 expedition, was a military mission led by British forces, which included 1200 men under the command of Admiral Sir Harry Rawson, who invaded Benin City, the capital of the Kingdom of Benin. The campaign lasted 17 days, and the invading forces took over total control of the kingdom.

The British expedition was primarily an act of reprisal for the attack suffered by a column of British officers led by the acting consul-general, James Philips, and indigenous soldiers disguised as porters and musicians who in 1897 attempted to reach Benin City to attack the city and depose the Obá. Only two officers survived the attack, which became known as the Benin Massacre. However, the expedition was part of the British attempts to control the region and annex Benin to exploit its resources.

Massacres in Congo

"Congo massacres during King Leopold's rule 1885 – 1908"

Atrocities in the Congo Free State refer to a series of documented atrocities perpetrated in the period 1885 to 1908 in the Congo Free State (now the Democratic Republic of Congo), which was a colony under the personal rule of King Leopold II of Belgium. These atrocities were mainly associated with the labour policies used to collect natural rubber for export. Together with epidemic diseases, famine and the drop-in birth rate caused by these interruptions, such atrocities contributed to a sharp decline in the Congolese population. The magnitude of the population decline over the period is disputed, but is believed to be between one and fifteen million.

King Leopold II of Belgium promised a humanitarian and philanthropic mission that would improve the lives of Africans. In return, European leaders, meeting at the Berlin Conference, granted him 2m² (770,000 square miles) to forge an individual colony where he could do as he pleased. He called it the Congo Free State. It quickly became a brutal and exploitative regime that relied on forced labour to grow and trade rubber, ivory and minerals. In addition, colonial administrators also abducted orphaned children from communities and transported them to "children's colonies" to work or train as soldiers. Estimates suggest that over 50% died there.

Murders, famine and disease combined to cause the deaths of perhaps 10 million people, although historians dispute the accurate figure. Leopold II may never have set foot there, but he poured the profits into Belgium and his pockets. He built the Museum of Africa on the grounds of his palace in Tervuren, with a "human zoo" on the grounds with 267 Congolese people.

Massacres in Ethiopia

"Yekatit 12, 19th February 1937"

This has been described as the worst massacre in Ethiopian history. This refers to the massacre and arrest of Ethiopians by the Italian occupation forces after an assassination attempt on Marshal Rodolfo Graziani, Marquis of Negele, Viceroy of Italian East Africa, on 19th February 1937. Graziani had led the Italian forces to victory over the Ethiopians in the Second Italian invasion of Ethiopia and was the supreme governor of Italian East Africa.

Estimates vary as to the number of people killed in the three days following the attempt on Graziani's life. Ethiopian sources estimated that 30,000 people were killed by the Italians, while Italian sources said only a few hundred were killed. The story of the massacre in 2017 estimated that 19,200 people were killed out of a population of 100,000, i.e. 20 per cent of Addis Ababa's population. The following week, numerous Ethiopians suspected of opposing Italian rule were rounded up and executed, including members of the Black Lions and other members of the aristocracy. Emperor Haile Selassie had sent 125 men abroad to receive a university education, but most of them were killed. Many more were arrested, including collaborators, who helped the Italians identify the two men who made an attempt on Graziani's life.

Massacres in Guiné – Bissau

- Pindjiguiti, 3 August 1959

Workers at the port of Pindjiguiti, in Bissau, organised a strike demanding a pay rise. Seamen, dockers and dockworkers, particularly those working for Casa Gouveia, an intermediary commercial monopoly of the CUF group (Companhia União Fabril), were violently repressed by colonial officials, police and military, and some civilians, repression that would result in fifty deaths and about a hundred injured. This was not the first strike of workers at the port of Bissau.

Massacres in Kenya

"Sotik Massacre, 1905"

Over 1800 Kipsigis people of the Talai clan were massacred by the British colonial government. The killing of men, women and children followed the refusal by members of the Kipsigis community to surrender heads of cattle alleged to have been stolen from the Maasai residing in the current Narok county.

His Excellency, Honourable Professor Paul Chepkwony, Governor of Kericho County, stated,

The Sotik massacre has been erased from the history books, not just of the United Kingdom but from Kenya as well. The slaughter of some 1850 men, women and children would today be classified as genocide and a crime against humanity. In 1905, Colonel Hennessey, used a Maxine Machine gun to conduct this slaughter. This massacre was used to terrorise the Kipsigi people and evict them illegally from their ancestral homeland. The colonialists justified this ethnic cleansing by stating that the "well-watered white Highlands were fit to raise a European child." Approximately 100,000 Talai people were forcibly removed to Gwasi, which they knew was unfit for human habitation. This was heartless racism of the highest order."

Mau Mau Uprising Massacres

The Mau Mau uprising began in 1952 as a reaction to inequalities and injustices in British-controlled Kenya. The response of the colonial administration was a fierce crackdown on the rebels, resulting in many deaths. By 1956, the uprising had effectively been crushed, but the extent of opposition to the British regime had clearly been demonstrated and Kenya was set on the path to independence, which was finally achieved in 1963.

Thousands of Mau Mau left their homes and set up camp in the forests of the Aberdares and Mt. Kenya, creating a base of resistance to the government. Hostilities were relatively subdued for the remainder of 1952, but the following year began with a series of violent killings of European farmers and loyalist Africans. This sufficiently shocked the white population into demanding that the government take more action to combat the Mau Mau, and so the Kenyan security forces were placed under the command of the British Army and began to surround the Mau Mau strongholds in the forests. This was accompanied by large-scale eviction of Kikuyu squatters from land that had been selected for European settlers. The government troops adopted a policy of collective punishment, which was again intended to undermine popular support of the Mau Mau. Under this policy, if a member of a village was found to be a Mau Mau supporter, then the entire village was treated as such. This led to the eviction of many Kikuyu, who were forced to abandon their homes and possessions and sent to areas designated as Kikuyu reserves. A particularly unpleasant element of the eviction policy was the use of concentration camps to process those suspected of Mau Mau involvement. Abuse and torture was commonplace in these camps, as British guards used beatings, sexual abuse and executions to extract information from prisoners and to force them to renounce their allegiance to the anti-colonial cause. The process of mass eviction furthered anger and fear among the Kikuyu who had already suffered through decades of land reallocation, and drove hundreds of squatters to join the Mau Mau fighters in the forest.

The uprising escalated further when Mau Mau fighters carried out two major attacks. The first was an assault on the Naivasha police station, which resulted in a humiliating defeat for the police and the release of 173 prisoners, many of them Mau Mau, from an adjacent detention camp. The second was the massacre of Kikuyu loyalists at

Lari, in which at least 97 Kenyans were killed. The incident was used by the government to further characterise the Mau Mau as brutal savages, and no official mention was made of a similar number of Mau Mau prisoners who were machine gunned to death by government troops in the Aberdare forest. These attacks began a pattern of Mau Mau raids against police and loyalists that continued throughout 1953. The gradual organisation of the rebel forces in the forests created military units, although they were limited by lack of weapons, supplies and training.

Massacres in Libya

"Battle and massacre at Shar al-Shatt, 23rd October 1911"

Italian troops were attacked by a 10,000-strong Turkish-Arab force while marching through the Mechiya oasis at Sciara Sciat. Some accounts stated that Turkish forces captured two companies of the Italian infantry in a nearby cemetery and massacred 250 men. Italian corpses were allegedly nailed to trees with their eyes and genitals mutilated, some claim in retaliation for sexual offences against local women perpetrated by the Italian troops.

The next day the Italians responded by attacking the population of the neighbouring Mechiya oasis, massacring about 4,000 people, including women and children, over three days. Though the Italians allegedly took measures to prevent news of this action from reaching the outside world, foreign press correspondents covered the event in detail. This negative coverage factored into the British Parliament's decision later that month to take a more pro-Turkish course, rejecting a proposed **Anglo-Italian-Mediterranean agreement.**

Massacres in Madagascar

- French colonial Massacre, 29th March 1947

The Malagasy people rose to free themselves from the colonial yoke. France responded to this uprising with a massive crime that left tens of thousands dead.

Several hundred insurgents, a column of poor peasants armed with old rifles, attacked the military camp in Moramanga, east of the island. This was the signal for an insurrection to set the French colony of Madagascar off the African coast of the Indian Ocean ablaze for almost two years. The creation, a few months earlier, of an elected assembly, with limited powers, was not enough to extinguish the nationalist flame that had been ignited on the Red Island, as large as France and Belgium, which had long been the scene of Franco-British rivalry before being placed under French colonial control in 1896. The return of Malagasy foot soldiers who had been enlisted in France during the Second World War, the miserable living conditions of the indigenous population and the activism of nationalist movements and secret societies fuelled the desire for independence and precipitated the outbreak insurrection.

Massacres in Malawi

"Chilembwe uprising, 15th January 1915"

This was a rebellion against British colonial rule in Nyasaland (modern-day Malawi). It was led by John Chilembwe a Black African Baptist minister. Based around his Church in the village of Mbombwe in the south-east of the protectorate, the revolt leaders were mainly from an emerging Black middle class. They were motivated by grievances against the white colonial system, including forced labour, racial discrimination, and new demands imposed on the indigenous population following the outbreak of World War I. The revolt broke out when rebels, incited by Chilembwe, attacked the A. L. Bruce Plantation headquarters at Magomero and killed three white settlers. A largely unsuccessful attack on a weapons store in Blantyre followed during the night. By morning, the colonial authorities had mobilized the white settler militia and redeployed regular military units from the King's African Rifles (KAR). After a failed attack by government troops on Mbombwe on January 25th, the rebels attacked a Christian mission at Nguludi and burned it down.

The KAR and militia took Mbombwe without encountering resistance on January 26th. Many of the rebels, including Chilembwe, fled towards Mozambique, hoping to reach safely, but many were captured. About 40 rebels were executed in the revolt's aftermath, and 300 were imprisoned; Chilembwe was shot dead by a police patrol near the border on February 3rd. Although the rebellion did not achieve lasting success, it is commonly cited as a watershed moment in Malawian history. The uprising had lasting effects on the British administration system in Nyasaland, and some reform was enacted in its aftermath.

After World War II, the growing Malawian nationalist movement reignited interest in the Chilembwe revolt. After the independence of Malawi in 1964, it became celebrated as a critical moment in the nation's history. Chilembwe's memory, which remains prominent in the collective national consciousness, has often been invoked in symbolism and rhetoric by Malawian politicians. Today, the uprising is celebrated annually, and Chilembwe himself is considered a national hero.

Massacres in Mozambique

Mueda, 16 June 1960

Massacre of Mueda, is one more among the tragedies caused by colonial exploitation in Africa. On that day, there was an administrative meeting between representatives of the Mueda district, in the north of the Mozambican territory, and the colonial government, with Portuguese headquarters. At the end of the event, the colonial authorities shot dead several Mozambicans. The number has not been counted to date. The meeting in question was allegedly a demand by MANU, the leading organization articulated for the independence of the district and separation of the territory from Mozambique. The event was of great significance among Mozambicans and was a relevant element in the development, two years later, of FRELIMO, the Front for the Liberation of Mozambique. The gratuitousness of the case and the Portuguese bloodshed demonstrated in the massacre were central to the movement's narrative during the early War.

- Wiriyamu, 16 December 1972

The Wiriyamu massacre was a case of structurally determined mass violence in the Portuguese colonial wars, not unlike similar massacres during wars of repression by white colonial and settler powers in Africa. An operation, code-named "Marosca," which involved aviation, commandos and PIDE/DGS agents, took place in the Tete area of Northern Mozambique, targeting five villages: Wiriamu, Juwau, Djemusse, Riacho and Chaworha. After bombs were dropped on the village of Wiriamu, the soldiers of the Comandos took action, and barbarity ensued. Hundreds of people were slaughtered, including women and children. The killing extended to the four villages along the Zambezi river in various inhuman ways. Many were locked inside cubicles where they were burnt to death by the action of incendiary grenades, and others were simply shot. Soldiers destroyed huts, infrastructures and villages, looted goods, opened fire on people whose bodies where then placed, with some alive in between, on funeral pyres to be consumed by fire.

Three hundred eighty-five people are said to have died, about a third of the 1350 inhabitants of the five villages. The list of the victims and the account of the events were compiled by Domingo Kansande and Father Domingos Ferrão, who passed on the information to Spanish and Dutch priests. The massacre would be divulged by the English priest, Adrian Hastings in the British newspaper "The Times" on July 10, 1973, days before the visit of Marcelo Caetano to London. The case would also reach the United Nations.

The episode reflects how the anti-colonial struggle had shades and other protagonists than those fixed in the official narratives. In this case, black Mozambican, Spanish or Dutch priests contributed to the liberation struggle of the populations. Officially, Portugal never assumed what had happened.

The massacre would have been lost to recorded history if it were not for the role played by data collectors, counter-reporting priests and fact-checking journalists in producing a list of the dead, mounting a concerted effort to verify and then publicise the massacre, and engaging in a daring rendition of a surviving eyewitness. On July 10th 1973, 206 days after the event, they managed to get their story on the front page of **The Times**. Five days later, the Sunday Times Insight team followed suit with extensive background coverage of the case.

Massacres in Namibia

-Genocide, 1884 – 1915

Germany ruled what was then called German South West Africa as a colony from 1884 to 1915. Colonial troops and settlers in 1904-1908 killed tens of thousands of indigenous Herero and Nama people. German soldiers targeted people of two ethnic groups - the Herero and the Nama - because they had resisted land grabbing by German settlers. The Africans were shot, hanged, abandoned in the desert and died in concentration camps. Survivors from the Herero and Nama population were forced into the desert and later placed in concentration camps where they were exploited for labour. Many died of disease, exhaustion and starvation with some subject to sexual exploitation and medical experimentation. It is thought up to 80% of the indigenous populations died during the genocide.

Descendants of the Herero and Nama, marginalised groups within Namibia, have kept the stories of their genocide alive through oral tradition and cultural events. A push to acknowledge the genocide began after Namibia's independence in 1990, and strengthened with the 100th anniversary of the atrocities in 2004.

Massacres in Nigeria

- Iva Valley, 18th November 1949

21 striking miners and a bystander were shot dead at a British government-owned coal mine at Enugu, 51 were injured. The miners were fighting for back-pay owed to them for a period of casualisation known as 'rostering', later declared illegal, and had been sacked following a work to rule. They occupied the mine to prevent a repeat of the lock-out they had suffered during the 1945 general strike. Because Enugu was home to the Zikist independence movement, which included Marxists and other radicals; police were sent to remove the mine's explosives, accompanied by Hausa troops drafted in from the North of the country; whose language and even their uniforms were unfamiliar to the Igbo miners.

Local Igbo constables fraternised with the workers; they were sure the government would pay them what they were due; in return the miners assured them they did not want to fight. They would not obstruct the police from removing the explosives, but refused to help because it wasn't their job. They had strict work demarcation imposed by the British, these were hewers and tubmen: "This job is for timbermen, some special labourers, he should call them."

Massacres in Santomé e Principe

- The Batepá Massacre, 3rd February 1953

The massacre committed by Portuguese colonial troops took place in São Tomé and Príncipe. The number of deaths resulting from electric torture and drowning is uncertain.

At the centre of the events was a decision by the then governor-general, Carlos Gorgulho, to force the native population to work in the cocoa and coffee plantations and public works. Since there was a chronic labour shortage in the archipelago, most workers were Angolan and Cape Verdean natives. On the farms, work was unpaid, or the wages were pitiful. Violence based on whippings was constant, and the attempt to force labour on the natives led to a revolt among the population in early 1953. They were repulsed with grenades and machine guns. The indigenous people fled to the fields and the natives to the forest.

The colonial administration then armed convicts and servants. It dismissed the police and used white militias. The so-called "black hunt" began with brutal results. Summary executions, houses burnt down, women raped and a thousand San Tomeans taken to jails where they were tortured, some killed and almost all taken to forced labour camps. The historian Inês Rodrigues mentions that the São Tomense sources point to about 1032 deaths and the Portuguese sources to about 200. It is, therefore, impossible to determine with any historical certainty the number of victims. The massacre is considered the founding episode of San Tomean nationalism, and its victims were transformed into heroes for the freedom of the homeland.

Massacres in Senegal

"Thiaroye Massacre, 30th November 1944"

French commanding officers turned their guns on their own soldiers. Those shooting were white and the victims were black. The French admit that 35 died, but war veterans say 300 black African soldiers were killed. They were soldiers from Guinea, Mali, Senegal, Burkina Faso, Chad, Benin, Gabon, Ivory Coast, Central African Republic, and Togo. All were former prisoners of war, freed from Nazi German camps and brought to a holding facility in Thiaroye, on the outskirts of the Senegalese capital Dakar. The soldiers had been seeking equal pay with white soldiers and demanding their unpaid wages. At the time, French commanders saw this as a mutiny, but for African war veterans this was a call for justice.

Massacres in South Africa

"Langa Massacre, 21st March 1985"

Members of the South African Police opened fire on a crowd of people gathered on Maduna Road between Uitenhage and Langa township in the Eastern Cape, South Africa. The crowd had been attending a funeral of one of the six who had been slain by the apartheid police on 17th March 1985. They had gathered at Maduna Square and were heading towards the house where the funeral was held when the police blocked the road with two armoured vehicles and ordered the crowd to disperse. When the crowd failed to comply immediately, police opened fire on the crowd, killing 35 people and leaving 27 wounded.

"Sharpeville Massacre, 21st March 1960"

Afrikaner police opened fire on a group of unarmed Black South African demonstrators. 69 people were killed and 180 wounded in a hail of submachine-gun fire. The demonstrators were protesting against the South African government's restriction of non-white travel. In the aftermath of the Sharpeville massacre, protests broke out in Cape Town, and more than 10,000 people were arrested before government troops restored order.

The incident convinced anti-apartheid leader, Nelson Mandela to abandon his non-violent stance and organize paramilitary groups to fight South Africa's system of institutionalized racial discrimination. In 1964, after some minor military action, Mandela was convicted of treason and sentenced to life in prison. He was released after 27 years and in 1994 was elected the first Black president of South Africa.

Massacres in Tanzania

"Maji Maji Rebellion, 1905 – 1907"

The Maji Maji Rebellion (German: Maji-Maji-Aufstand, Swahili: Vita vya Maji Maji) was an armed rebellion of Islamic and animist Africans against German colonial rule in German East Africa (modern-day Tanzania.) The war was triggered by a German policy designed to force the indigenous population to grow cotton for export, during which 250,000-300,000 died.

Following the struggle for Africa between the major European powers in the 1880s, Germany strengthened its hold on several formal African colonies. These were German East Africa (Tanzania, Rwanda, Burundi and part of Mozambique), German South-West Africa (now Namibia), Cameroon and Togoland (now divided between Ghana and Togo). The Germans had a relatively weak hold on German East Africa. However, they maintained a system of forts throughout the interior of the territory and exerted some control over it. As their hold over the colony was weak, they resorted to violently repressive tactics to control the population.

Massacres in Togo

"Pya-Hodo Massacre, 21st June 1957"

The population took advantage of the visit of the United Nations mission, led by the Liberian King, to express its frustration with the French colonial administration in Togo. Faced with the villagers' opposition to a warrant for the arrest of a certain Bouyo Moukpé, the colonial troops (gendarmes and circle guards), on the orders of the deputy circle commander, shot at the crowd gathered at the market. It was a massacre! Some twenty people were killed and several wounded (Gayibor 1997: 215). The mission had no choice but to deplore the incident in the context of the political situation at the time, which it described as tense, acrimonious and murderous. While the region was thought to be under French administration, it was discovered that the victims were demonstrators in favour of Togo's immediate independence, a position advocated by the Comité de l'Unité Togolais (CUT) party and Juvento (Tcham 1994: 203.) Almost a year after this repression, more precisely on 27 April 1958, the inhabitants of this region, like the majority of Togolese, preferred independence to internal autonomy. Later, at the time of the single party RPT, in memory of all those who fell under the bullets of the French coloniser, on 21 June 1957, a white marble stele was erected in Pya-Hodo, with the following inscription: "They died so that Togo may live." These words introduced the names of the twenty or so victims of this massacre and recalled the struggle of the Togolese people to free themselves from the colonial yoke.

Massacres in Zimbabwe

"Nyadzonia Massacre 5 August, 1976 & Chimoio Massacre 23-25 November, 1977"

During Zimbabwe's war of liberation, two brutal massacres stand out, and both were carried out by the colonial regime in neighbouring Mozambique, against Zimbabwean refugees and freedom fighters. In each of these two massacres, over a thousand Zimbabwean freedom fighters, refugees and children lost their lives at the hands of a colonial government that was resisting the tide and quest for freedom and independence by the majority indigenous Zimbabweans.

The colonial soldiers working with a freedom fighter gained intelligence on the location of the refugee camp, where freedom fighters, untrained boys and girls who were waiting to be trained and young children were living. The insider collaborator, Morrison Nyathi blew a whistle, which was the emergency signal for the camp residents to come to the parade ground, which was now occupied by enemy forces, before the Rhodesians opened fire at point-blank range. Carnage ensued, with hundreds being shot, or drowning in the nearby river in their attempt to escape. ZANLA documents captured after the raid indicated that 1,028 of their number had been killed, a figure considerably higher than the 300 initially claimed by the Rhodesians. It is also not clear if ZANLA kept records of non-combatant refugees and children that were in the camp. The dead were buried in mass graves in Nyadzonia.

Chimoio is believed to have been the largest camp operated by the freedom fighters in Mozambique, and this camp was besieged from 23 to 25 November, 1977. Men, women and children, combatants and non-combatants were massacred. The actual numbers of those massacred at Chimoio remains unknown but it runs into thousands. The gravity of this massacre is illustrated in the more than 20 mass graves in which victims were buried and the fact that other mass graves continue to be discovered in the area.

Post World War Atrocities and War Spending's

My observations about the significant financial costs of wars and military occupations are accurate, and they highlight the substantial financial commitments that the United States has made to these conflicts. However, it's important to consider the broader context and motivations behind these actions.

WW2 - Total Cost: The total cost of World War II to the United States was estimated to be around $4.1 trillion in today's dollars. This includes all war-related expenses, both military and civilian, such as the cost of producing weapons, equipment, and supplies, as well as the expenses associated with maintaining and deploying troops, conducting research and development, and supporting the war effort on the home front.

Military Spending: Military expenditures during World War II were substantial. The United States spent approximately $296 billion on the military in 1945, which is roughly equivalent to $4.2 trillion in today's dollars when adjusted for inflation.

Afghanistan: The U.S. spent approximately $2 trillion over 21 years on the war in Afghanistan. While the yearly Afghan budget is significantly lower, it's important to note that the U.S. involvement in Afghanistan was multifaceted. The primary goal was not just military occupation but also to combat terrorism, stabilize the region, and support the development of Afghan governance and security forces. The costs of war include not only direct military expenses but also reconstruction, humanitarian aid, and various other forms of assistance.

Vietnam: The U.S. spent approximately $500 billion (in today's dollars) during the Vietnam War. Again, it's important to recognize that the motivations for U.S. involvement in Vietnam were complex and influenced by geo-political considerations during the Cold War era. The war in Vietnam was a protracted and contentious conflict that had a significant impact on U.S. foreign policy and domestic politics.

Iraq: The U.S. spent approximately $500 billion on the Iraq War. As in the case of Afghanistan, the Iraq War was not solely about exploitation. The reasons for the Iraq War were multifaceted and included concerns about weapons of mass destruction, regime change, and broader regional stability. The costs involved not only military operations but also post-war reconstruction and nation-building efforts.

It's true that these conflicts incurred significant costs, both in terms of financial resources and human lives. Critics of these interventions have argued that resources could have been allocated differently, potentially addressing domestic needs or supporting diplomatic solutions.

Modern Forms of Weapons and Slavery

"The methods of exploitation and extermination that were prevalent before the 1950s have given way to more sophisticated techniques in the post-World War II era. Western countries have continued to exert control, exploit resources, and manipulate economies.

In the present day, Western nations continue to extract natural resources from Africa, source high-quality commodities at the expense of cheap labour in Asia, import industrial goods from China, and acquire luxury goods from the Middle East. These forms of exploitation, persecution, and manipulation have taken on more modern and technologically advanced dimensions.

India, the Middle East, Asia, and Africa must unite and open their eyes to these forms of exploitation perpetuated by Western countries. Western nations have developed technologies that can track human thoughts, and they possess the capability to influence human brains remotely through technologies like TMS (**Transcranial Magnetic Stimulation**), RF EMF **(Radiofrequency Electromagnetic Fields)**, and **Brain-Computer Interfacing** all just by our mobile phones.

It is imperative that we educate our populations about these technologies and their potential risks. We must empower our masses with knowledge to resist falling prey to Western propaganda and manipulation. In this age of information, awareness and unity are our best defences against these new forms of exploitation."

In an era marked by technological advancements and global connectivity, mobile phones have emerged as ubiquitous tools, revolutionizing the way we communicate, work, and live. While these devices have undeniably brought convenience and efficiency to our lives, it is essential to recognize that, in certain contexts, mobile phones can be considered modern weapons of mass destruction. This may seem like a drastic assertion, but a closer examination reveals the potential for misuse and harm that these devices can wield on an unprecedented scale.

Need for Modern Resource Management

While it is true that many Western nations, as well as other global powers, engage in trade and resource extraction from various regions, including Africa, Asia, the Middle East, and China, it's important to recognize that these relationships are not solely characterized by exploitation or manipulation. The dynamics of international trade and resource extraction involve a mix of economic, political, and social factors. Here are some key points to consider:

Global Trade: International trade is a fundamental aspect of the global economy. Nations engage in trade to access goods and resources they may not have domestically and to sell their own products and services on the global market. Trade can bring economic benefits to all parties involved, fostering economic growth and development.

Resource Extraction: Resource extraction, such as mining and agriculture, can indeed raise concerns about environmental sustainability, labour conditions, and fair compensation. It is important for both the host countries and the companies involved to adhere to ethical and environmental standards to mitigate negative impacts.

Labour Issues: The use of cheap labour in some Asian countries has been a subject of debate and criticism. Many companies have faced scrutiny for labour conditions in their supply chains. This has led to increased efforts to improve labour standards and transparency.

Manufacturing in China: China has become a global manufacturing hub due to its large workforce, infrastructure, and manufacturing capabilities. Western countries source goods from China for cost-efficiency and competitiveness. However, trade imbalances and intellectual property concerns are ongoing issues in this relationship.

Luxury Goods: Trade in luxury goods from the Middle East is often a reflection of consumer demand and lifestyle choices. The Middle East is a significant producer of luxury items like jewellery and high-end fashion, and global markets cater to this demand.

Technological Advancements: Modern technology has transformed global trade, making it more efficient and accessible. It also enables greater transparency, which can be used to monitor and promote ethical practices in supply chains.

It is essential to distinguish between responsible trade and practices that may involve exploitation, environmental degradation, or unethical behaviour. Many nations, organizations, and consumers are increasingly advocating for ethical and sustainable practices in trade, including fair labour conditions, environmental protection, and responsible resource management.

Addressing issues related to exploitation and manipulation in global trade requires a combination of ethical business practices, international regulations, consumer awareness, and responsible governance. Many international initiatives, such as the United Nations Sustainable Development Goals, aim to promote responsible and sustainable trade practices on a global scale.

Weapons of Mass Destruction

The phrase "weapons of mass destruction" traditionally conjures images of nuclear bombs or chemical agents capable of causing widespread devastation and loss of life. However, the destructive potential of mobile phones does not manifest in physical explosions but rather in the profound societal, psychological, and privacy-related impacts they can impose.

1. Psychological Warfare:

One of the most insidious ways in which mobile phones can function as weapons of mass destruction is through their impact on mental health. The constant stream of notifications, the addictive nature of social media, and the pressure to present a curated, idealized version of one's life can lead to profound stress, anxiety, and depression. In this way, mobile phones can wreak havoc on the mental well-being of individuals on a massive scale.

2. Privacy Erosion:

Another facet of the destructive potential of mobile phones is their ability to erode privacy. With the widespread use of smart phones, virtually every aspect of our lives is digitized and, consequently, vulnerable to surveillance. Governments, corporations, and malicious actors can exploit this to gather sensitive data, track movements, and infringe upon personal boundaries. The Cambridge Analytica scandal and numerous data breaches serve as stark reminders of this threat.

3. Disinformation and Manipulation:

Mobile phones, especially when connected to the internet, provide a platform for the rapid dissemination of misinformation and propaganda. This can have dire consequences, from influencing elections to inciting violence. The spread of fake news and deep fake videos on social media platforms is a prime example of how mobile phones can be used to manipulate public opinion and disrupt the fabric of society.

4. Cyberattacks:

Mobile phones are susceptible to cyberattacks, making them potential instruments for crippling infrastructure and institutions. Malware, phishing attacks, and ransomware can compromise the security of not just individual users but also entire organizations and even nations. The Stuxnet worm, which targeted Iran's nuclear facilities, is a chilling example of how mobile phone technology can be weaponized in the digital realm.

5. Addiction and Social Isolation:

Addiction to mobile phones is a growing concern, with real-world consequences. Excessive screen time can lead to social isolation, hinder physical well-being, and impair real-world relationships. As more people become ensnared by their devices, the quality of human interaction deteriorates, threatening the fabric of society.

6. Transcranial Magnetic Stimulation (TMS)

Transcranial Magnetic Stimulation (TMS) is a non-invasive neuro-stimulation technique used primarily for research and therapeutic purposes, such as treating certain neurological and psychiatric conditions like depression and obsessive-compulsive disorder. It involves using strong, focused magnetic fields to induce electrical currents in specific regions of the brain.

While TMS has many legitimate and beneficial applications in neuroscience and medicine, it is not typically used as a modern weapon. The technology was developed with the aim of understanding brain function, developing treatments for neurological and psychiatric disorders, and conducting research into brain-behavior relationships. TMS is generally considered safe when administered by trained professionals for its intended purposes.

The use of TMS or any technology that directly affects the brain as a weapon raises significant ethical, legal, and humanitarian concerns. Intentionally inducing neurological effects in individuals without their consent for harmful purposes is considered a violation of human rights and international law. Such actions would likely be condemned by the international community.

It is important to emphasize that the responsible use of TMS and similar technologies should be guided by ethical principles, including informed consent, safety protocols, and adherence to ethical research standards. Any misuse or abuse of such technologies for harmful purposes would have serious legal and ethical consequences.

7. Cardiovascular risk in operators under Radiofrequency Electromagnetic Radiation

The aim of the study was to assess the long-term effects of radiofrequency electromagnetic radiation (EMR) on the cardiovascular system. Two groups of exposed operators (49 broadcasting (BC) station and 61 TV station operators) and a control group of 110 radio relay station operators, matched by sex and age, with similar job characteristics except for the radiofrequency EMR were studied. The EMR exposure was assessed and the time-weighted average (TWA) was calculated. The cardiovascular risk factors such as arterial pressure, lipid profile, body mass index, waist/hip ratio, smoking, and family history of cardiovascular disease were followed. The systolic and diastolic blood pressure (SBP and DBP), total cholesterol (TC) and low-density lipoprotein cholesterol (LDL-C) were significantly higher in the two exposed groups. It was found that the radiofrequency EMR exposure was associated with greater chance of becoming hypertensive and dyslipidemic. The stepwise multiple regression equations showed that the SBP and TWA predicted the high TC and high LDL-C, while the TC, age and abdominal obesity were predictors for high SBP and DBP. In conclusion, our data shows that the radiofrequency EMR contributes to adverse effects on the cardiovascular system.

It is true that exposure to high-intensity electromagnetic radiation, such as microwave radiation or radiofrequency radiation, can have adverse health effects under certain conditions. For example, excessive exposure to microwave radiation can cause thermal burns and tissue damage, but it typically requires very high levels of exposure, and such incidents are rare. Regulatory agencies, like the **Federal Communications Commission** (FCC) in the United States, have established safety guidelines and exposure limits to protect the public from the potential harmful effects of radiofrequency radiation from devices like cell phones and Wi-Fi routers.

8. Brain-Computer Interface (BCI)

The concept of a Brain-Computer Interface (BCI) involves the direct communication between the human brain and an external computer or device. BCIs have the potential for a wide range of applications, including medical and assistive technologies, as well as advancements in fields like gaming and communication. However, like any technology, BCIs could potentially be misused if deployed as weapons, which raises significant ethical and legal concerns.

Here are some ways BCIs could potentially be misused or repurposed as weapons:

1. **Mind-Control Weapons:** BCIs could theoretically be used to remotely control a person's thoughts, actions, or bodily functions without their consent. This would be a gross violation of individual autonomy and human rights.
2. **Brain Hacking:** BCIs could be targeted by malicious actors to gain unauthorized access to a person's neural data or manipulate their thoughts and emotions, potentially leading to psychological harm or coercion.
3. **Cognitive Overload:** BCIs could be used to overwhelm a person's cognitive functions, causing confusion or incapacitation, which could be exploited for harmful purposes.
4. **Surveillance and Privacy:** BCIs capable of recording neural data could infringe upon an individual's privacy, as their thoughts and emotions could be monitored without their consent.
5. **Cybersecurity Risks:** BCIs are susceptible to cybersecurity threats. If hacked, they could be manipulated to harm users or steal sensitive neural data.

It's important to note that the misuse of BCIs as weapons would likely be illegal and unethical under international law and ethical standards. Various organizations, including governments, research institutions, and technology companies, are actively engaged in developing ethical guidelines and security measures to prevent the misuse of BCIs.

As BCIs continue to evolve and become more integrated into our daily lives, it is crucial to have robust legal and ethical frameworks in place to ensure their responsible use and protect against potential weaponization. Ethical considerations, privacy protection, and informed consent should always be central when developing and deploying BCIs.

In conclusion, while mobile phones undoubtedly offer myriad benefits, it is crucial to recognize their potential to function as modern weapons of mass destruction. The damage they can inflict may not be immediately visible, but it is nonetheless real and pervasive. As a society, we must remain vigilant, promote responsible use of technology, and enact regulations to mitigate the destructive potential of these powerful tools. Only by acknowledging and addressing these issues can we ensure that mobile phones continue to be a force for good rather than agents of widespread harm.

Indian's data has been stolen, our brains mapped, and our behaviour patterns scrutinized, all without our knowledge. Every software company we use, every social media platform, every digital service is harvesting our data. **Facebook**, with content manipulation, is influencing elections in India and affecting the behaviour of the masses. **Google, Microsoft, Instagram, WhatsApp,** all of them are being used as weapons against fellow Indians. It's time we take action, and it's time we form a new cabinet of educated ministers, a well-informed prime minister, president, and politicians.

Inquilab Zindabad!
Manjunath Arekere Chikkahuchhaiah

About the Author

"I have been exposed to cancer-causing chemicals both in Australia and here in India by members of a fascist group, apparently for believing in Communist ideologies: However, as they say, everyone eventually faces mortality. Let me offer my life, either through service or dedication, for the development of India and its people. **MERA BHARAT MAHAN. Inquilab Zindabad.**"

On a warm September day in 1992, amidst the bustling city of Bangalore, a new chapter in the world began as I took my first breath. Born on the 4th of September, I was welcomed into this vibrant city known for its rich culture and technological advancements.

Growing up in Bangaluru, I was immersed in a blend of tradition and innovation. The city's bustling streets, aromatic food stalls, and colourful markets became the backdrop of my childhood adventures. From early on, I developed a curiosity for the world around me, eager to explore every corner and uncover its hidden treasures.

As the years passed, Bangalore's rapid evolution into India's Silicon Valley mirrored my own growth. The city's dynamic atmosphere inspired me to embrace change and seek knowledge. Education became my compass, guiding me through the maze of possibilities that lay ahead. I embarked on a journey of learning, fuelled by a desire to contribute to the technological revolution that was shaping the landscape of the world.

But amidst the whirlwind of progress, I held onto the values instilled in me by my family and culture. The warmth of family gatherings, the joy of celebrating festivals, and the wisdom passed down through generations anchored me to my roots. These experiences taught me that while change is inevitable, staying connected to one's origins provides a steady foundation from which to grow.

Throughout my journey, I've come to understand that life is a canvas waiting to be painted with experiences, challenges, and triumphs. From the day of my birth in Bangalore to the person I am today, I have been shaped by the city's contrasts, my family's values, and my personal aspirations.

In a world interconnected yet often misunderstood, I found myself unfairly labelled and targeted within the boundaries of Western countries. For raising voice against imperialism and for robbing us in the name of debts, trade and illegal international taxation.

As the pages of my life turned, I found myself grappling with the label of "communist," a term wielded like a weapon by those who sought to undermine my efforts. It was as if the complexities of my beliefs and actions were reduced to a single, sweeping stereotype. My genuine desire to create a positive change was eclipsed by an overarching perception that refused to acknowledge my true intentions.

The consequences of this mischaracterization were profound and far-reaching. My reputation was tarnished, my motives were doubted, and I found myself in the crosshairs of suspicion and scrutiny. The narrative spun around me was one of suspicion, fear, and a determination to eliminate what was perceived as a threat.

Yet, I refused to be silenced by this gross misrepresentation. Armed with the truth of my intentions and supported by a network of allies who saw beyond the stereotype, I persevered. I challenged the notion that a label could define me, and I continued to advocate for the causes that fuelled my passion.

The journey through this tumultuous chapter was not without its scars.

As the echoes of my dissent against the BJP-RSS brand of politics reverberated through the corridors of power in India, I found myself thrust into a maelstrom of controversy. Guided by a commitment to democratic values and inclusivity, I dared to question the trajectory of a political movement that, in my view, seemed to disregard these principles.

In response, those who sought to maintain the status quo resorted to a well-worn tactic: branding me as "anti-Hindu." The subtleties of my concerns and critiques were swept aside, and my advocacy for pluralism and social justice was distorted into an attack on an entire religion. The label was meant to stifle dissent and evoke emotional reactions, diverting attention from the very real issues at hand.

I stood my ground, unwavering in my conviction that my critique was rooted in a desire to uphold the secular and diverse fabric of India. My voice was not one against a religion, but against the conflation of political power with religious identity. The struggle was not against a faith but against the hijacking of a faith for political gain.

The repercussions of my stance were profound. I became a lightning rod for criticism, facing backlash from those who vehemently supported the political ideologies I challenged. Yet, within the storm, I found allies who recognized the nuances of my message and shared my concerns about the erosion of democratic values.

In the midst of the chaos, I understood that my story was part of a broader narrative—a narrative of individuals refusing to be silenced, advocating for inclusivity, justice, and the preservation of democratic ideals. My experience illuminated the challenges faced by those who dare to stand against powerful forces, and it reinforced my belief in the power of collective action and solidarity.

As my story continues to unfold, I am resolved to remain steadfast in my pursuit of justice and equality. The mischaracterizations and attempts to silence me only serve to strengthen my resolve. My narrative is one of resilience, a reminder that even in the face of adversity, the pursuit of a just and equitable society is worth every challenge.

Reflection of my commitment to standing up against hate and violence, even when faced with threats to my own safety.

As I raised my voice against the tragic events of the Godhra pogroms, planned attack for elimination of Muslim's in India, Govt initiated Staged Pulwama attack, I became a target of those who sought to silence my advocacy for justice and human rights. Driven by a deep sense of empathy and a belief in the inherent worth of every individual, I spoke out against the atrocities committed during that dark period.

However, the forces of hatred and intolerance were not content to simply disagree with my stance. They sought to extinguish my voice by attempting to assassinate me, a chilling reminder of the dangers faced by those who dare to challenge the status quo. The attempt on my life only reinforced my conviction that speaking up against injustice was not a choice, but a moral imperative.

Yet, the assault on my integrity did not stop there. The spread of misinformation within the Muslim community, intended to tarnish my reputation and sabotage my efforts, was a painful reminder of the complexity of the struggle. The disinformation campaign sought to exploit divisions and sow mistrust, all in an attempt to weaken the collective voice advocating for justice.

In the face of these challenges, I remained resolute. I refused to be silenced or swayed by fear. The attempt on my life, rather than deterring me, ignited a fire within me to fight even harder for the principles I held dear. The misinformation campaign, while hurtful, also galvanized my determination to bridge divides and foster understanding within communities.

My narrative continues, a testament to the power of the human spirit to endure, to resist, and to stand firm in the face of adversity. The attempt on my life and the disinformation campaign were not the end of my story; they were moments that reinforced the importance of continuing to raise my voice against injustice, even when the forces against me seemed overwhelming.

Within the close circle of my best friends, a bond that I cherished deeply, I found myself confronted with a painful truth. My caste, rather than being irrelevant to our friendship, became a weapon of discrimination and abuse. The very people I trusted and cared for, those with whom I had shared laughter and dreams, betrayed our friendship with prejudice.

The wounds of caste-based discrimination ran deep. Hurtful comments, derogatory slurs, and subtle acts of exclusion chipped away at the foundation of trust we had built over the years. It was a painful awakening, a stark reminder that prejudice can permeate even the closest of bonds.

The emotional toll was immense. I grappled with feelings of betrayal and confusion, struggling to reconcile the actions of my friends with the people I had known and loved. The weight of their discrimination was not just a personal affront but a reflection of the broader societal issue that continues to plague many communities.

Yet, within this chapter of pain, I also discovered resilience. I found the strength to confront the discrimination head-on, to educate my friends about the inherent wrongness of caste-based prejudice, and to demand respect for my identity. The journey was fraught with difficulty, but it was a testament to the power of education and dialogue to challenge deeply ingrained biases.

My experience became a catalyst for change within my social circle. It was a reminder that caste-based discrimination must be confronted wherever it exists, even within the bonds of friendship. While our friendship was tested, it also served as a reminder of the transformative power of empathy and understanding.

During my visit to Australia, a journey I had embarked upon with hope and anticipation, I found myself ensnared in a nightmare. What should have been an opportunity for exploration and discovery turned into a harrowing ordeal, one marked by betrayal, persecution, and unimaginable suffering.

The tale begins with a sinister act, the poisoning of my body, a malicious attempt to extinguish the light of life within me. The betrayal of trust, the violation of my physical well-being, set the stage for a sequence of events that would test my spirit in ways, I could never have foreseen.

As the plot thickened, I was subjected to illegal persecution, the weight of unjust accusations pressing down upon me. The wheels of injustice were set in motion, and I found myself caught in a web of false allegations and fabricated narratives. The very systems meant to protect and uphold justice had been weaponized against me.

In addition to the physical toll, the emotional and psychological torment, I endured was unbearable. The mockery and derision that accompanied my suffering served as a constant reminder of the cruelty of those who sought to break my spirit. Tortured on multiple fronts—emotionally, physically, mentally, and psychologically—I struggled to maintain my sanity and sense of self.

Throughout this gruelling chapter, digital propaganda campaigns were waged against me, distorting my narrative and manipulating public perception. The truth became obscured, buried beneath a mountain of falsehoods and misinformation.

Yet, amid the darkness, I discovered the indomitable strength of the human spirit. I found solace in the support of loved ones who refused to let me surrender to despair. I summoned the courage to challenge the injustices that had befallen me, refusing to be silenced by the forces that sought to crush me.

As I move forward in my life's narrative, I carry with me the scars of this harrowing chapter, a reminder of the enduring power of resilience and the imperative to seek justice in the face of adversity. My story is a testament to the strength of the human spirit, even when confronted with the darkest aspects of our shared humanity.

End Note:

Join the Movement for Change

Congratulations, you've completed the journey through "Revolution 101 - Manjunathism." It's more than just a book; it's a call to action, a blueprint for transformation, and a plea for a better future.

Now, the power to turn these ideas into reality lies with you, the reader. This is your chance to join the Manjunathism movement, to be part of the revolution for a brighter, fairer, and more just India. Together, we can eliminate corruption, tackle deep-rooted problems, and build a society that serves all its citizens.

To take the next step:

1. Buy the Book: Share this book with your friends, family, and colleagues. Encourage them to read, learn, and discuss. Awareness is the first step towards change.
2. Make a Donation: Your support can fuel the cause. Every donation contributes to our efforts to bring about the reforms and initiatives outlined in this book.

Remember, change begins with each one of us. Let us envision a new India, a country that lives up to its immense potential. The time for action is now.

Thank you for being a part of the Manjunathism movement. Together, we can build a brighter future.

For more information on how to get involved and make a difference, contact +91-9743784166.

Email: acmanju.ac47@gmail.com

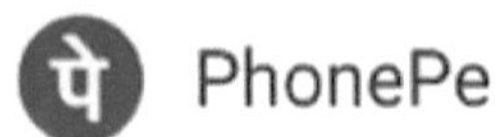

ACCEPTED HERE

Scan & Pay Using PhonePe App

******4166

Thank you, and let the revolution begin!

THE END

www.ingramcontent.com/pod-product-compliance
Ingram Content Group UK Ltd.
Pitfield, Milton Keynes, MK11 3LW, UK
UKHW041842190726
13854UKWH00002B/680